Advocating for Children in Foster and Kinship Care

Advocating for Children in Foster and Kinship Care

A Guide to Getting the Best out of the System for Caregivers and Practitioners

MITCHELL A. ROSENWALD

AND

BETH N. RILEY

Columbia University Press   *New York*

Columbia University Press
Publishers Since 1893
New York   Chichester, West Sussex
Copyright © 2010 Columbia University Press
All rights reserved

Library of Congress Cataloging-in-Publication Data
Rosenwald, Mitchell.
Advocating for children in foster and kinship care : a guide to getting the best out of the
system for caregivers and practitioners / Mitchell A. Rosenwald, Beth N. Riley.
p.   cm.
Includes bibliographical references and index.
ISBN 978-0-231-14686-9 (cloth : alk. paper) — ISBN 978-0-231-14687-6 (pbk. : alk. paper)
— ISBN 978-0-231-51935-9 (ebook)
1. Foster home care—United States. 2. Foster parents—Services for—United States.
3. Foster children—Services for—United States. 4. Foster children—Legal status,
laws, etc.—United States. 5. Child welfare—United States.   I. Riley, Beth N. II. Title.

HV881.R675 2010
362.73'3—dc22   2009026894

∞
Columbia University Press books are printed on permanent and durable acid-free paper.
This book is printed on paper with recycled content.
Printed in the United States of America
c 10 9 8 7 6 5 4 3 2 1
p 10 9 8 7 6 5 4 3 2 1

References to Internet Web sites (URLs) were accurate at the time of writing. Neither the
authors nor Columbia University Press is responsible for URLs that may have expired or
changed since the manuscript was prepared.

To my parents, who gave me my roots and my wings.—MR

To all the families who have taught me so much about advocacy, especially
Scott, Shane, Colin, and Ian.—BR

Contents

viii

Contents

Foreword

GERALD P. MALLON

After working many years in the field of child welfare, I decided to put my money where my mouth was and to become a foster parent for the child who is now my daughter, Leslie. She and I had known each other for more than five years: I met her when she was nine, when I was a childcare worker in her cottage. At the time I became her foster father, Leslie was fifteen years old, both developmentally and emotionally challenged, and had lived all of her life—since twelve weeks of age—in institutional settings. I thought then—and I am sure now—that she deserved to live in a family, even a family as imperfect as mine.

I believed back then that I knew child welfare and the systems in which one must operate as a foster parent, but in fact I was totally unprepared for being on the other side of social services. Delivering child welfare services is very different from being the recipient of child welfare services; as a foster parent, even though you are "part of the team," you are also in many ways, like the child you care for, a client. Like many foster parents who have familiarity with the child welfare system, I thought I knew all there was to know. But I was wrong. It's very challenging to be the client, to be the one who is "visited" and not the one who does the visit. It is very difficult to parent a child who spent fifteen years in foster care and who had her own separate life before coming to live with you in your world. It is also at the same time joyful to know that what you are doing in becoming a foster parent will change another person's life—and it has. Being a foster parent is not always easy or smooth, and advocating for an emotionally and developmentally challenged child is, even for a skilled practitioner, a challenge.

There have been many books written about foster parenting, but I have never read any like this one. As I read this wonderful book, *Advocating for Children in Foster and Kinship Care*, written by Mitchell A. Rosenwald and Beth N. Riley, I could not help but think, "I wish this book had been available when I was a foster parent—I could have used some help in advocating for my child and for myself as a foster parent!" Co-authors Rosenwald and Riley make a compelling case for why advocacy in child welfare remains such a critical issue for practitioners, policymakers, and foster parents. In ten succinct chapters, separated into three overarching organizing sections, the co-authors discuss a range of issues within the realm of advocacy, from advocacy in the family court and social services systems to advocacy on the level of policy change and legislation. In utilizing case studies and providing clear and realistic questions to guide the child welfare worker or the foster parent (both kinship care providers and nonrelative care providers), this book promises to be a valuable tool for both foster parents and professionals who are engaged in child welfare practice. It offers advice that is grounded in practice wisdom and in empirically based evidence.

All these years as a foster parent later—Leslie, now 41, was adopted by me as an adult when she was 37 (proving that you're never too old for a family) and is working on her associates degree at the Brooklyn Institute of Technology—I marvel at what a wonderful gift Dr. Rosenwald and Ms. Riley have given to the child welfare profession, to current and to old foster parents like me!

Preface

The fact that you are reading this book suggests that you are particularly invested in helping improve the lives of children who have vulnerabilities that they themselves in no way chose to have. Children in foster care (care by adults who are nonrelatives) and kinship care (care by adults who are relatives) need the assistance of professionals and guardians who have competent knowledge and skills, a strong sense of ethics, and a big heart. Because of your current or future primary role in the lives of these children, we would like to point out that advocacy will be a central part of your work in helping these youth who rely on you for their care.

In this book we refer to "children in care" because we are including children who reside in both foster care and kinship care. Additionally, when we discuss those in foster care particularly, we refer to them as youth "in care"—rather than as "foster children"—because from a strengths perspective, it is vital for readers to remember that these youth are children first; while they may inhabit a child welfare system at a particular time in their life, this is merely an *aspect* of their identity and development as children rather than the *central focus*. To this end, when we crafted these words (contrary to those in the literature), we strove for this orientation. We will also refer to foster parents and kinship care providers collectively, at times, as "care providers." Finally, "practitioners" are those current or future professionals who typically have degrees or a background in social work, human services, or related fields.

"Advocacy," as defined in a social work context, can be broadened to apply to everyone's work in advancing the cause of youth in care; it "is the exclusive and mutual representation of a client(s) or a cause in a forum, attempting to systematically influence decision-making in an unjust or unresponsive system(s)" (Schneider and Lester 2001:64–68). It is essential for foster parents and kinship care parents as well as for practitioners to focus on influencing decision-making, if they are to become an effective voice for the youth entrusted to their care.

This book is structured on and adapted from a specific model of advocacy—Rae and Nicholas-Wolosuk's "action-strategy model." This model is based on six factors: (1) "solution-based incrementalism," (2) a "bottoms-up approach," (3) "macro social work practice for direct service workers," (4) "savvy workers–strong clients/consumers," (5) "social work values and the Code of Ethics," and (6) "a systematic process" (2003:42). In adapting these principles to our book, we place emphasis throughout the text on how the process of advocating for youth in care: (1) can address needs, often one small step at a time; (2) is most often initiated by foster parents and practitioners, who are on the front line of service delivery; (3) considers the larger context in which needs emerge; (4) expects knowledgeable foster parents, kinship care providers, and practitioners on the front line to emphasize the strengths of the youth in their care and collaborate among themselves and with others (including the youth themselves as possible) to address youths' needs; (5) resides in an ethical context and includes a respect for diversity, and (6) achieves its ends by following a series of steps (Rae and Nicholas-Wolosuk 2003).

Regarding this last point, Rae and Nicholas-Wolosuk describe the four steps of the action-strategy model: (1) dream about agency policy change; (2) analyze the policy situation related to the change idea; (3) develop a plan of action related to the change goal/idea, and (4) implement change strategy to accomplish approval of agency policy change (2003:49). Using these four steps as a foundation, we have structured each chapter below to include the following steps/subsections: identify the need; analyze the context; develop the plan; implement the plan. Additionally, each chapter includes a vignette at its beginning that is referred to throughout the chapter. While the vignettes vary in discussing the foster care or the kinship care context, we believe that the general points of advocacy remain the same for both foster parents and kinship caregivers; we note points of difference when they do exist. Finally, every chapter contains an advocacy checklist (which reflects the structural sections of that chapter), discussion questions, and relevant Web sites giving further information.

The substantive areas of advocacy into which this book is organized reflect the hierarchy of the overall system that foster parents, kinship care providers, and practitioners inhabit and have the opportunity to advocate within. These correspond to the micro systems-interventions of the caregivers, the mezzo systems-interventions of organizations, and the macro systems-interventions of agencies, government, and community. The first two chapters (part I) address preparation for advocacy as foster parents and kinship caregivers, with practitioners' assistance, work both to verify for themselves that they are ready to become foster parents and kinship caregivers and to assess the range of youth issues they feel comfortable dealing with in parenting. Chapters 3 through 7 (part II) address advocating with organizations, that is, those service providers who are "part of the system" and yet so central to the lives of youth in care. These organizations, examples of where direct advocacy occurs, include the court system, the social services system, the educational system, the health and mental health systems, and interdisciplinary teams comprised of representatives of multiple systems. Finally, the last three chapters (part III) focus first on advocacy through policy change at the agency and legislative levels and then on the role of the community in supplementing, or often leading, advocacy efforts.

This book is written for four audiences: foster parents, kinship caregivers, service practitioners, and undergraduate and graduate students intending to pursue careers in child and family services. While social work is the principal profession that focuses on advocating for youth in care, it is not the only one that works with these youth, and therefore the scope of this book has been expanded to include *all* practitioners who work with children, including essential professional volunteers known as "court-appointed special advocates" (CASA). And while we focus on issues for practitioners to consider when working with foster parents and kinship caregivers, this book can also aid practitioners working with youth in care who reside in "higher levels of care"—group homes and residential treatment facilities (RTFs).

Regardless of your role—as practitioner, as kinship caregiver, as foster parent, as student in a child welfare course and/or field placement—knowing how, when, and among whom to advocate on behalf of the children and adolescents who are disenfranchised and residing in the foster care system—or with relative caregivers—will be crucial to your effective work. The presence and quality of advocacy by care providers and practitioners can make or break a placement. You are both empowered and obligated to pursue the best advocacy that you can.

We hope that this book guides you in "getting the best out of the system" for the children you have decided to work with and are charged with helping. We wish you every success in your efforts.

Acknowledgments

We would like to thank the following individuals for their assistance with this book, which has been transformed through the many talents possessed by the following collective. Laura Bronstein's writings, research, and resources are an asset to this book. We recognize as well Johanna Byrd's careful review and guidance of the legislative chapter; Donna Corbin's provision of numerous documents on the current state of foster care; Brian Manganaro's review of the mental health and developmental disabilities information; Lynne Masland's contributions and review from the foster parent perspective; Nancy Moss's contribution as another talented and experienced foster parent; Antonio Nunez's helpful research assistance; Dianne Oakes' contribution of her legal knowledge; Amber Riley's review of some of the earliest drafts; Shirley Rolison's coauthorship of table 4.2; and Debbie Winters' insight regarding the services offered for youth in foster care in schools.

A special "thank you" is extended to Dr. Gary Mallon, both for his mentorship over the years and for the foreword he has written for this book.

Finally, we thank Lauren Dockett, editor for social work at Columbia University Press, for her initial idea and support throughout the book's creation, and the editorial staff at the press, for their assistance in bringing this book to publication.

Advocating for Children in Foster and Kinship Care

[Part I]

Preparing for Advocacy

In the Beginning

Assessing Commitment and Family Resources

Children are our most valuable natural resource.

—Herbert Hoover

Vignette

A couple, Mr. and Mrs. Johnson, are thinking about becoming foster parents. They have raised three children: one son is married, age 24, and on his own; the other son is age 22 and on his own; and their daughter is in college, age 18, and comes home to visit during breaks from college. The Johnsons have been thinking about fostering for some time but wanted to wait until their own children were grown and able to be accepting of the Johnsons' sharing their love and their lives with additional children. Now seemed like the time to do more research on the topic. They wanted to make sure they were doing this for the right reasons, so they did some soul-searching. Part of this process was to ascertain that they had the emotional commitment, time, money, and physical space that were necessary to foster.

With respect to commitment, they differed. Mrs. Johnson was enthusiastic. She was so excited that she had been researching youth programs that a child might like to join. Mr. Johnson, however, was unsure. He questioned whether he wanted to give up his free time—he had raised three children and was not sure he had the energy for more. He liked having time for his hobbies and time with his own family. Mr. Johnson was concerned, too, because they both worked: she as a receptionist and he as a mechanic at his business. He, then, wanted to consider this decision carefully. Moreover, they both shared some concern about whether they would feel truly comfortable working with children who were ultimately in someone else's custody. Because they still were finding their answers, they called Mrs. Thomas, a practitioner at their local children's agency, for guidance in their quest to assess their decision to foster.

Key

Mr. and Mrs. Johnson: potential foster parents.
Mrs. Thomas: foster care worker.

Mr. and Mrs. Johnson and Mrs. Thomas have several important considerations to confront. This first chapter provides information that can help them and other potential caregivers explore their readiness to accept children into their care. For practitioners and foster parents, for example, this means ensuring that they can and will give their all to making a foster care placement successful; for foster parents, it specifically means standing by the youth (children and adolescents) in the long term and thereby minimizing any placement disruption. Placement disruptions undermine the efforts of child welfare agencies to promote safety, permanency, and child well-being (Price, Chamberlain et al. 2008). In our vignette, therefore, it was essential for the Johnsons, with Mrs. Thomas' assistance, to understand the ramifications of the decision before them. Ensuring that foster parents are ready to foster is the first step of advocacy. Advocacy must be completed at each step along the way, and such advocacy requires energy and stamina. If the care providers are not ready, the children may suffer, either because the care providers might change their mind or because their skills might not be sufficient to handle those children's specific needs.

Advocacy Checklist

- Assess commitment to providing foster/kinship care.
- Examine existing resources.
- Evaluate motivation to foster.
- Understand the precertification process.

Assess Commitment to Providing Foster/Kinship Care

Identify the Need

Choosing to parent a child who is not biologically your own is a huge decision and an even greater commitment. It means committing oneself to the time, attention, and level of care that a young person needs, as well as the time it takes, as the premise of this book suggests, to advocate for that youth. Some children have greater needs than others, which could involve more supervision, coaching, and medical attention. Foster parents must believe that other nontangible rewards exist; financially, no amount of money can adequately compensate for the strife and ache that come with caring about another human being in pain, emotional or physical. Mrs. Thomas, our practitioner, knew that many potential foster parents give up within the first year (Rhodes, Orme et al. 2003). And yet, for those who continue to foster, there is great joy when a small child smiles at you or a teenage youth feels victorious because you have helped her obtain her first job. Committing to fostering or providing kinship care means following through on an obligation to stay with a child long after it becomes emotionally difficult for everyone involved. For a foster or kinship caregiver, that means agreeing to parent the child(ren) until a permanent family can be found. That "permanency" is achieved when the child returns to his or her parents, or after the child's parents' rights have been terminated and either an adoptive family has taken over your responsibilities or you yourself have chosen to adopt the child. Other options for a permanent placement can include the youth participating in an independent living (IL) program and becoming emancipated at a state-recognized age.

During an initial information session, prospective foster parents are sometimes asked if they can make this type of commitment. Deciding if one can make a long-term commitment to an unknown child may take some soul-searching. For couples, the question may be: do you both have the same level of commitment? In our vignette, we met the Johnsons, potential foster parents, who are exploring this decision.

Analyze the Context

For our discussion throughout this text, we are defining both sets of caregivers, foster parents and kinship caregivers, as adults who care for youth who have been temporarily or permanently removed, under court order, from their biological parents' care, typically as the result of maltreatment (physical abuse, sexual abuse, neglect, emotional abuse). To distinguish these two groups further: Foster parents are adults who wish to provide care for youth to whom they are not biologically or legally related. They may or may not end up adopting the child. Kinship caregivers are adults who have some familial relationship to youth other than being his or her biological or legal parent through adoption; they are typically grandparents but can also be great-grandparents, aunts, uncles, and other relatives. Sometimes kinship care providers serve in a temporary role as they step in to care for their "kin" while the child waits for her/his parent(s) to improve their parenting skills and provide a safe and nurturing home. Other times they serve as "permanent" caregivers by adopting the child, serving as a legal guardian, or acting in other court-approved capacities.

During the early assessment of commitment, kinship and foster parents' perceptions of factors that promote or inhibit successful fostering must be considered (see Buehler, Cox, and Cuddeback 2003). Inclusive in this decision is an assessment of their emotional commitment to this role as well as an assessment of their family resources (spouse/partner, children in home already, finances, household management, physical space, skills) and subsequent commitment of these resources for fostering. Part of this process involves honestly assessing the family's ability to care for children in specific developmental ranges and children with extremely challenging behaviors and/or challenging birth family members. The job of the practitioners is to assist potential foster and kinship parents in this assessment and in the resulting decision to enter this role and take the initial training.

Let's first turn specifically to this decision for potential foster parents. Such a decision is first based on having a fundamental knowledge of foster care and the role of foster parents. What is foster care? According to the National Foster Parents Association: "Foster care is the temporary placement of children and youth with families outside of their own home as result of abuse or neglect. The goal is to provide a safe, stable, nurturing environment" (http://www.nfpainc.org/content/?page=FOSTERPARENTINFORMATION).

What is the scope of responsibilities for a foster parent? The National Foster Parent Association states:

> A foster parent is a person who cares for children/youth who are not in their custody, children and youth who have entered the foster care system. Foster parents care about children and are willing and able to provide care and nurturing for the duration of the child's stay in foster care. Foster parents are asked to complete an application, submit to family/home assessments and attend training. Foster families must demonstrate financial and emotional stability, responsibility and a willingness to work with the agency that supervises their home. (http://www.nfpainc.org/content/?page=BECOMEAFOSTERPARENT)

Potential foster parents mull over fostering for a long time before they finally decide to inquire (Love and Velasco-Nunez 2004:30). Nonkinship foster families make up 75 percent of the caregiver applicants (Orme, Buehler et al. 2004). The need for foster homes, and the wonderful people who fill the roles of foster parents, is immense. For the last two decades or more, a push has occurred to shift treatment for children in care from the "therapist to the caregiver (foster parent) with appropriate training and development programs" (MacLean 1992:62). This means that foster parents are faced with more responsibility than ever before. Likewise, greater attention, commitment, and time must be given to the educational needs of youth in care with disabilities by both education and child welfare professionals (Geenen 2006).

Ethically, we do not want to place a child with a foster parent who will give up at the first sign of adversity, for it would be unfair for a child to become bonded with a foster parent only to have that person decide that fostering is too hard and ask the practitioner to remove the child. Or, worse yet, we would not want a foster parent who decides to foster a child and then finds some characteristic(s) of the child that differs from the foster family (e.g., race, religion, or other cultural factors) too difficult to reconcile and therefore asks for the child to be removed. Such action breaks with the

National Foster Parent Association Code of Ethics (2008), which believes in: "Recogniz[ing] the rights of children and youth to safe, nurturing relationships, intended to *last a lifetime.*"

Here are some comments of foster parents that imply this type of commitment.

> Before I took that seventeen year old, my husband was like, "That's it, no more" and I said "Okay, well [name] wants us to go meet her and just tell her what we think about her," and we weren't two minutes out the door when he goes: "Okay, when's she moving in?"

> I spent every day with him on the porch, moving his arms, moving his legs, making him look this way, keeping him alert all the time . . . 'cause I just felt determined that this innocent child was not gonna be brain damaged just because [name] shook him, you know?

> It's like just when you feel like "Ugh, I want to quit," you know, something sort of miraculous or out of the blue thing happens.   (Rosenwald and Bronstein 2008:291)

Commitment involves foster parents not just working with youth, but mentoring birth parents as well. Indeed, partnering with birth parents to work toward the return of the children to their home ("family reunification"), or another permanency plan, is a requirement of many agencies. Birth parents are, of course, a very valuable resource for children in care, children, who despite the circumstances of removal from their family of origin, generally remain very emotionally attached to the birth family. It is the practitioner who informs the potential foster parents that they (both the practitioner and the foster parents) have important roles in assisting the birth parents, who are working toward family reunification. This can be challenging, as birth parents vary on their own motivation and the pace of that motivation in working toward family reunification. As a result, the long-term options, referred to as "permanency" options, range from children in care returning home to safer and more nurturing environments ("reunification") to being "freed" for adoption after parental rights have been terminated (known legally as TPR).

Now we will consider kinship (relative) caregivers' commitment to serving in the role of foster parent. Kinship care is a quickly increasing trend among child placement options. Kinship caregivers are more likely to promote contact between the children and their parents than nonrelative foster parents (LeProhn 1994), and children who are cared for by relatives rather than nonrelatives have less behavior problems (Rubin, Downes et al. 2008). While some 6 million youth under 18 are being raised by a nonparent relative (Lugaila and Overturf 2004), when we discuss kinship caregivers, we are specifically referring to those kinship care providers who are caring for youth because they do not want the child to be in the temporary care of "unfamiliar" foster parents and potentially at risk for being permanently removed from family contact.

Aside from facing considerations similar to those of potential foster parents, relative caregivers find that this enormous decision is made more complicated by a factor unique to them—the reality that they are related to the biological parents, who are not viable parent options at the time. Even though kinship caregivers love their children and may be extremely relieved that they are keeping the children from having to enter the foster care system (though sometimes there is an overlap, wherein relatives serve as temporary guardians of children in foster care), they still may feel enormous stress when faced with, and after accepting, an obligation to raise their relative children. This stress can arise from the sheer responsibilities of caring for, at an older age, one or more young children. It is often a result of the disruption of later-life plans, including changing notions of what retirement means. It also relates to continuing difficult emotions of anger, sadness, and/or disappointment that kinship caregivers may still feel and be trying to resolve toward the children's parents for being unable or unwilling to parent themselves. Reasons for these parents' absence include the inability or deliberate choice to not parent (often due to substance dependency, mental health challenges, or incarceration).

Consider just one real story of a married couple in their sixties who have legal custody of their daughter's two grandchildren and are pursuing custody of the third child (Rosenwald, Kelchner, and Bartone 2008). The couple had continued to hope that their daughter, who had a long history of drug dependency, would be able to successfully raise her children, but they were disappointed.

> Their lives have not been easy nor has their "retirement" been what they expected. They are saddened by their daughter's continued use of drugs and alcohol, by her frequent arrests and hospital stays, and by the damage

done to the children both physically and emotionally. Mary is also sad-
dened by the fact that she has not been able to be a "grandmother," as
she is now their [her grandchildren's] parent. She misses being able to
"spoil them" as she had envisioned, but knows that parenting requires a
different level of responsibility. Even with the disappointments and the
expense both financial and emotional, Mary and Paul believe, as do other
grandparents interviewed, that parenting their grandchildren has been a
"blessing."   (Rosenwald, Kelchner, and Bartone 2008:12)

For kinship caregivers, while the child(ren) may wish to live with
them, they (the adults) need to consider their ability for maintaining
objectivity. As the grandparent, cousin, aunt, uncle, or other relative of
the children involved, they must ask themselves, "Do I have the ability
to maintain objectivity when deciding what is in the best interest of the
child(ren) or am I torn to make decisions that are best for the child's
parent(s)?" Indeed, some of kinship care's pressures include "pressures
from the agency, the community, the foster child, and his or her parents
[that] affect the way in which [the] family style functions" (McFadden
1996:545). These pressures can impact the commitment level of the kinship caregivers.

Therefore, whether considering foster or kinship care, potential caregivers need to honestly assess their commitment to this vitally important
responsibility. Youth who have experienced maltreatment must be able to
rely on stable, consistent caregivers.

Develop the Plan

Recalling the Johnsons, the potential foster parents from our vignette: two years
had now passed since they initially started discussing the idea of bringing foster children into their family. Understanding the commitment was an important factor to consider, and they wanted to develop a plan to help them decide
if they could commit to a child for a lifetime. Therefore, each planned to spend
a weekend thinking about the following questions: What does it mean to commit to fostering? Do they see this as a trial run? Do they want to try fostering
out by initially providing respite care (temporary care of youth to provide relief
to the full-time foster parents)? What will happen when they feel they cannot
commit themselves in accordance with the agency's mission or the National

Foster Parents Association Code of Ethics? Can they really make the necessary commitment?

Mrs. Johnson knew that the Child Welfare League of America recommends that children should be with and grow up with their own parents if at all possible (Child Welfare League of America 2003b). Her husband did not always believe that; he assumed that once a parent has abused or neglected a child, her or she might do it again and therefore could not be allowed to continue raising the child. He did not realize that

> A primary goal of the foster care system is to reunite foster children with their biological parents. Keeping foster children connected to their biological parents, through visiting and other forms of contact, is essential for reunification because it helps to reestablish and maintain family ties during out-of-home placement. Parent-child contact can also increase the child's well-being while in care. Although foster parents are expected to help foster children stay connected to their biological parents, their actual involvement in this process remains problematic. (Sanchirico and Jablonka 2000:185)

Concerned about Mr. Johnson's level of commitment to the requirement of working with a child's birth parents, Mrs. Thomas asked them both to consider this difference in opinion as they gauged their commitment.

Implement the Plan

Mr. and Mrs. Johnson put the plan into play. During their usual weekend activities, they each thought about their ability to commit to providing the emotional resources of love and nurturance to an unknown child, or set of siblings, for a lifetime. Although fostering ends when the child is 18 years old (or 21 years old, or even older in fewer cases), the Johnsons contemplated what it would mean to follow the National Foster Parent Association Code of Ethics and make such an emotional commitment for a lifetime. They compiled a list of potential challenges that might make their commitment wane, including: repeated acting out by the youth that places their family members in danger; repeated acting out by the youth that puts the child him- or herself in danger; and challenging birth parents showing up unannounced or threatening their family or property.

Mrs. Johnson found a book chapter that addressed foster parent commitment. This chapter, entitled "The Role of Caregiver Commitment in Foster Care: Insights from the 'This Is My Baby Interview,'" helped them determine how strong their commitment was (Dozier, Grasso et al. 2007). They also reviewed other books and films that gave them insight into issues related to child welfare and foster care. They read *Three Little Words: A Memoir* by Ashley Rhodes-Courter, which chronicles her courage as a child in the face of first being removed from her home as a result of maltreatment and then experiencing further abuse by her foster family. The Johnsons also examined *Wounded Angels* by David Kagan and *A Child Called It* by David Pelzer, which familiarized them with further traumatic yet courageous stories about people who had survived child maltreatment. They viewed a documentary, *The Beat Down Club* (produced by the Freddie Mac Foundation), that showcases perspectives on foster care from individuals who were actually in the system. Finally, they watched *White Oleander* and *I Am Sam*, two films that address issues with child welfare and specifically with foster care. (For relative caregivers, two helpful books can provide more information about kinship care: *Relatives Raising Children: An Overview of Kinship Care*, edited by J. Crumbley and R. Little, and *Grandparents as Parents: A Survival Guide for Raising a Second Family*, by S. de Toledo and D. E. Brown.)

On Monday morning, the Johnsons met with agency personnel, including Mrs. Thomas, to further discuss their thoughts about commitment, which included their concerns about safety factors. Mrs. Thomas reviewed potential safety plans (plans set by the caregivers and practitioners to ensure a safe environment for the child) they could put in place with the help of their assigned worker. (Mrs. Thomas may or may not be the worker assigned to work with the Johnsons; the particular staff assigned to the case depends on the individual agency.) The examples of safety plans reassured the Johnsons that they would not be alone, and as a result, the Johnsons decided they had the fortitude to see fostering through with a solid commitment. Yet with this commitment they needed to review other components before their decision process would be complete.

Examine Existing Resources

Identify the Need

When considering fostering, potential foster parents and kinship caregivers must evaluate their resources and assess if they have enough to share with children placed in their home. Resources include social support, parenting skills, finances, physical space, and time. The Johnsons now faced the large task of examining these resources.

Analyze the Context

The first resource—social support—plays a key role in helping foster and kinship parents to feel like they made the right choice. Because fostering can be stressful, both emotional support and tangible support are important. What family members, both inside and outside of the home, are available to provide support to the foster parents, to help defuse feelings of frustration? Social support can come from family members' friends, neighbors, work colleagues, and clergy, among other individuals who are available as a sounding board to foster parents when they (the foster parents) want to share a joy, when their last nerve is frazzled, and when they need advice. It is helpful to gauge the extent to which relatives in the home can provide such support. In the case of kinship caregivers, discovering whether there are additional relatives to help them with child raising is important.

Another consideration for social support relates to the relationship between the foster parent/kinship caregiver and the agency practitioner. A positive relationship is vital; it is the charge of the practitioner to initiate such relationships, and both the practitioner and the foster parent must work to maintain them. Having negative relationships with professional child welfare agency staff, for example, can lead foster parents to consider quitting (Roger, Cummings, and Leschied 2006). Chapter 7 discusses the importance of collaboration in greater detail, but it is important that one of the practitioners patiently and effectively work with potential caregivers even through the initial decision-making process under discussion here.

Foster and kinship parents feel supported when they have family, friends, and neighbors who can provide tangible support both to them and to the youth in care. This support includes providing assistance with transporting children to appointments and extracurricular activities, tutoring, and, depending upon their circumstances, helping supply day care on days that the child(ren) are home from school. Occasional last-minute assistance with running errands and providing supervision may seem minor yet this is an extremely helpful component of social support.

The second resource to be examined is parenting skills. The full component of skills must be determined to be present before foster parents are certified or relative caregivers are approved. Five crucial skill areas are identified by the PRIDE model, a nationally recognized training program developed for potential foster parents. Potential caregivers must be competent in

1. Protecting and nurturing;
2. Meeting developmental needs and addressing developmental delays;
3. Supporting children's relationships with their [biological] parents;
4. Connecting children to safe and nurturing lifetime relationships;
5. Working as a member of a professional team.   (Leighton et al. 2003, as cited in Mallon and McCartt Hess 2005:668–669)

While all of these skills are essential, the first—"protecting and nurturing"—provides the bedrock that supports the rest; it therefore requires particular attention. This skill relates to the potential foster parents having "room in their heart"—this is otherwise known as "capacity." These individuals will need to have the capacity to love and care for the child placed with them—recall that it is precisely the difficulties that the children's biological parents had in showing them love or care that account for why the youth are in foster care or awaiting kinship care in the first place. Caregivers must have the patience and tenacity to cope with the myriad of details related to parenting children with damaged bonds and, perhaps, special needs.

Part of the decision-making process is for caregivers, with the assistance of practitioners, to be honest in this assessment; although it may not be easy, they must be ready to admit to themselves that they are not ready to become foster parents or relative caregivers, at least at the current time.

This also relates to foster parents' readiness to acquire skills that they may not have, or wish to possess, in order to foster children with particular needs. For example, if the family cannot deal with a child who has a history of verbally aggressive behavior (cursing, yelling) and they are not interested in developing/refining their parenting skills to work with a child with this behavior, then the foster parents may not want an adolescent or youth who demonstrates that behavior. However, if a family is willing to learn the skills necessary to handle children with behaviors they are unaccustomed to, then it is possible they can become that next resource family for such a child. No one individual possesses every skill necessary to work with every child—the point is for the individuals to be honest about their parenting skill levels. It is important to note that it is normal for foster parents to not always have all skills for all children; however, it is crucial to honestly identify their skill level. Stating they can foster when they do not have or wish to learn the necessary skills is a profound disservice to children and a waste of system resources that can be avoided. (This discussion is continued in chapter 2.) When the alternative is foster care, kinship caregivers may not feel like they have the luxury, or a choice, to refuse to raise a relative's child.

A third resource to consider is finances. While all foster parents receive a stipend for children's basic material needs, often this stipend is not enough and the foster parents pay for some items out of their own pocket. Additionally, foster parents, depending on the jurisdiction, may have to expend money at first and then be reimbursed sometime later. Therefore, a careful consideration of their budget—their family's monthly income and expenses—and a consultation with the practitioner on estimated additional expenses and the stipend will help with financial planning.

For example, usually when children come into foster care, they have few, if any, belongings. They may be delivered to the foster parents with only the clothes they are wearing, or an infant may be dressed in just a diaper (Rosenwald and Bronstein 2008). If they do have belongings, they are sometimes dragged behind the child in a plastic garbage bag. Therefore, foster parents may need to purchase some initial clothing for the child before being reimbursed by the agency. Aside from clothing, they may need to have the financial resources to pay for incidentals (toothbrush, etc.), toys, equipment, and activities above and beyond what the agency stipend will reimburse. Subsequently, having a reasonable amount of surplus money to devote to the care of the child is important. Kinship care providers do not always have the same financial support as foster parents, because states and counties vary on the existence, type, and amount of stipend provided to kinship caregivers in raising their relative children.

A fourth resource is physical space. Having adequate sleeping arrangements, living space, and efficient kitchen and bathrooms is important. Additionally, sufficient furniture (bed, desk/table, closet/wardrobe, and other items) is needed for the youth in care. Of course, attention to safety and sanitation is paramount as well. Part of the screening process for becoming foster parents includes a required safety check (which may be conducted by the fire company as well as the local health department). The appropriateness of relative caregivers' space will be examined as well by practitioners.

A final resource to consider is time. Childhood is brief; potential foster parents and relative caregivers should make sure they can "invest" in the development of the child throughout their childhood by making time to show their care. Time must be devoted to such core components as love, nurturing, and responsible discipline, and to practical matters such as transportation and attending activities. Practitioners can ensure that there is congruence between foster parents' goals for the child's life and the amount of time they have necessary to meet those goals. For example, foster parents who work more than full time may not have much time or energy to devote to a child in need. Therefore, potential foster parents must decide if they are ready to give up free time or time that cuts into what they currently do for their own children. Their sleep may be disrupted. Their social life may diminish. As with the arrival of a new baby, it is difficult to anticipate the impact a new child will have on the home and family; they should anticipate an increased need for time management. This time challenge is particularly relevant for relative caregivers, because often they have not deliberated as long as foster parents in making the decision to raise children at the present moment in their lives. It is necessity rather than choice that creates a new kinship care family.

Several tools exist to assist potential foster parents in assessing their decision to serve in this role. One is a psychometrically sound measure called the "Casey foster applicant inventory–applicant version" (http://www.fosterfamilyassessments.org/pages/takeassess/cfaiassess_index. htm). A second is the "Should I Become a Foster Parent?" series of questions included below in table 1.1. These and other instruments can provide important feedback to potential foster parents.

TABLE 1.1 Should I Become a Foster Parent?

YES:

1. I enjoy being around children.
2. I have the time and energy to devote to working through behavior problems of children.
3. I want to contribute to the life of a special needs child/youth.
4. I enjoy teamwork and working with other people.
5. I am naturally optimistic and embrace the many challenges of life.

NO:

1. I have a full-time job and other time-consuming commitments.
2. I have a job that will not allow me to occasionally miss work or phone calls because of the foster child's/youth's needs (e.g. school meetings, emergencies, medical appointments).
3. I am going through a major life change (e.g., divorce, marriage).
4. I prefer to work through problems alone and do not like others to suggest or ask too many questions.
5. I have difficulty coping with stress and excessive demands.
6. I am not ready or willing to experience the huge change in lifestyle or decrease in personal time that working with an abused or neglected child entails.

National Center for Children and Families (2003) as cited in Mallon & Hess (2005), p. 673

Develop the Plan

In developing their plan, the Johnsons already felt adequately prepared in regard to a number of the resources. While it was just the two of them and their dog in the home, they knew that their older children, along with two neighbors, supported them and had stated they would be willing to help as needed. For physical space, they had a spare bedroom as well as enough general living space (including a spacious yard) in their home for up to two children. Because they were a two-income family with adult children outside of the home who were financially independent, the Johnsons had sufficient funds to cover any items that the stipend did not cover.

However, their plan development still required them to assess the impact on their time. Mrs. Thomas had suggested they examine how their life would change in terms of time. These questions framed the process that would help Mr. and Mrs. Johnson evaluate what it would *really* mean to foster. They planned to sit down and write out their weekly schedule; once it was completed, they would review it and plug in all the times that a child would need attention.

With respect to the skills identified by the PRIDE model, they felt that theirs were already sufficient. Mrs. Johnson had a reservoir of patience in regard to scheduling appointments, transporting to appointments, helping with homework, reminding children of their expected behaviors, praising them, and showing love in other ways. Mr. Johnson was skilled at teaching children how to do everything from household chores to playing games. Additionally, he also was the one who had found it easier to follow through with consequences with the children they had already raised. On top of all that, he was a wonderful cook and specialized in "children's favorites" like pizza and making ice cream.

Mrs. Thomas asked the Johnsons to think about their potential ability to work with, not against, the birth family, for example, in coordinating rules and visits. This is one of the skillsets identified by the PRIDE model. Although Mrs. Johnson had no issue with this, Mr. Johnson was still hesitant about the idea of working with a child's birth parents. Therefore, he and Mrs. Johnson planned to take this training, based on Mrs. Thomas' recommendation, even though they had not fully committed yet.

Implement the Plan

The two items identified in their plan that the Johnsons needed to implement were assessing how their schedule would be impacted and waiting to attend the PRIDE training (once they were in the precertification process—see next section). For the first issue, as mentioned above, the Johnsons wrote down their typical weekly schedule. For brevity, we have taken an excerpt of Saturday, which appears in table 1.2.

When they were adding in activities that included a child, they decided for the sake of the exercise to pretend they would have a child or siblings between the ages of 6 and 10, in order to have "actual" examples for determining the amount of time and attention the child/children would need. The adjusted schedule is given in table 1.3.

TABLE 1.2 Tentative Schedule without Fostering

MORNING

- Wake up
- Make and eat breakfast/read the newspaper
- Bathe and get dressed
- Go to bowling or golf league

NOON

- Make and eat lunch
- Do housekeeping and gardening chores
- Visit with the neighbors
- Watch TV or work on hobby or home repair

EVENING

- Make and eat supper
- Go out to movies, sporting events or visit friends or relatives

TABLE 1.3 The Johnsons' Tentative Schedule with Fostering

MORNING

Wake up.

Help the child get going for the day.

Make and eat breakfast/read the newspaper while helping and talking with the child (*this would take longer*).

Bathe and get dressed.

Help or encourage the child to bathe and get dressed.

Take the child bowling or to dance or to an activity of their choice (*not covered by stipend*).

NOON

Make and eat lunch.

Help the child with lunch and clean-up.

Do housekeeping and gardening chores.

(*continued*)

TABLE 1.3 The Johnsons' Tentative Schedule with Fostering (*continued*)

Teach the child how to help the family with chores intermingled with playing with the child.

Visit with the neighbors.

Take the child to a friend's house or host a friend at our house.

Watch TV or work on a hobby (*there might not be time for this*) or work on home repair.

EVENING

Make and eat supper with the child or help with homework while cooking.

Coach the child on behavior issues.

Go out to movies or sporting events or visit friends or relatives with the child; or hire a sitter and go out without the child.

The Johnsons knew they would need to evaluate the accuracy of their proposed schedule. To do so, they showed it to an already certified foster parent, who suggested that they might need to transport the child to a visit or that the schedule could be disrupted when a child was sick. Additionally, the schedule would be evaluated when they started doing respite (providing other foster parents with a break from parenting by temporarily caring for those foster children), which they had decided might be a good way to try out foster care. After researching the amount of the stipend, they decided they had the time and money for the scheduled activities.

They signed up and looked forward to attending the PRIDE training.

Evaluate Motivation to Foster

Identify the Need

The Johnsons also needed to identify why they *really* wanted to foster. Assessing commitment addresses whether they wanted to foster, and they knew they did. But it was also important to focus on *why* they wanted to foster—that is, to assess their motivation. Identifying and evaluating motivations provides not only information but also "clues" that represent individuals' deeply held (and sometimes subconscious) values.

Analyze the Context

There are positive and negative reasons to foster. The most frequent motivations for becoming a foster parent are: "intrinsic, altruistic motivators of wanting to make a difference in children's lives and a desire to have children in the home" (MacGregor, Rodger et al. 2006:351). In one study, successful foster parents were motivated by wanting to be loving parents to children and saving children from harm (Roger, Cummings, and Leschied 2006). The negative reasons for fostering have more to do with the adult wanting to satisfy some inner narcissistic need. Fostering for the money is another self-fulfilling need that does not work out very well for the children. Wishing that someone had helped them when they were young and wanting children to keep them company are not sufficient motivations on their own.

This difference between positive and negative motivations centers, therefore, on whether the motivation is child-centered or self-oriented (Rhodes, Cox et al. 2006:105). It behooves potential foster parents to critically self-examine their motivations. Agencies need adults who have sufficient positive motivation to carry them through tough times. For example, children with special needs can make progress at a pace slower than others in their age group, which takes a strong motivation to work with. Therefore, it greatly behooves individuals to understand their underlying motivations to foster.

Develop the Plan

The Johnsons developed a plan—after they attended an information session for potential foster parents, they decided each would go away for a private weekend (apart from each other) and think about how they were raised and their motivations to foster. They would then compare lists with each other. The questions in table 1.4, suggested by Mrs. Thomas, provided them with much "food for thought."

TABLE 1.4 Questions to Assess Motivation to Foster

- How were they raised?
- What was their relationship to their parents/caregivers?
- Were they, themselves, in foster care or adopted?
- What values were instilled in them?
- Did they have compassion for a child they knew growing up?
- Did they feel guilty that they had a "good" upbringing or a "bad" upbringing and therefore wish they had been in foster care?
- If they reflect on their life, what is it about fostering that makes them want to go the extra mile? Is it for philanthropic reasons?
- Is the "empty nest syndrome" something driving them since they have time on their hands now?

Implement the Plan

The Johnsons did take some private time from each other to reflect on these questions. During their weekend, they each sat down and listed his or her motivations for fostering. When they returned from the weekend and met at home, at the top of their lists was giving back to the community. Mrs. Johnson was feeling the effects of the empty nest syndrome—now that her children were grown, she wanted children in her home again. Fostering could fill that void for her. Mr. Johnson desired to make his wife happy but knew that was not a strong enough reason to foster. He also recognized that when he was a child, he had felt sorry for the children in the family down the street. There seemed to be domestic violence in that home, and Mr. Johnson always had wished his family could take care of the other children so they did not suffer as much. Besides all this, Mr. Johnson enjoyed teaching children how to do things, seeing the wonder in their eyes, and laughing with them. Both Mr. and Mrs. Johnson knew that raising children also meant illnesses, temper tantrums, sleepless nights, and additional stress; but in their minds, the joys outweighed the pains. Their lists appear as table 1.5. On Monday after their weekend, they contacted Mrs. Thomas to share their thoughts on their motivations. Mrs. Thomas applauded their work. Together, they learned that they had mostly positive motivations to foster (e.g., giving back to community, making a difference, teaching).

However, Mrs. Thomas wanted to be thorough. She was still concerned about motivation, as she would be with any foster care candidates, and she

TABLE 1.5 The Johnsons' Lists	
Mrs. Johnson's lists	Mr. Johnson's list
1. Giving back to the community.	1. Give back to society
2. Empty nest syndrome—want children in the home.	2. Want to make wife happy.
3. Make a difference in a child's life.	3. Enjoy teaching children.

wanted to establish that the Johnsons were not trying to foster simply so they could look good in the community. Moreover, Mrs. Thomas wanted to make sure they could handle losing some independence, so she questioned them about her concerns. The Johnsons assured Mrs. Thomas that they saw fostering as a way to give back. They did recognize that "the empty nest syndrome" was what Mrs. Johnson was experiencing and that she wanted to give that time to a child or children in need. She clarified to herself and the others that it was about helping a child rather than filling up her time that served as her motivation. Additionally, Mr. Johnson recognized that he had come a long way since they had first considered foster care. He now understood the importance of working with birthparents when necessary. He attributed this to the education they'd received from Mrs. Thomas and to his wife's determination to "do the right thing" by giving their time and talents to children in need.

Additionally, even though they had not been through the foster parent training yet, Mrs. Thomas described some of the eventualities that could occur while they were caring for someone else's child. It can be difficult to work with someone who sexually abused a child, or beat a child, or chose to party with drugs over caring for the child. Even after all the stories that Mrs. Thomas shared and that the Johnsons heard from other foster parents, however, they still thought they had the motivation to work with the children and their parents because they were patient and caring people.

Understand the Precertification Process

Identify the Need

All potential foster parents need to complete a precertification process, which typically includes a home study, an information session, education and training, and a criminal history check, including fingerprinting. Potential kinship caregivers also undergo a screening process, but the parameters for such a screening widely vary: relative caregivers should consult with their caseworker for further details. (The National Resource Center for Family-Centered Practice and Permanency Planning provides some of states' requirements for kinship care—see the list of Web sites at the end of this chapter.)

Because the home study is the most comprehensive component of this process, we will place the most emphasis on it. After all the soul-searching and lists the Johnsons had made, Mrs. Thomas decided it was time for the Johnsons to be educated about the home-study process. This could help the couple gain a better understanding of the time involved, allowing both of them to do more research. For the Johnsons, they could gather information about procedures—it would be an exploration for both the Johnsons and Mrs. Thomas, as the agency representative, because the agency would also gain more information about the Johnsons. Mrs. Thomas had also conducted research about assessment tools used by practitioners to decide if potential families are ready to foster; she relied on the "Casey foster applicant inventory–applicant version (Orme, Cuddeback et al. 2007) (mentioned earlier) and a book entitled *Adoptive and Foster Parent Screening: A Professional Guide for Evaluations* (Dickerson and Allen 2007). Even though the home-study process could be a daunting undertaking, the Johnsons decided to proceed with whatever it was necessary to do to be able to foster.

Analyze the Context

The home-study process is an extensive series of interviews and other data collection that serves as the principal tool for potential foster parent assessment. Home-study requirements and processes vary from agency to agency. Table 1.6 provides a summary of some areas that applicants can expect to be part of the home-study process. As you can see, it covers information that ranges from physical and mental health history to financial stability and house safety. (The criminal history check can be included with the home-study process or can be separate.)

This process has changed over time as child welfare has evolved. Initially, "courts used adult probation departments to investigate families" to decide

TABLE 1.6 Components of the Home-Study Process

1. *Education.* Foster and kinship parents rule in an agency or rule it out. The agency does the same with the applicant.
2. *Interview.* This may take place in the home, possibly over two or three sessions.
3. *Home Visits.* Safety checks are an important part of this clearance process. Additionally, home visits help the worker gather information about the culture of your home as well as the neighborhood where you live.
4. *Health Statements.* These ensure that the foster and kinship parents are physically and mentally fit enough to attend to the needs of children who may be placed with their family.
5. *Criminal History Checks.* This process begins with taking fingerprints of potential foster or kinship parents and uses those fingerprints to check for a history of criminal activity.
6. *Income Statements.* Foster and kinship parents must show financial stability. Foster care stipends do not always cover the full cost of caring for another person.
7. *Autobiography.* This statement may include a photo album to be shown to the child and family of the child to be placed with the foster family.
8. *References.* These are a necessary part of the process to round out the information shared by the potential foster family. Some states require an in-person interview with references.
9. All of the above are written into a document that may be broken down into the following categories:
   a. Family Background
   b. Education/Employment
   c. Relationships
   d. A Typical Day
   e. Parenting Style and Skills

Source: Adapted from Bayless and Craig-Oldsen 2004 and "The Adoption Home Study Process" (http://www.childwelfare.gov/adoption/adoptive/homestudy.cfm).

if they were "fit to adopt" (Love and Velasco-Nunez 2004:222). Later, social service agencies were asked to perform this service and placement decisions were based more on "physical characteristics than matching the psychosocial needs of the child with the parenting capabilities" of the family (Love and Velasco-Nunez 2004:222). Because the home-study process can be the source of great anxiety, foster and kinship parents should be prepared to answer the questions in table 1.7, which are typical of a home study.

Foster parents may even have to assist the home-study worker in writing their own professional development plan. As in any work setting, the development plan is an agreement between you and the agency; it lists who will do what to assist you in developing the skills needed to do the job of fostering.

Although much focus is needed to address the home-study process, education and training form another essential part of the precertification process. These are an excellent way for potential foster parents to get to know the child welfare system and for the child welfare practitioners to get to know the potential foster parents. The National Resource Center for Family-Centered Practice and Permanency Planning has assembled a listing of state training requirements. It appears in table 1.8.

TABLE 1.7 Questions in the Home-Study Process

- How do you think having a child in your home will impact your social life and lifestyle in general?
- How do you think a child will impact how you express your emotions?
- How would chores be divided up in your family?
- Who do you turn to for help when having a crisis (financial, emotional, physical)?
- What does that person think about your fostering?
- What is your plan for child care after a child is placed with your family?
- How would the child be treated by your friends, relatives, neighbors?
- What experiences have you had with other races and cultures?
- What age range of youth have you experienced?
- What behaviors are you willing to address?

TABLE 1.8 State Training Requirements for Precertification of Foster Parents

REQUIRED HOURS	STATES
6 hours	Minnesota, Pennsylvania*
8 hours	Nevada
10 hours	Alaska*, Georgia (IMPACT), Idaho*, New Mexico
12 hours	California, Colorado*, Michigan (PRIDE), Mississippi (PATH)
14 hours	South Carolina
16 hours	Wyoming
18 hours	Hawaii, Montana
20 hours	Indiana (Fosterparentscope)
21 hours	Florida (GPS-MAPP)*, New Hampshire, Nebraska
24 hours	Maine, Massachusetts (MAPP), Ohio*
27 hours	Delaware (PRIDE), New Jersey, Illinois (PRIDE), Maryland, Missouri (STARS), North Dakota (PRIDE), Oklahoma (OK PRIDE)
30 hours	Alabama*, Arizona (PS MAPP)*, Arkansas*, District of Columbia (PS MAPP)*, Iowa (PS MAPP), Kentucky (GPS-MAPP), Louisiana (MAPP), North Carolina, Rhode Island*, South Dakota, Tennessee (PATH), Texas (PRIDE)*, Vermont, Washington*, West Virginia (PRIDE)
32 hours	Utah (CCBT)
45 hours	Connecticut (PRIDE)*
# of hours not specified	New York*
No preservice requirement	Oregon* (orientation, prior to or within 30 days of placement), Virginia, Wisconsin

*Exceptions and Explanations, by state:
* Alabama: 30 hours over 10 weeks of group preparation or 7 weeks of individual sessions if family cannot participate in a group.

(continued)

TABLE 1.8 State Training Requirements for Precertification of
Foster Parents (continued)

* Alaska: Requires 10 hours for a one-parent household, or 15 hours per household for a two-parent household.
* Arizona: Or 7 consultations using the PS Deciding Together program.
* Arkansas: CPR and First Aid training are required.
* Colorado: 12 hours plus CPR and First Aid. Additional 15 hours completed within 3 months of placement.
* Connecticut: 45 hours of training must be completed within the first 18 months of licensure.
* District of Columbia: All public and private agencies in the District of Columbia must use a federally recognized training modality, i.e., PRIDE or PS-MAPP.
* Florida: The Administrative Code standard is 21 hours, but also requires use of GPS-MAPP, which consists of 30 hours.
* Idaho: Not less than 10 hours of training no later than 1 year following the issuance of an initial foster care license.
* New York: Requires certain content areas, but not number of hours. Many counties and agencies use the Model Approach to Partnerships in Parenting/Group Preparation and Selection (MAPP/GPS) Precertification Training Program. Although it is not required by the Office of Children and Family Services, it is the recommended selection and preparation program.
* Ohio: A person seeking certification to operate a pre-adoptive infant foster home shall complete a minimum of 12 hours of preplacement training. A person seeking certification to operate a treatment foster home shall complete a minimum of 36 hours preplacement training.
* Oregon: Applicants and certified families must complete the Foundations of Relative Care, Foster Care, and Pre-Adoptive Care (Foundations) training, or have written documentation of completion of equivalent training content from another licensed child-caring agency within two years of an applicant,'s dated application for a Certificate of Approval from the Department.
* Pennsylvania: 6 hours minimum preservice orientation is required. Many counties require additional preservice training hours.
* Rhode Island: Requires 27 hours of preservice training for state foster parents. Some contracted child placing agencies require fewer hours of preservice but have mandatory training requirements after licensing. In order to insure that all of the agencies deliver the same basics in their training, State has developed core competencies, based on the CWLA core competencies, and the agencies have to demonstrate when/how the competency is delivered.
* Texas: DFPS's Residential Child Care Licensing (RCCL) division is responsible for licensing and monitoring child-placing agencies (both DFPS and private). It is the child-placing agencies that are responsible for verifying families. RCCL requirements are 8 hours of preservice training. DFPS requires 30 hours of PRIDE training for its homes.
* Washington: Also must complete first aid/CPR and blood-born pathogens course.

Source: http://www.hunter.cuny.edu/socwork/nrcfcpp/downloads/policy-issues/Foster_Parent_Preservice_Training.pdf.

Develop the Plan

The Johnsons planned to complete the paperwork for the home-study process and to continue with their precertification training. They knew it would take time and were looking forward to the process of telling their own stories. One concern they had, however, was that "skeletons in their closets" might be found. Mr. Johnson had an uncle that abused alcohol, while Mrs. Johnson had been sexually assaulted as a teenager. Mrs. Thomas assured them that based on how they had handled these challenges, those experiences could help develop skills that would help them foster children with similar challenges. Subsequently, she scheduled a screening appointment.

Implement the Plan

Implementing their plan included learning about and completing the home-study; the Johnsons enjoyed the process of talking with each other and Mrs. Thomas about their answers. At times, they needed assistance on how to interpret some of the questions on the written forms; Mrs. Thomas was happy to help them and asked that they examine the questions and realistically answer the questions based on fact rather than perception.

Additionally, they consented to criminal background checks and attended the PRIDE training in their state, which counted as the required education and training. (They had attended an information session several months ago.) After they completed the education and training, Mrs. Thomas checked in with Mr. Johnson on where he was with working with birth parents. (Mrs. Johnson was already on board.) The three discussed this issue at length. From the training, Mr. Johnson had learned that a parent's abuse or neglect of a child does not automatically lead to a termination of a parent's rights and that in fact much of the work when a child is in care is focused on family reunification as appropriate. As a result, he felt much more comfortable about working with birth parents because if family reunification was the goal, then the birth parents had been determined by practitioners to be "motivated"—and that was good enough for him. Mrs. Johnson was proud of her husband. Mrs. Thomas typed up the home-study and provided the Johnsons with a copy of it as well as an evaluation of the home-study, and the education and training. She followed up with another evaluation six months after the Johnsons began to foster their first set of siblings.

Summary

This chapter outlines issues that practitioners, foster parents, and kinship caregivers should assess when deciding to take the initial step toward advocacy by become a stable caregiver for children through fostering or kinship care. Foster and kinship parents must commit themselves and other resources to the goal of raising someone else's child. This is a monumental undertaking and one to be taken on with great seriousness. It is the responsibility of the practitioner to make sure that potential foster parents consider all the important factors, including assessing commitment, resource, and motivation and undergoing the precertification process. Practitioners can assist with the precertification process through information sessions, training, and the home-study process. Relative caregivers will also benefit from practitioners who are sensitive to the additional needs of these caregivers. Proper assessment and honest reflection go a long way in strengthening foster parent and relative caregiver retention and increasing placement stability.

This all illustrates that the decision to caregive is indeed the first step in advocating for children in care.

Discussion Questions

1. How would you handle a situation in which a married couple who were considering fostering disagreed with each other on their motivation? Would your answer be different if the married couple were grandparents considering raising their grandchild? Why or why not?
2. Describe the components of the home-study process and why it is an important assessment tool.
3. Five resources were discussed that contribute to foster parent readiness. Can individuals increase some of these more easily in preparation for the role? Are some more difficult? Why?
4. If potential foster parents or kinship caregivers are found not to have sufficient commitment, in what other ways might their talents be utilized and still make them feel good about their contributions?

Web Sites

- Child Welfare Information Gateway: http://www.childwelfare.gov
- Foster Care Support Network: http://www.impact-publications.com/category/general_info_fcsn
- Kinship Training: http://www.hunter.cuny.edu/socwork/nrcfcpp/dow loads/policy-isues/kinship_training.pdf
- National Child Abuse and Neglect Data System: www.ndacan.cornell.edu
- National Foster Parent Association: www.nfpainc.org
- National Resource Center for Family-Centered Practice and Permanency Planning: http://www.hunter.cuny.edu/socwork/nrcfcpp/

Knowing Limits

Finding the Right Match Between the Children in Care and the Foster Parents and Kinship Caregivers

Service is what life is all about.

—Marian Wright Edelman

Vignette

Mr. and Mrs. Ninan decided they wanted to become foster parents. They consulted with Mrs. DeMarco, a home finder. Although they knew there were many challenges ahead of them, they were excited as well. As part of their precertification training, they needed to determine what characteristics children might have whom they believed they could foster successfully. Mrs. Ninan had some nursing training; consequently, she was comfortable with most medical situations. Mr. Ninan, however, was not. He was an engineer by trade and although he was used to interacting with a variety of people, he was not comfortable with some of the messier parts of parenting (like toileting challenges such as bedwetting/enuresis or inappropriate defecation/encopresis) and medical emergencies that included things he found frightening, like convulsions. The agency for which they would serve as foster parents was required, by its accreditation, to supply training for the full variety of challenges the children might present after placement. Therefore, one of the concerns Mr. Ninan indicated was his level of discomfort with babies who were medically fragile.

Two more areas of concern existed for the Ninans. For one, they were not certain they knew how to handle children with severe developmental delays; subsequently, they did not include that as part of the profile of the child(ren) they desired to foster. Second, because they could not biologically have children themselves, it was difficult for them to understand why someone, other than a young teen, could give up a baby into foster care. For this reason, they stated that they would have difficulty partnering with the birth family. They thought they might have some anger toward the birth parents of a baby when they could not have their own babies. Mr. and Mrs. Ninan also knew it would be difficult to give children back after fostering them.

The Ninans thought they might be able to help a child who had attention challenges like attention deficit disorder, and believed they could help a child, regardless of gender, race, or sexual orientation, who had been sexually assaulted, but only if they had enough training to develop the skills needed for this type of challenge. With these initial thoughts in mind, they looked forward to exploring more information about the types of medical issues that are most common in children coming into foster care.

Key

Mr. and Mrs. Ninan: potential foster parents.
Jessica and Brendan: siblings in foster care.
Darrell: child in foster care.
Mrs. DeMarco: home finder.

As part of their precertification process, the Ninans and Mrs. DeMarco have questions to be answered and information to consider. Once individuals commit to serving as foster parents, they need to determine the types of children they feel comfortable in fostering (Rosenwald and Bronstein 2008). Preparing for advocacy includes foster parents articulating for themselves and their family the profile of the children they would want. This is based on both parents' particular demographic preferences (e.g., children's age/gender/race, developmental ability) and their desire and level of skill in parenting children with cognitive, medical, and mental health issues. Practitioners play a key role in assisting foster parents in this process because of their extensive study and practice.

The information presented in this chapter is also relevant to kinship caregivers. Although they may try to convince themselves that they "have" to take in a relative child as an alternative to foster care, it is of paramount importance that kinship caregivers understand their capacity to foster relative children with particular characteristics. Practitioners can help relative caregivers in their decision-making process, wherein they try to balance the obligation they feel to raise the child with the match between the child's needs/characteristics and the potential caregiver's capacity to raise that child.

Advocacy Checklist

- Determine type and level of fostering to provide.
- Self-assess fostering preferences.
- Identify comfort with fostering children with major medical needs.
- Identify comfort with fostering children with mental health needs.

Determine Type and Level of Fostering to Provide

Identify the Need

For potential foster parents, deciding what type of care and level of care they have the skills to provide care can be tricky. In our vignette, the Ninans are concerned about this and need more information. Mrs. DeMarco, their home finder (the person who places children with foster families), is concerned about making the right match between foster parents' strengths and children's needs. Together, they hoped to find the right children for the Ninans. The needs and strengths approach to fostering children is taken from the GPSII/MAPP ("group preparation and selection II/model approach to partnerships in parenting") training developed for foster parents (2003:34).

Analyze the Context

Respite and long-term foster care are two different types of fostering. Respite care is when the children in care stay with another family temporarily (for a day or two, or even a week or so) because the main foster family needs a break or cannot care for children temporarily. An example of this might be a family emergency that takes the foster parents away from caring for children. The biological children of the foster parents might go stay with aunts and uncles, but children in foster care may need to stay with a respite family. Respite is also a strategy for foster parents to try out caring for children with a variety of personalities and needs while providing a valuable service to other foster families. Within this same vein, respite can be a way for children to visit other families overnight and further try out other families in case of disruptions or emergencies where the children need to spend time away. The children can develop bonds with more adults than just those in their foster family, thus bringing more positive influences into their lives. Finally, respite supports collaboration because it allows respite parents the opportunity to meet other foster parents and often build lasting relationships, which become supportive and educational for both the adults and the children.

Respite can be contrasted to long-term fostering, which is divided into three levels by the amount of care required. The first level is the "entry level," which is the most common level for children coming into care. This is quite often handled by the least experienced foster parents or those wanting the "easiest" children to care for (if we can define any child as being easy to care for). The next higher level of care is called "specialized" or "special rate." This level is for children needing more than average care, such as specialized interventions and additional supervision. Examples at this level of care might be a child with developmental delays, a child who needs more supervision due to a history of running away, and/or a child who requires a very high-energy foster parent to raise him or her. The third level is most commonly called "therapeutic" or "treatment" foster care (TFC). This level is for those youth with significant mental health, cognitive, or medical challenges that require major supervision and intervention. Examples at this level include children with a history of fire starting or other physically aggressive behavior or children who have autism. The Foster Family–Based Treatment Association is the leading resource devoted to this level of care.

If foster parents elect to serve at a level of care requiring less of them than their skills could provide, then some children coming into care will be deprived of the opportunity to be placed with foster parents who could provide them with a wonderful home life, and the fostering system will suffer as well. If, on the other hand, foster parents select a level that is higher than their ability, they may not be able to care for children adequately and satisfy the children's needs; such children might then have to be moved from their home to another placement, which can cause them to trust less willingly, build emotional walls, or trust too quickly. Choosing the right level of care is considered advocacy because the right choice will provide what is best for the children involved.

Qualified foster parents are in high demand. According to the Child Welfare League of America (2008), in 2004, although there were some 513,000 children in care, only 153,000 licensed foster homes (including both relative and nonrelative) were available—a ratio of more than three children to one foster parent.[1] With such a high demand for foster parents, home finders (practitioners who secure foster placements) often ask foster and kinship parents to agree to foster children outside the profile they have completed; this is especially true for kinship parents, where the existing bond is so important.

Foster parents should not choose the level of care based on the amount of money paid—for again, ability is the most important factor when deciding on the foster care level. In some states, the cost/benefit analysis shows that more money can be saved when children are kept in stable placements. "Historically, foster parents have been reimbursed at low rates for the care they provide" and they have been expected to subsidize the funds used to care for children with their own money (Barbell and Freundlich 2005:508). Higher levels of care may (or may not) bring with them higher levels of money for foster parent stipends. However, some foster parents report that their stipend is not sufficient to compensate for their work (Brown and Calder 2002; Rosenwald and Bronstein 2008). For example, one foster parent is quoted as saying, "Look how much money you're making. Break that down. You make like less than two dollars an hour" (Rosenwald and Bronstein 2008:291).

We also know that when children come into care they often have mental and physical healthcare needs that have yet to be labeled or identified for treatment. Because these youth enter care at higher risk for developmental delays and medical problems, Mr. and Mrs. Ninan have been told, chances are that one out of every three children will have an undiagnosed problem. Indeed, Landsverk and Garland (1999) estimate that between one-half and two-thirds of the children coming into foster care are described as having behavioral or emotional problems in general. This need for mental health

---

1. Number of licensed foster homes based on 2004 data; number of children in care based on 2005 data (http://www.cwla.org/programs/fostercare/factsheet.htm).

treatment means foster parents and kinship parents must be prepared for the responsibilities that go along with caring for a child with such needs. (See chapter 6 for more information on children in care with mental health needs.)

It is much easier if the children with such mental health challenges come in already classified as "special needs/specialized." However, that can also mean the children have been in care long enough to have had to leave a foster home because of a failed placement. Therefore, it would seem that foster parents give up "one for the other"—either they have the opportunity to shape the child from the beginning or the child comes into care already classified, which then saves the foster parent much time and work in getting them classified. If foster parents find out the youth have special needs, it is difficult and time-consuming to gather the information needed to qualify children for higher levels of care payments and the services that come with that level of care.

Developing the Plan

Mrs. DeMarco believes the Ninans' strengths, their medical training, and their flexibility could be a good match for many children. Therefore, the Ninans are planning to build upon their strengths and state they could take on respite care of two children who are at either the entry level or the specialized level of placement. With this agency, the local Department of Social Services, the second level of placement is called a "special needs" placement. Although fostering at this level may be a stretch for the Ninans, Mrs. DeMarco encourages them to try. They decide to do some research into fostering children with special needs, with a specific emphasis on learning about children with challenges like bedwetting/enuresis and convulsions. They believed that it would be helpful both to consult an experienced pediatrician, a children's psychologist, and other foster parents, and to review research at the library/online.

Implementing the Plan

Mr. and Mrs. Ninan wanted to foster at the entry level of foster care first, to test out their abilities, and then try the second level of care later. They felt unprepared for teens and worked too much to care for an infant. Therefore, they decided to put in their profile that they wanted children age 5–11, with no restrictions on race and gender. Little did they know that eleven-year-olds can sound like teenagers and even have the habits of teenagers (e.g., they continuously talk on the telephone and experience mood swings). Mrs. DeMarco, their home finder, suggested they be open to fostering the next level of care, "special needs." Remember, this level is for children who have needs beyond what entry-level foster care can meet. Mr. and Mrs. Ninan thought it over and decide that they might be able to handle some children at this middle level of care—children with special needs.

Self-Assess Fostering Preferences

Identify the Need

The match between children in foster care and their foster parent(s) is critical (Ridding, Fried, and Britner 2000). You can have wonderful foster parents and a lovely child, but if there is no chemistry, the placement can fail. Because "foster parents play a pivotal role in the child welfare system," they possess the awesome power to make or break a placement (Rosenwald and Bronstein 2008:287). They make decisions about their comfort based on such variables as a child's gender, age, race, sexual orientation, and ability (both mental and physical). (Youth and their abilities are specifically discussed in later sections of this chapter.) For some foster parents, teens or babies are more or less desirable; others may be supportive of or uncomfortable with youth who are questioning their sexuality, or with fostering children of a different race.

As mentioned earlier, kinship caregivers typically do not have the luxury of leisurely reflecting on the type of child they would consider caring for—in fact, the majority likely would prefer not to raise a child at all if they had their choice. Yet because they want to prevent the youth from entering foster care with strangers, they often step up to care for the youth. Even in these situations, however, assessing their ability to raise children with certain characteristics is a worthwhile endeavor before they make the decision to commit to raising a child; the possibility that the placement will be disrupted later must be avoided.

Analyzing the Context

When our potential foster parents from the vignette, the Ninans, first met their home finder, Mrs. DeMarco, she suggested they be prepared to answer a number of questions about their "ideal child." These questions appear in table 2.1.

It is vital that foster parents are honest in their reflection and foster only youth to whom they can fully commit—children who do not feel like they fit in may exhibit behaviors reflecting their feelings of inadequacy. This can become problematic if the behaviors are unsafe, such as hitting and punching, cutting, and suicidal gestures. One study showed that "volatile placement histories contribute negatively to both internalizing and externalizing behavior of" children in foster care, and that those same children who "experience numerous changes in placement may be at particularly

---

TABLE 2.1 Questions for Gauging Interest/Comfort Level Regarding Diverse Children in Foster Case

Can you foster a child whose first language is one other than English?
How difficult would it be to help a child participate in a religion other than your own?
How comfortable are you with a child who is a different race than you?
Could you be supportive and helpful to a child who identifies as lesbian, gay, bisexual, transgender, or a child who is questioning (LGBTQ) his or her sexual orientation?
How will you help a child maintain connections with people from cultures similar to his or her own?
Could you help a child who faces a physical or mental challenge, such as being hearing-impaired or having separation anxiety?
Do you have strong feelings about fostering a boy or a girl?
How do you think having a new child placed with your family who has the above differences will impact your relationship with family and friends?

Source: Partially adapted from GPSII/MAPP (Love and Velasco-Nunez 2004).

high risk for" problematic behaviors (Newton, Litrownik, and Landsverk 2000:1295). Quinton, Rushton, Dance, and Mayes add:

> One of the most problematic groups of children in care—older children with disrupted pasts where return home is undesirable or has already failed and where placement with relatives is not possible or appropriate . . . these children's interests may be best served by permanent family placement with approved, alternative parents, through adoption or long-term fostering arrangements.   (1998:xi)

Another study provided data from foster parents, who discussed their "experiences and concerns about difficult-to-place children," including those youth who are lesbian, gay, and bisexual:

> Foster parents expressed a range of concerns about the placement of a lesbian, gay, or bisexual (LGB) child in their home and tended to hold homophobic beliefs about the population in general. Analysis of the focus group data found that this group of foster parents had significant fears about the placement of a child who was LGB in their home.   (Clements and Rosenwald 2006:57).

The above example, therefore, suggests that a well-versed practitioner serving as a home finder should initiate the discussion with potential foster parents about the types of children they would feel comfortable fostering.

Developing the Plan

In order to construct a plan to assess the type of child that would be the best match, foster parents, with the assistance of practitioners, should begin a deliberate and honest self-examination of their interest and comfort levels with various types of children. To complete the profile of the "future" child that they might foster, Mr. and Mrs. Ninan asked if they could meet more foster parents to discuss some of the children who had been referred to their foster care program. During the Group Preparation and Selection/ Model Approach to Partnerships in Parenting (GPSII/MAPP) training they would also be introduced to similar challenges raised by children coming into foster care (Love and Velasco-Nunez 2004). Such training better meets the needs of foster and kinship parents. Studies demonstrate that "foster children fare better when their foster parents have received training" (Czerwinskyj 2003:23). Preparation programs for adoption, foster parents, and kinship parents helps the adults to develop better insight into the reasons for children's actions. They can then decide about the children and behaviors they can come to accept (Schein 1984).

Between the two—talking to foster parents and hearing about children during the certification training—Mr. and Mrs. Ninan hoped to learn more about the issues and needs that children bring with them; from that they would figure out their own requirements for helping a child placed with their family. They decided to take as much training as possible to broaden their abilities to care for children who need fostering. They wanted to know more about ages that they had no experience fostering, so they could at least provide respite. The Ninans also wanted to learn about other races so they could help children maintain ties to their own culture. Moreover, they believed that if they had children placed with them that had a challenge for which no training is offered, such as those who identified as lesbian or gay, they would advocate to receive training to meet their needs.

Implementing the Plan

Implementing their plan meant first having a full discussion with each other before they talked with Mrs. DeMarco about their comfort and preferences. We already reported on their decision about age range (5–11 years old, mentioned in the previous section). Thinking about gender, the Ninans liked the idea of fostering both boys and girls and were comfortable with both; they were open to having children of either gender placed with them. Additionally, the Ninans learned that the majority of children in care are African-American and Latino (http://www.acf.hhs.gov/programs/cb/pubs/cw005/chapters/chapter1.htm). Because the Ninans were also part of a racial minority group, they thought they would do a fine job of fostering someone struggling with feeling like an "outsider," even though they knew that if they fostered a child who was African-American (they were Indian-American), they would need to be able to expose the child to African-American culture. Could they foster a child who identified as gay or lesbian or transgender? The Ninans had no qualms about fostering these children. While the Ninans were largely open, this is by no means the case with all foster parents.

Mrs. DeMarco approached the Ninans with a request for them to provide respite services for siblings Jessica, age 12, and Brendan, age 10. She asked the Ninans to get to know them through respite and consider fostering them on a long-term basis. Bed-wetting, asthma, and anger were just a few of the challenges that awaited the family who took in these children. While the children, on paper, were not 100 percent what they had hoped for (Jessica was 12 years old), they were more or less comfortable with the descriptions of Jessica and Brendan, and so the Ninans decided to get more information by meeting the children. They realized that a gap would always exist between the ideal characteristics and reality.

The Ninans learned that both youth also experienced health and behavioral challenges. For example, Jessica startled easily and wet the bed. Brendan had asthma and got into fights easily. Mr. and Mrs. Ninan had little experience with such issues. Additionally, they learned that Jessica and Brendan's mother had been diagnosed with depression.

The Ninans decided to serve as respite parents to see how they could manage the health and mental health challenges of these youth. While they were determined to persevere with the children, they knew they needed to understand more about these issues.

It is to these last two areas that we now turn.

Identify Comfort with Fostering Children with Major Medical Needs

Identify the Need

When Jessica and Brendan came for respite, Jessica felt embarrassed about wetting the bed, even though she really could not help it. She watched how much she drank in the evening, and the doctors determined there was nothing wrong with her physically. The Ninans understood that some youth struggled with bed-wetting even into their older youth years, but they wanted more information (even after having met with the pediatrician) about how to help Jessica break the habit, if possible. Bed-wetting (enuresis) and asthma are common enough problems that there was some research available to meet Mr. and Mrs. Ninan's need for information.

Analyze the Context

The percentage of all children in care who have had a chronic health condition is 27 percent (ACF/HHS: http://www.acf.hhs.gov/programs/opre/abuse_neglect/nscaw/reports/special_health/special_health.html#fig1).
Table 2.2 provides a checklist of some of the most common medical issues to be considered that may be present, although often undetected, when children come into care. These medical conditions can also include cognitive and developmental challenges.

Foster and kinship parents must ask themselves tough questions. These medical conditions can impact the children's emotional growth and development. For example, children with juvenile diabetes are sometimes less mature than their counterparts (and this difference can manifest in how they get along or do not get along with their peers) well into adulthood. Children with other medical conditions sometimes grow up faster than

TABLE 2.2 Medical Issues That May Appear Among Youth in Care	
Asthma	Hydrocephalus (enlarged skull with
Bed-wetting	atrophy of the brain)
Blood disorders	Kidney disease
Brittle bones	Microcephaly (small head)
Cancers	Multiple sclerosis
Cerebral palsy	Muscular dystrophy
Cleft palate	Nutritional deficiency
Club foot	Rheumatoid arthritis (juvenile)
Diabetes	Shaken Infant Syndrome
Down Syndrome	Sickle cell anemia
Epilepsy	Spina bifida (bones of the spine do not
Fetal Alcohol Syndrome	form correctly around the spinal
Hearing loss/deafness	cord)
Heart murmur	Visual disturbances
HIV/AIDS	

Note: See AFCARS (Adoption and Foster Care Analysis and Reporting System) for a complete listing of childhood illnesses to consider. This listing can be found at http://www.acf.hhs.gov/programs/cb/systems/specneeds.htm.

their peers in that they have to be responsible for self-care. Some medical conditions limit children's abilities to play with other children, and thus lead them to spend more time with adults. For example, it is common for children who wet the bed to stay home instead of participating in sleepovers with other children. When children spend more time with adults, they begin to talk and act more like an adult than a child. Children who sound grown-up may be treated like a grownup before they are ready for grown-up decisions or interactions—those who have been responsible for siblings sometimes fall into this category. It is then often difficult for the child to be trained to let adults worry about adult decisions and for the child to simply focus on children's issues (playing, creating healthy peer relationships). Children at higher levels of care are in this category because they need more attention than the average child. This can include children with extraordinary medical situations that take more time to attend to. Further, children with medical issues will require more transportation to doctor's appointments, more time attending to their physical ailments, and lots of help to feel "normal."

From an ethical perspective, practitioners should help foster parents determine the number of resources that should be invested in children in foster care who have special medical needs. For some parents, this is an agonizing question. Some people lose their homes by seeking the best specialists and treatments. For children in care, the medical bills are covered by the government or agency. Therefore practitioners' careful assessment of a youth's medical needs is a strong factor in the level of care in which that child is placed. On a related note, children with major medical challenges who may be terminally ill need to have their religious practices respected when it comes to medical treatment. Training for practitioners, as well as foster parents and kinship caregivers, is an important consideration here.

Develop the Plan

Mr. and Mrs. Ninan need more information to determine if they can commit to fostering children long-term who have medical needs (such as Jessica with her enuresis). They have some understanding of typical developmental issues for children, but Mr. Ninan has neither Mrs. Ninan's medical knowledge nor her comfort level with medical illnesses. Mrs. Ninan can certainly benefit from her medical training, although she has not had to care for someone all day and night, every day. Mrs. DeMarco suggested they try providing respite for other foster families who have children with more significant medical needs to provide them with insight.

Implement the Plan

This Ninans continued to serve as respite parents for Jessica and Brendan and decided to serve as a respite parent for one more child—eight-year-old Darrell, a precocious youth who had juvenile diabetes. The Ninans worked with Mrs. DeMarco in learning about juvenile diabetes, as well as enuresis and asthma.

They learned that enuresis remained the most challenging of the three medical issues because of both the practical housekeeping issues involved and the psychological impact it was having on Jessica. Some of the information they found out about bed wetting/enuresis indicated that "bed-wetting is not a mental or behavior problem. It doesn't happen because the child is too lazy to get out of bed to go to the bathroom" (Familydoctor.org). Mr. Ninan was feeling impatient with Jessica before he read this information from the Family Doctor Web site. Once he had a better understanding of bedwetting, he felt more patient and more inclined to assist Jessica in whatever way he could. The Ninans even tried a moisture alarm on the bed Jessica slept in—this alarm seemed to be helpful.

They also learned that helping Darrell with his juvenile diabetes care and ensuring that Brendan had his inhaler were not that demanding. When they saw the satisfaction on the faces of all three children, they knew that their concerns were small compared to the joy they received. They decided to continue to serve as respite parents for youth with somewhat major medical issues. Darrell returned to his foster parents after two weeks.

Identify Comfort with Fostering Children with Mental Health Needs

Identify the Need

The Ninans were still considering whether they wanted to provide only respite for Jessica and Brendan or make the move toward serving as the siblings' foster care placement until a permanency plan could be developed. They were not sure they were prepared to foster youth with the mental health needs these two children demonstrated.

Jessica complained that she frequently felt sad and had bad dreams. She wanted to stay happy when she was happy, and wanted the dreams to go away. Additionally, Jessica wanted to visit her mother, but did not want to have the visits in their home (although she could not articulate why). Mrs. DeMarco suspected it was due to the abuse that had occurred in the home, and that visits reminded Jessica of the abuse. Of course, this bothered Jessica and Brendan's mother.

Additionally, Mr. and Mrs. Ninan thought it was odd that Jessica did not want to talk about her future. In fact, Jessica stated she did not expect to have a career, have a family, or live as long as most people live. Finally, they noticed that Jessica seemed "jumpy"—she startled quite easily. Taking all of their concerns into consideration, Mr. and Mrs. Ninan consulted with Jessica's pediatrician to gather more information. The pediatrician discovered that Jessica no longer desired to play with the toys she had played with before she came into foster care, and referred the Ninans and Jessica to a child psychiatrist for both a full assessment and education.

Analyze the Context

In determining which mental health professional to consult, foster parents and practitioners have a range of options. Differentiating between them is necessary to provide further direction. The difference between counselors, social workers, doctors, psychologists, and psychiatrists are outlined in table 2.3.

It is important to know that "child maltreatment is a significant risk factor for adult mental disorders and physical illnesses" (Kessler, Pecora et al. 2008:625). Jessica's social worker suspected she was suffering with posttraumatic stress disorder (PTSD). PTSD is very common in children in care and the symptoms can look like other psychiatric disorders. According to the *Diagnostic and Statistical Manual* (DSM IV-TR), PTSD is:

the development of characteristic symptoms following exposure to an extreme traumatic stressor involving direct personal experience of an

TABLE 2.3 Guide to Professionals Who Commonly Treat Mental Health Issues*

Counselors: any professional who provides psychotherapy. They are typically graduate-level trained mental health professionals, but the category can likewise include volunteers with a minimum amount of training.

Psychiatrists: physicians who specialize in treatment of mental disorders. They can prescribe medications.

Psychologists: typically have graduate-level training and provide therapy, counseling, and testing of personality, intelligence, emotions, etc. They usually cannot prescribe medication.

Social workers: graduates of schools of social work. They may earn Bachelor,'s, Master,'s, and/or Doctoral degrees in the field. Social workers use their knowledge to provide a range of mental health and social service interventions by working to increase their clients,' capacities for problem solving and coping within their environment.

*Other professionals are pediatricians, psychiatric nurses, and physician assistants.
Source: Summarized from Barker 1996:83, 301, 302, 358.

event that involves actual or threatened death or serious injury, or other threat to one's physical integrity; or witnessing an event that involves death, injury, or a threat to the physical integrity of another person; or learning about unexpected or violent death, serious harm, or threat of death or injury experienced by a family member or other close associate. (pp. 463–467)

PTSD can "look like" generalized anxiety disorder (GAD), attention deficit hyperactivity disorder (ADHD), or attention deficit disorder (ADD). One study found that children in foster care are more likely to be treated for ADHD or ADD than the general population of children not in foster care (Zito, Safer et al. 2008).

When determining if a child's maladaptive behavior is normal or not, it is important to take into consideration what the child has experienced in his or her prior environment(s). Generally, it is quite traumatic for children to be taken from their family. Further, we may not know the birth family history of mental illness—a youth may have a family history of bipolar illness or depression and not know it. If the youth shows symptoms of depression, anxiety, and/or PTSD, these can be very difficult to sort through and treat properly. Subsequently, it takes an extensive period of time for the foster family to be able to help the youth through their challenges; for example, coaching the youth before trips that are anxiety provoking, although necessary, can be time-consuming. Kinship caregivers will likely have an advantage over foster parents in this area because often they are aware of a family history of mental health challenges (just as they would typically have more knowledge of family medical history).

Having reviewed information on mental health challenges for some youth in care, what are foster parents' interests in taking in these youth? The majority of foster parents are willing to take children with a range of mental health and behavioral challenges, although those who set fires, exhibit other destructive behavior, or act out sexually are often the least acceptable (Cox, Orme, and Rhodes 2003).

During one of our interviews with an experienced foster mother, the foster mother was asked to review a list of mental health issues and identify which mental health challenges she thought she could live with and which ones she could not. The foster mother told the author it did not matter what the label was or what the diagnosis meant—what was important was the type of emotional bond between the child and the foster family. The child could have one of the most difficult mental health challenges and still be a good fit for the family. Therefore, the context of the behavior was more important than the label. This foster mother and her family found, over time, that they could not ethically deny caring for a child they fell in love with. Indeed, they entered the world of foster care to make a difference in the life of a child and this mattered more than any particular "diagnosis" (pers. comm., Lynne Masland, Sept. 8, 2008).

We might agree that children need mental health services, but getting those services can be difficult, even impossible, without the proper advocacy:

> Despite the importance these child welfare professionals attribute to the mental health needs of foster children, and the burgeoning acknowledgment of the impact of trauma on abused and neglected foster children, access to mental health services has remained elusive.   (Collado and Levine 2007:134)

Therefore, for foster parents like the Ninans, advocating for the youth in their care would require a further level of advocacy as they consider whether they can seriously commit to foster children with mental and cognitive needs. Only they, with the practitioners' assistance, can decide which mental health challenges in youth they believe they can manage. (For an extensive listing of mental health needs of children in foster care, see chapter 6.)

Develop the Plan

Mr. and Mrs. Ninan decided to learn as much as they could (so they could advocate effectively for Jessica and Brendan) and therefore planned to seek the advice of other foster parents by joining their local chapter of the National Foster Parent Association. In response, the other foster parents suggested the Ninans document their observations of Jessica's behavior, as the psychiatrist had. In the meantime, they decided to start identifying a list of behaviors of concern, ranging from nightmares to her having unusual experiences and sharing them (e.g., telling respite and foster parents she did not want to have visits at home).

Kinship care providers and the practitioners that work with them can connect with resources and consult with other kinship care providers and the professionals that advocate for them in the particular state in which they reside. The following Web site details this information: http://www.grand-factsheets.org/state_fact_sheets.cfm. The resource is a collaborative effort between six organizations: the American Association of Retired Persons, the Brookdale Foundation Group, Casey Family Programs, the Child Welfare League of America, the Children's Defense Fund, and Generations United.

Foster parents like the Ninans can advocate for children (Jessica and Brendan) because they have spent so much of the time with the children. They have the knowledge and the firsthand observations that others (including practitioners) lack by not having experienced the children's behaviors directly. In cases like these, where foster parents need to advocate with mental health professionals, one foster parent recommends:

List symptoms and behaviors and learn about whatever the disorder is. . . . Letters with [clear] facts on where the behaviors are seen, work better than a long, rambling letter or email. Is it just happening at home or is it happening at home, in school, and in the community? [The letter) needs to be short and clear—look at your developmental guide and make the list with that in mind.   (Masland, pers. comm., Sept. 8, 2008)

The practitioner can help to advocate by assisting the foster parents with such a letter and possibly clarifying the wording. Practitioners can also advocate by meeting with the psychiatrist and psychologist during their regular agency consultations. The above method of documenting observations can be quite helpful to a practitioner during the assessment and diagnosis phase of treatment.

Implement the Plan

After collecting this information, and after much thought and reflection, the Ninans decided they could foster children with some mental health issues, but not the more severe medical challenges (e.g., spina bifida). While the Ninans provided respite for Jessica and Brendan, Mrs. Ninan started by listing Jessica's behaviors of concern (for brevity we have examined only Jessica's needs here). They put them all in a letter to the psychiatrist before actually scheduling a consultation. Below is a summary of their concerns about her mental health:

Agitation
Angry outbursts
Easily startled
Lack of desire to return home (though wants to visit mother)
Nightmares
Pessimism about living a long life
Sadness
Traumatic experience of being taken from her birth family

In addition, the Ninans gained a great amount of knowledge from the Foster Parent Association. They took their observations to the treatment team, which was a great way to advocate for Jessica to receive additional services (see chapter 7 for more information on treatment/multidisciplinary teams). The foster parents encouraged the Ninans to pursue seeing the child psychiatrist and going prepared with their letter listing their observations.

Once Mr. and Mrs. Ninan had met with the treatment/multidisciplinary team and presented their concerns about Jessica, the team supported the foster parents' recommendation to attend a consultation with the child psychiatrist. Their recommendation, along with the medical doctor's recommendation, encouraged the Ninans in thinking they were on the right path. To summarize, the Ninans:

1. Consulted with a medical doctor, who recommended they see a child psychologist and/or a child psychiatrist;
2. Attended an appointment with a child psychologist, who encouraged them to document the behaviors they observed, including what had happened directly before the behaviors (the antecedent) and what happened directly after the behavior (the consequence);
3. Met other foster parents at the Foster Parent Association, who suggested they write a bulleted letter with all their observations of concern, not just the ones the doctors suggested they document;
4. Wrote the letter, listing the specific issues;
5. Delivered the letter to the agency child psychiatrist, who examined the letter and met with both the Ninans and Jessica.

The psychiatrist completed a comprehensive evaluation of Jessica. While some of her feelings and behavior fell within the "typical range," her other symptoms were diagnosed as posttraumatic stress disorder (PTSD). The psychiatrist recommended play therapy as a way for Jessica to deal with her feelings, including her fears on entering foster care and not living with her mother. In the end, the Ninans decided they wanted to move beyond serving in a respite capacity and foster Jessica and Brendan in their home until a permanency plan could be put in place.

Summary

With so many diverse children in foster care and kinship care who experience a range of major medical and mental health needs, foster parents will likely be asked to foster children with varying demographic characteristics as well as medical and mental health challenges. These needs may fall within a range of higher levels of care (e.g., needing a higher level of supervision, coaching, or medical interventions), and foster parents, with practitioners' assistance, need to determine the type and level of care they can and wish to provide. This chapter has presented resources for potential and current foster parents and kinship caregivers who care for children with many challenges and the process of deciding to foster children with those challenges (or not). Such resources include their home finder, other foster parents (including the local foster parent association), pediatricians, social workers, and other mental health professionals.

Discussion Questions

1. What information would you need to decide about which child(ren) to whom you could provide foster or kinship care with respect to their: Demographic characteristics? Mental health issues? Medical issues?
2. Make two lists of children's characteristics that you think would be, respectively, easier for a caregiver and more challenging for a caregiver. What is the rationale behind your lists?
3. What is the role of the practitioner with respect to assisting the Ninans, the couple from the vignette, in their decision? To what extent should a practitioner's assessment of the foster parents' abilities influence the foster parents' decision to foster children with particular characteristics?
4. Let's say the Ninans, the couple in the vignette, really disagreed in regard to the types of children they wanted to foster. One was more ready to be a therapeutic foster parent, while the other wanted to be an entry-level foster parent. Who should prevail? Why?

Web Sites

- American Academy of Family Physicians: Familydoctor.org
- American Academy of Pediatrics: www.aap.org
- Children's Aid Society: www.ChildrensAidSociety.org
- Children's Bureau, Administration for Children and Families, and the Department of Health and Human Services: www.adoptUSkids.org
- Foster Family–Based Treatment Association: www.ffta.org
- National Foster Parent Association: www.nfpainc.org
- National Kidney Foundation, definitions for kids: www.kidney.org/patients/bw/BWkidsglossary.cfm

- Nemours Foundation: http://kidshealth.org/kid/health_problems/bladder/enuresis.html
- North American Council on Adoptable Children: www.nacac.org
- State Fact Sheets for Grandparents and Other Relatives Raising Children: http://www.grandfactsheets.org/state_fact_sheets.cfm

[Part II]

Advocacy with Service Providers

[3]

Advocating Within the Social Services System

Many are attracted to social service—the rewards are immediate, the gratification quick. But if we have social justice, we won't need social service.

—Julian Bond

Vignette

Shanika, Angelina, and Tanya lived with their mother, Mrs. Brown, who was addicted to heroin, and who had conceived the girls by three different men. Child Protective Service (CPS) workers were contacted by school officials when a teacher found the children sleeping in a nearby park one night. Angelina had handprint-shaped bruises on her arm while Tanya had what looked like cigarette burns on her abdomen. The workers found the children to be in imminent danger, and therefore took them immediately into care. The Family Court ordered that the children be placed in foster care (all in the same family, if possible), and required rehabilitation and parenting classes for Mrs. Brown; she entered the rehabilitation facility and successfully transferred into a halfway house.

Unfortunately, the three sisters could not stay together in foster care. Shanika (age 11), who was African-American, was placed with the Loeffler family in an upper middle-class, all-white neighborhood in a suburban section just outside of the city where they had been found. Angelina (age 6) and Tanya (age 5) were placed in a same-race home with Mrs. Wheeler, an African-American woman who lived in the middle-class school district where the children had lived before they entered placement.

Unsurprisingly, the children cried when they were separated into two different homes. They immediately asked when they would see each other again. Mrs. Lewis, the case manager from the county social service unit, knew that the court had ordered supervised visits with the mother and her children. She knew it would be difficult for the foster families to coordinate their schedules with Mrs. Brown's schedule so that everyone could visit together. Ms. Michie, the social worker from the contract agency, advocated for joint visits. Mrs. Brown attended visits sporadically and sometimes planned activities for the children in advance of their visits. As the visits progressed, they were expanded to include Mrs. Brown's mother, Ms. Barrett, on a monthly basis. Ms. Barrett showed fantastic skills in handling all the children together and the three siblings looked to their grandmother with adoration and respect. Unfortunately, their mother, Mrs. Brown, relapsed and disappeared onto the streets, thus changing the permanency goal from "return to parent" to "return to grandmother."

Key

Shanika, Angelina, and Tanya: siblings brought into foster care.
Mrs. Brown: the children's mother.
The Loefflers: Shanika's foster family.
Mrs. Wheeler: Angelina and Tanya's foster mother.
Mrs. Lewis: county case manager.
Ms. Michie: contract agency social worker.
Ms. Barrett: Mrs. Brown's mother, and grandmother to the children.

The adults in our vignette need to consider the children's best interests and how to advocate for them. This chapter describes areas in which practitioners as well as caregivers can develop advocacy skills with social service agency staff (e.g., social workers, caseworkers, parent aides). Also discussed are the various groups the staff might enlist for the welfare of the children in care (e.g., parents and other family members, extended family support systems, and mentors), with strategies for intervention. Finally, the importance of collaboration and documentation is highlighted.

Advocacy Checklist

- Partner for advocacy.
- Understand the different roles and authority of social services staff.
- Identify the supervision "chain of command."
- Advocate for material needs.

Partner for Advocacy

Identify the Need

For foster parents, kinship caregivers and practitioners, partnering with teammates can help increase their knowledge about social services and the agencies providing services for the children in their care. The agency awarded custody by the Family Court is the "custody agent"; its title varies by jurisdiction, but it is sometimes referred to as the Department of Social Services (DSS), as Health and Human Services (HHS), or as the Department of Children and Families (DCF), among other possibilities. Depending again on jurisdiction, it may be at the city, county, or state level in most regions.

This was the second placement of children in her care for Mrs. Wheeler, Angelina and Tanya's foster mother. Over this earlier period, Mrs. Wheeler had noticed that some of the foster parents she most admired had built relationships with their team of workers, who then supported their advocacy. She decided that she wanted to learn how to advocate better with the Department of Social Services, including Mrs. Lewis, and needed to learn more about the agency and the case manager for the children now placed with her. The girls were used to having Mrs. Lewis as their case manager because she was the one adult who had been consistently involved in their lives throughout their placement process and even before, during the Child Protective Service (CPS) investigative stage.

This need to partner had been highlighted in regard to a meeting planned recently to discuss the three girls' permanency plans. Mrs. Wheeler became quite irritated when she realized who was *not* invited for the up-coming DSS meeting. It turned out that DSS decided to have a meeting about the family to discuss the family's progress and set goals relating to visitation and a permanent plan. Although Mrs. Wheeler and the Loef-flers (Shanika's foster parents) were invited, neither Ms. Barrett, the grand-mother, nor any of the children was invited. When Mrs. Wheeler discov-ered that the family members were not to be invited, she was upset and spoke with her worker, Ms. Michie, who agreed that the family should be part of the meeting. Together they decided to advocate for family members, so that they would included in decision making directly related to the goals to be set for them. (Additional information on advocating within an agency is the focus of chapter 8.)

Analyze the Context

At times, a deeply adversarial divide can grow between the custody agent and an agency that works with the child(ren). This can also be true for care-givers and practitioners.

The context of social services includes competing interests and conflicts that can impede advocacy efforts. Having agencies partner with each other helps produce environments in which children can flourish, but unresolved conflict between the agencies can be detrimental (see Rosenwald and Bron-stein 2008). Mrs. Wheeler understood the need for children to thrive and prosper but believed that the friction between the two agencies could spill over into the creation of a noncoordinated permanency plan and ultimately affect the three girls. What Mrs. Wheeler could not understand was why the agency for which she served as a foster parent and the Department of Social Services (DSS) for Children and Families seemed to have competing values—in this case, regarding the priority of including the birth family for consultation. Her agency believed in asking the parents (kinship, birth, and foster parents) to be involved about goals and treatment plans, and regularly followed this as a protocol to help the family grow and plan for themselves. By contrast, DSS seemed to ignore the relatives' desires and input. DSS workers would discuss their goals for the family members and then tell the family what they thought their goals ought to be. This often left the parents at odds with the department, and the children felt caught in the middle.

Partnering with our teammates is great role modeling for our children—and it also builds trust and efficiency. A comprehensive book on building professional relationships is *First Among Equals* by Patrick McKenna and David Maister (2002). McKenna and Maister address the importance of becoming inspirational, influencing people to accept your guidance, and working in diverse ways based on individuals' needs. They also discuss juggling relentless demands while serving as a group leader among teammates, interacting with "annoying professionals" with "attitude" problems, and attending group meetings that lack purpose. (See more on collaboration with interdisciplinary team members in chapter 7.) This is the context of professional interaction and partnering in the social service system, which can have similar dynamics.

They discuss the important set of perceptions and interpersonal skills listed in table 3.1 (adapted from McKenna and Maister 2002). By drawing on this foundation, relationships can be built to improve agencies' relationships—and, by extension, those of practitioners' and caregivers,'—by partnering with one another.

TABLE 3.1 Important Perceptions and Skills in Relationships

Be *truly* interested in the person's life. For example, if they tell you about something significant in their life, make a note and follow up.

Deal with your colleagues with the same sort of delicacy and phraseology you would use in working with your most important clients.

Fuel interactions by active and regular communication.

Drop in regularly to talk with your team mate/colleagues, but not at their busiest times.

Spend time talking about non—work-related items.

Go out for tea or a meal together.

Give of yourself.

Be sensitive to the fact that people will observe your first few unscheduled or non—work-related visits with skepticism.

Understand your colleague's style. There are several good books available related to personality style. For instance, recognize that some people are philosophers, some doers, some are expressive, some just want to get along, etc.

Don't let first impressions take over your thinking. Continue to absorb new information about each person's style.

Develop the Plan

Mrs. Wheeler and Ms. Michie planned to speak with Mrs. Lewis, the case manager in DSS, about having the meeting include the grandmother, Ms. Barrett, and the children to an extent. They thought they might be able to convince Mrs. Lewis, but they were not sure she had the authority to decide about the attendees. Therefore, they planned to speak with Mrs. Lewis first and then Mrs. Lewis' supervisor if necessary. While Mrs. Wheeler and Ms. Michie had a cordial relationship with Mrs. Lewis, they knew it could be improved and they believed it would be quicker to build up their partnership with Mrs. Lewis than to go over her head, likely with unfavorable results. They hoped this could occur sooner rather than later because the meeting was scheduled in one month.

Their development of this plan was informed by the perceptions and skills suggested by McKenna and Maister (2002). In addition, to avoid creating any kind of divide, Mrs. Lewis and Ms. Michie drew on the following suggestions:

1. Make friends with the "enemy." They say "one can catch more flies with honey than vinegar," and this is true with relationships.
2. Be kind to your partner.
3. Show appreciation for their work.
4. Speak respectfully at all times especially with a respectful tone. Then practice this approach.
5. Build a therapeutic alliance with your partners just as a social worker or therapist might build a therapeutic alliance with a client. This is done by "allowing clients space to talk, (showing) empathy, demonstrating positive regard" and by establishing "a set of rules of working together, usually delineated in the initial meeting."   (Kets de Vries and Carlock 2007:20)

Implement the Plan

Mrs. Wheeler, with Ms. Michie's support, knew that in order to advocate efficiently and effectively, she would have to get to know Mrs. Lewis as a person, not just a worker. Mrs. Wheeler crafted "conversational" emails to Mrs. Lewis to learn about Mrs. Lewis's family, hobbies, and things that were important to Mrs. Lewis. The purpose of this was to get to know her better as a human being.

At first Mrs. Lewis was guarded, but after a while they talked and spent more time together. Mrs. Wheeler always made sure to share with Mrs. Lewis how grateful she was for Mrs. Lewis' effective work with the children, and to tell her how much good feeling the children expressed when Mrs. Lewis's name came up. This led to even more positive regard between Mrs. Wheeler and Mrs. Lewis. These interventions improved their relationship with each other and led to more open communication and a better understanding on both sides of how the world of social services works. If your partners in the case receive you openly, "you can make a lot of mistakes and still have a big impact" (McKenna and Maister 2002:28).

Since Mrs. Wheeler had forged a partnership, Ms. Michie called Mrs. Lewis while Mrs. Wheeler was right there in her office. Knowing there was "strength in numbers," Ms. Michie asked if both she and Mrs. Wheeler could speak with her over the speaker phone. They were right. Based upon the genuine rapport that Mrs. Wheeler and Mrs. Lewis had created, Mrs. Lewis agreed that Ms. Barrett should be invited to the meeting. She did say that the girls could be invited for the last portion of the meeting. Mrs. Lewis immediately called Ms. Barrett to invite her to the meeting, and Ms. Barrett stated she would be thrilled to attend.

This collegial partnering might seem minor, but it is a crucial example of advocacy in the social services system.

Understand the Different Roles and Authority of Social Services Staff

Identify the Need

The Loefflers (the foster parents for Shanika) would become quite confused when they needed to call their worker. After all, Shanika had two people working on her behalf (Ms. Michie and Mrs. Lewis), plus substitutes who would act for them in their absence. Sometimes the Loefflers felt overwhelmed about "Who was who?" and "Who did what?"; they needed clarification for the entire process. They reached out to Mrs. Wheeler, Shanika's sisters' foster mother, for assistance in this regard when they wanted to learn how they might get authorization for all the foster parents to take the three sisters to a local amusement park.

Analyze the Context

Indeed, it can be confusing for all the parents involved (birth, foster, and kinship) to understand the roles of the various social service practitioners; this can delay advocacy efforts in various ways, such as if the wrong person is contacted. Table 3.2 attempts to provide clarification by providing common titles and brief descriptions of the many roles played by practitioners; actual titles and job descriptions vary by jurisdiction. You can consult your caseworker or social worker for further information and investigate your state's Foster Parent Bill of Rights.

Beyond working to distinguish the positions of these staff and volunteers, when you are developing relationships with your partners in social services, one of the most important things for you to know is *who* has the power to make *what* decisions. Therefore, it is critical that practitioners and professional foster parents alike know both who has the authority (to make decisions, to give written or verbal consent) and what the authorizing process is.

TABLE 3.2 Social Services Titles and Positions

Caseworker/aide: professional working for the county social service unit and/or the subcontracted agency; either entity could be the custody agent, depending on locale. Central responsibility is case management.

Commissioner or director: the representative of the governmental authority in a district, state, province, or other unit; often has both judicial and administrative powers.

Deputy commissioner: the assistant commissioner or second in command to the commissioner.

Foster parent: primary care provider for the children placed in a family care setting.

Parent aide: a person who assists the birth parent in developing parenting skills (e.g., budgeting, age-appropriate work activities with the children). Sometimes they help supervise visitation.

Social worker: professional who holds a bachelor's or master's degree in social work. Responsibilities vary, but usually provides case management, crisis intervention, counseling, information and referral, and advocacy.

Supervisor or case manager: the practitioner responsible for overseeing the case and approving the foster care plans.

Practical matters—such as signing consents, school papers (including field trip forms), medical procedures, clothing allotments, and other expenditures—may require the authorization of different parties' authorization, or one person may have the authority to sign for everything. For example, in some agencies, money (e.g., for clothing allotments and reimbursement for transportation) can only be authorized by the supervisor. However, *who* does the transporting can sometimes be decided by a caseworker.

A wide range of variation exists with respect to consent. It is possible that authority has been set by policies at the county/parish level, but it is also possible that authorization levels have set by state regulations. For example,

> The rights accorded to parents include the right to make medical decisions for their children, but this right is subject to numerous exceptions, such as a minor's right to be tested for sexually transmitted diseases, including HIV, to receive necessary treatment without parental consent, and to terminate a pregnancy without parental consent. In addition, a state may under certain circumstances override a parent's medical choices when intervention is deemed necessary to safeguard a child. (Stein 1998:80)

In some organizations the process may begin with a social worker, secretary, or other teammate, while in others the worker or parent may need to start at a higher level and simply notify the teammates that an authorization is in process. Sometimes paperwork has to go through two or more organizations for authorization. Complicating this further is the reality that sometimes practitioners and foster parents may need to request a full set of agency policies and procedures as well as a full set of state and county regulations that would explain authorization processes. Be aware that some agencies will not provide copies of policies and procedures to those outside their agency.

The answers vary too widely by jurisdiction to provide any consistency—you simply have to find this out on your own. So if you are a practitioner, foster parent, or kinship caregiver who does not know the answers—ask! Make sure you find out who makes the decisions, and who might be able to persuade the authorizing agent when she is making decisions about approvals. For example, the deputy commissioner may be the authorizing party, yet it is possible that he only listens to his directors when deciding whether to authorize something. Table 3.3 provides a model grid for a series of questions and answers to help make sense of this sometimes

TABLE 3.3 Authorization and Social Services			
AUTHORIZATION	WHO CONSENTS?	WHO ARRANGES?	WHO SUBMITS THE PAPERWORK?

Who pays for
  transportation to appointments?
  the child's allowance?
  clothing for special events/activities?			

Who pays for medical/dental procedures not covered by Medicaid?			
Who authorizes medical procedures?			

Who authorizes activities such as
  media coverage?
  sports?
  summer camp?
  fieldtrips?			

Who is responsible for advocating for material needs such as
  Health care payments?
  Money for items not covered by any other funds, etc.?			

Who advocates for the needs of the parents?			
Who advocates for the needs of the children?			
Who decides where visits are held and for how long?			

Who completes forms for
  Referrals?
  Applications for holiday baskets?
  Toy drives?
  Summer camp?
  School registration?			

Who writes
  Social service reports?
  Legal reports?			

TABLE 3.3 Authorization and Social Services			
AUTHORIZATION CONCERNS	WHO CONSENTS?	WHO ARRANGES?	WHO SUBMITS THE PAPERWORK

Who advocates for the children
  with the custody agent?
  with the court?
  with the school?
  with the medical team?
  with the multidisciplinary team?			

dizzying bureaucratic hierarchy; you can list who is authorized to consent, who facilitates the authorization, and who (if different from the facilitator) submits the paperwork for the authorizations.

Develop the Plan

Mrs. Wheeler and Ms. Michie clarified for the Loefflers what each worker's role was, so that initial inquiry was solved. When it comes to advocating for the children, the ideas of partnering from the previous section are always relevant, because even finding out "who can authorize what" can take patience and good interpersonal skills. Additionally, the practitioner who works as the custody agent and the practitioner from the contract agency might have very different ideas about what is in the best interest of the child. An innocent request by the Loefflers and Mrs. Wheeler to take the children to the amusement park was met, in fact, with an initial "yes" by their workers at the contracted agency but no response from Mrs. Lewis. The reason, according to Mrs. Lewis, was that her supervisor had not yet responded to her, although two weeks had elapsed since the initial request.

Developing a plan of advocacy when it comes to identifying the roles and authority to consent can thus either be fairly direct or, as in this case, quite complex. The foster parents and contract workers might give up in defeat. But Mrs. Wheeler and Ms. Michie had made inroads with Mrs. Lewis and believed that partnering with Mrs. Lewis might have an influence on finding out what was taking her supervisor so long to get back with a decision. (Recall that they wanted to change the type of relationship between the agencies and therefore the amusement park consent was partially symbolic.) Ms. Michie, on Mrs. Wheeler and the Loefflers' behalf, committed to finding out more about the authorization delay. To do this, Ms. Michie proposed that she and Mrs. Lewis "shadow" each other for half a day to gain more information about how each agency worked, including its authorization procedures.

Implement the Plan

Ms. Michie and Mrs. Lewis obtained approval to each shadow each other for a few hours in the coming week. This gave both workers a better understanding of the information that needed to accompany authorization forms. They also figured out which forms needed original signatures and which forms could be faxed. Both processes worked more efficiently with this newfound information. Additionally, although neither of their agencies was willing to release a policy and procedure manual to the other, Ms. Michie and Mrs. Lewis agreed to make their manuals available to each other whenever one had a question about the other's policies or procedures. This also sped up authorization procedures.

This intensive review of authorization procedures revealed that the request that Mrs. Lewis had put in on Ms. Michie's behalf was missing a form from the pediatrician; neither Mrs. Lewis herself nor Ms. Michie had known it was needed. Mrs. Lewis' supervisor, inundated with requests, had seen that the request was not complete but had simply forgotten to get back to Mrs. Lewis, who admittedly had not followed through either.

The pediatrician note was obtained; Shanika, Angelina, and Tanya, with their foster parents, went to the amusement park. The partnering relationship had allowed for increased knowledge of the authorization process, and Ms. Michie and Mrs. Lewis' authorization requests went through much more quickly in the future.

Identify the Supervision "Chain of Command"

Identify the Need

For this section, "supervision" refers to who is responsible for decisions about the child in care when key players, such as caseworkers or supervisors, are unavailable (due to court obligations, or out for personal reasons such as vacation or illness). Practitioners sometimes forget to notify caregivers and children about what practitioner is in charge when workers and supervisors are unavailable. The need for this information may be particularly relevant in the winter and summer months, when illness and vacation occur more. This can leave caregivers wondering which agency to contact when decisions need to be made about the child(ren). It can also cost caregivers additional time contacting other workers as they try to figure out who is covering. Although the foster parents may be resourceful enough to locate a worker who can assist in the absence of the social worker, caseworker, or supervisor, children (and sometimes the caregivers and parents) may not have the skills to identify the chain of command or other resources that they can tap into to get some answers when needed.

Remember from our vignette that the permanency plan was for all three children to live with Ms. Barrett (the grandmother). For this to occur, supervised visits of Ms. Barrett with the children were required (Ms. Barrett was also going through the precertification process). However, a potential glitch arose with the visits. Because Ms. Barrett wanted to take her granddaughters to church and sing with them, she knew she had to be supervised at the church. While Mrs. Wheeler and the Loefflers (the foster parents) agreed to supervise this one visit (and possibly more) at the church, they needed approval of the party responsible for supervision to make this change in visit venue from Ms. Wheeler's home to the church. Ms. Barrett did not consider that someone would need to approve this change in venue and time. All she knew was that she had to get the approval of someone to supervise the visit (preferably the foster parents, and maybe the social worker).

Analyze the Context

As was noted earlier, departments of social services (or their counterparts) are given license via law and regulation to ensure the safety of children. The dynamics of supervision change once the children are brought into care, whether that is kinship care or other family foster care. The supervision shifts from CPS (child protective services) to the units that oversee foster care, when the children are placed with foster families. Federal, state, and local laws as well as agency best practices govern visits; for example, the requirements for maintaining supervision via home visits came from a federal mandate (per email from Michelle Rafael, OCFS, to executive directors of Voluntary Foster Care Agencies, Aug. 21, 2006).

From an agency perspective, best practice regarding authorization requires close communication among teammates; this includes communication between the family teammates (birth and foster families) and workers from all supervising agencies involved with the families. It also includes communication about who would cover for workers in the event of their unavailability. If a worker is out for a day and there is an emergency, the name of the covering worker should be readily available for anyone who tries to contact the missing worker. However, sometimes voicemail and email notifications are not updated in a timely way. Therefore, the supervising worker may be unknown to someone (for instance, the birth family members, such as Ms. Barrett) trying to contact the person in charge of the case. It helps communication when a substitute is assigned at the same time the case is assigned to a worker (in the beginning). If that does not happen, the second-best form of communication is to notify teammates at some point so they know who in the future will cover during absences. A third option is to list the name of the substitute in places where teammates may try to contact the worker (i.e., via email or in voicemail).

To put all this into context, let us examine what happened next. Shanika, Angelina, and Tanya's foster parents, the Loefflers and Mrs. Wheeler, agreed to supervise the visits at the church. However, since they needed the caseworker in charge of supervision to approve this change, Ms. Barrett was supposed to contact that worker or supervisor to get approval. Getting approval could be very difficult if that person was out and no information was readily available about to whom Ms. Barrett should go in their absence.

Ethically, the best place to start for questions of supervision (or policies related to supervision) is with the worker most closely involved with the family. As in cases of teamwork, it is important to work through the system one contact at a time. The sequence of contact (who gets contacted first, second, and so on) depends on the structure of the relevant agency.

Develop the Plan

Having secured the foster parents' agreement to supervise the visits, Ms. Barrett planned to contact someone with the authority to approve the change in venue. She decided to call Ms. Michie; if Ms. Michie was not available, she would contact Ms. Michie's supervisor and then Mrs. Lewis. Ms. Barrett knew that all this needed to happen quickly; it was Thursday and she only had a day and a half to get approval for the Sunday visit with her grandchildren at church. This process of seeking approval in multiple places can at times seem nonsensical, both because at the higher levels some of the people doing the approving are not even familiar with the case and because of the logistical difficulties.

Implement the Plan

Ms. Barrett started by calling Ms. Michie for permission to change the visit that week from home to church. She learned that Ms. Michie was out sick; neither the message on Ms. Michie's voicemail nor the unit secretary identified who was covering for her. Ms. Barrett partnered with the unit secretary, by dividing up how they would find out who needed to authorize this change. The secretary would inquire within the agency about who could authorize a change in visitation venue while Ms. Barrett contacted the agency with custody (custody agent) to inquire about its authorization process. The secretary discovered that no one was covering for Ms. Michie that day and that the decision could be made directly by Ms. Michie's supervisor rather than having to go higher, to the custodial agent. The supervisor contacted Mrs. Wheeler and the Loefflers to make sure they had agreed to supervise the visit at church and then checked her supervision notes and the visit documentation to assess whether any reason existed not to allow the visit to be moved to the church for this Sunday. After finding no such reason, she stated that Mrs. Lewis, the case manager, needed to be called to confirm the visit at the church.

Ms. Barrett contacted Mrs. Lewis and left a similar message about the proposed change, stating she had received permission from Ms. Michie's supervisor. Mrs. Lewis also checked her documentation just to make sure there were no reasons why the visit venue should not be changed. After calling Ms. Michie's supervisor and learning of her support as well as finding no problems in the notes, Mrs. Lewis took the request to her own supervisor, who approved the change.

As we see at this point in the vignette, decisions have to be made within both agencies—first the contract agency, and then the custody agency. It is important to note here that an ethical issue raised by this scenario is the creation of accurate and timely documentation of "visit data" notes, which are crucial to system improvement and change. If the notes had not been current or had not accurately reflected prior visits content, the workers involved would have run out of time and would have been forced to break the news that the change in venue could not occur. This would have been very disappointing for the family. However, the change was approved, and Ms. Barrett and her three granddaughters sang together that Sunday.

Advocate for Material Needs

Identify the Need

Suppose we have a child who wishes to go to camp—in this case Shanika, who lives with the Loefflers. The cost of the camp would create a hardship for the foster family, and the birth family is not in a financial position to help. She had expressed a desire to go to a dance camp, because she showed some talent in that activity. Her dance coach sent the Loefflers some information about one of the best in the area, one which could really help her build upon her skills. Shanika did not know how much it cost but was so excited when she heard about it that she cheerfully talked about the camp with the Loefflers, her mother, and even her teacher at school. After inquiring about the camp, the Loefflers learned how expensive it was and that, unfortunately, scholarships were not offered. They were willing to pay for some of the camp costs. At the next home visit, Mr. Loeffler mentioned to Ms. Michie that Shanika really wanted to attend the dance camp, but that it was cost-prohibitive. When he asked Ms. Michie for suggestions, she told him that the Department of Social Services had a special fund for activities just like the camp. While they were glad to know of this fund, the Loefflers knew that using their own money and drawing on the DSS fund still would not be enough.

Sometimes children in foster care, like other children, really excel in something, or simply express a strong interest in one area or another. They deserve to have the same opportunities to be exposed to skill-building environments that children who are not in foster care have. But those skill-building environments often cost money, money that foster parents and agencies do not always have. Consequently an opportunity arises for workers and foster parents, and the child, to advocate for material needs—in this case, money for camp.

Analyze the Context

Focusing on the bigger picture, we understand that funds need to be dispersed equally and realize that not all children can be given the most expensive items or opportunities. However, sometimes special circumstances exist in which a child could progress in an exponential way. For example, there are those special occasions, like a senior prom, that are typical "rites of passage," anticipated norms in which the majority of youth would like to participate. For various reasons (such as when the child has moved to a new foster care placement and a new high school and did not have the opportunity to engage in the fund drives other students benefited from), the funds may not necessarily be available to allow the child's participation. One of the authors is familiar with one agency policy that divides responsibility for a youth's material needs into thirds: one-third of the cost must be earned by the youth; one third of the cost is the responsibility of the foster parent(s); and the last third is absorbed by the agency. A fourth source of funds is local community organizations.

One of the dynamics that affects funding for material needs is the relative popularity of social service programs as perceived by both the taxpayers and government representatives. As this book goes to print, states from New York to California are considering cutting social service budgets (http://www.californiaprogressreport.com/2008/09/fifth_in_a_seri .html). In June 2008 California reportedly looked at cutting 840 social workers across the state, which would result in higher caseloads and less time per child. However, the plan was voted down in September (http:// www.californiachronicle.com/articles/view/73591). During the Clinton Administration, the budget for preventive and foster care services doubled (http://eir.nicwa.org/law/fcia/PL106–169_summary.pdf), increasing from 70 million to 140 million dollars. During the Bush Administration, news agencies across the country reported budget cuts for social services (http:// www.detnews.com/2004/specialreport/0409/26/a01–284666.htm). If an agency has had a financially solid year, the foster care budget might contain more funds for activities/programming than the year before. If an agency has had a financially rough year, no money may exist for summer camps or for any other activities, for that matter. Typically, states that vote for "anti-tax and anti-government policies place children at greater risk" for child abuse and poverty, among other issues (Stoesen 2007:1).

Another factor that comes into play when youth are in their later teen years is the need to prepare them for adulthood. In regard to foster care service delivery, this means that foster agencies provide foster parents and practitioners with the necessary staffing, funding, and programming to help these teens acquire life skills (e.g., job training, managing a house-hold, personal budgeting) to prepare them for independence.

The John H. Chafee Foster Care Independence Program (title I of the Foster Care Independence Act of 1999) (discussed further in chapter 9) supplies funding to the states to assist youth in foster care. Some of this money is set aside for youth residing in independent living programs, while some is earmarked for youth in foster home care. By focusing on independent living skills, foster parents are expected to help the youth in their care in obtaining job skills. That may mean helping them to enroll in a job training program, apply for a job, manage the interview process, and successfully secure a job. Some of the Chafee money can also be used for college or college supplies such as computers.

It is important to note that the above discussion of available funds refers to monies for youth in foster care. When relative caregivers raise youth, they may serve as adoptive parents, legal guardians, temporary caregivers, or some other configuration. As such, the amount of funding available to kin-ship caregivers and the youth in their care can vary widely. In general, the availability and equity of funds provided for kinship care is not as developed or as organized as formal foster care. The children may be adopted by them, or may not be in formal foster care —all of which leaves relative caregivers identifying financial assistance as one of their largest needs (Rosenwald, Kelchner, and Bartone 2008). (Youth in either care situation qualify for their state's children's health insurance or other medical assistance program.)

Develop the Plan

In the case of Shanika and her dance camp, Mrs. Lewis of DSS might ask for the price of camp to be split. Ms. Michie decided to ask Mrs. Lewis for part of the money so that Shanika could attend the camp and believed it would be helpful if Shanika helped write a letter requesting the money. Sometime a request from a child in care is honored more quickly than one from the foster or kinship parent, because it shows that the youth is truly invested in the request. In this case, Shanika was very invested and excited about the possibility of attending this camp. Additional strategies to consider could be contacting nonprofit family service agencies, religious organizations, and civic clubs (Kiwanis for example) that provide scholarships, toy drives, etc., for youth.

Implement the Plan

Shanika worked with the Loefflers to compose a letter asking for money to go to camp. Despite her young age, she was willing to do extra chores and to help neighbors and relatives with chores to earn extra money to help with the costs. Her descriptions of this work activity in her letter impressed those who read it (for example, she sent the letter to the DSS, the head of the local Kiwanis, and the deacon of the church) impressed with her work ethic and goal of attending camp. The letter also contained a summary of what Shanika planned to do with her new talents after the camp concluded. A determination of the effectiveness of the letter would come when Shanika found out if DSS, the Kiwanis, or her church had decided to help pay for camp or not. The three administrators who reviewed the applications marveled at Shanika's dedication, and all three granted funds. With the money from the Loefflers as well as the money she had earned, Shanika attended and enjoyed dance camp.

Summary

Edwards and Yankey remind us that "contemporary managers must contend . . . with rapidly changing political, economic, and social conditions" (1991:5). Their apt words can easily extend to practitioners, foster parents, and relative caregivers, who should be equipped "with a broad range of knowledge, skills, and abilities to perform in a competent, effective manner (Edwards and Yankey 1991:5). In this chapter we have outlined several key skills and interventions that can be used to build relationships that can lead to a greater understanding of the dynamics of social service agencies. The four advocacy needs: partnering for advocacy, identifying the different roles of social services staff, understanding the supervision "chain of command," and advocating for material needs, all relate to issues in social services that demonstrate that parents (foster, birth, and kinship) and workers must partner effectively to advocate for the birth families. Gaining that understanding may appear to be much work. However, once the knowledge has been gained, parents and practitioners can function much more efficiently and effectively.

Discussion Questions

1. Was it ethical for the Department of Social Services to hold meetings without the family members present? Why or why not?
2. If you could not reach the caseworker, who would you go to in the chain of command for consent for agency funds to be spent?
3. Should Shanika be allowed to go to an expensive summer camp? Why or why not?
4. If visits between the children and the birth parents cannot be safely held in the home and must therefore be held someplace else, what locations would you recommend?

[4]

Advocating Within the Family Court System

Justice delayed is justice denied.

—William E. Gladstone

Vignette

Mary, Jason, and Sara were placed in foster care after Mary reported to school officials that her father, Mr. Randolf, had sexually abused her. Mrs. Randolf, their mother, is developmentally delayed, and the court determined that she could not be a "protective ally" (provided of appropriate supervision) for her children. The three children faced a variety of developmental and medical problems that impacted their health, such as microcephaly (a small head), low IQ, and delays in acquiring motor skills. Because the local department for social services home-finding unit was unable to locate a family for all three children together, Mary was placed with the O'Donnell family, and Jason and Sara were placed together with the Palowski family (also Caucasian).

After the children were placed in care, Mrs. Randolf left Mr. Randolf to live on her own. Mr. Randolf was convicted of the charges and subsequently had his parental rights terminated. Mrs. Randolf began to work at McDonald's and consistently visited the children as often as these visits were allowed.

Mary (age 13) resided with the O'Donnell foster family, which included two mature foster parents. Mrs. O'Donnell always made sure visits were convenient for the children's mother. The O'Donnell foster parents worked together and helped Mary make presents for Mother's Day. On birthdays and Christmas, Mary always had gifts for Jason, Sara, and their Mom, as well as for the foster family members. Staunchly Irish, they also loved celebrating St. Patrick's Day.

The Palowskis, foster parents for Jason (age 4) and Sara (age 2 1/2), were new, energetic foster parents who immediately enrolled Jason in soccer and Sara in a library reading course for toddlers; they were kept busy with this schedule. Unable to have biological children of their own, they wanted to adopt Jason and Sara.

The two sets of foster parents' agency worker, Ms. Danby, was new to the agency and eager to help. Visits with the children were scheduled in such a way that Mrs. Randolf had one visit with Mary and a separate visit with Jason and Sara. Mrs. Randolf asked if the children could visit together to continue bonding. The Palowskis did not see the point of joint visits; in their minds, the children would only be separated after the adoption was final anyway.

Ms. Danby knew the importance of having the siblings maintain contact and therefore suggested to the Palowskis that visits with all three siblings occur. In the context of these visits, Ms. Danby also suggested that their mother attend, for this would be good for the children's bonding process. The Palowskis were persuaded and decided to make their schedule a little more flexible. While Ms., Danby was pleased that the two sets of foster parents had come to a visitation agreement, she knew that the ultimate course for these children rested in the decision of the court.

Key

Mary, Jason, and Sara: the children who came into care.
Mr. and Mrs. Randolf: the birth parents of the children.
Mr. and Mrs. O'Donnell: Mary's foster family; fostered Jason and
    Sara later; subsequently adopted all three children.
Ms. Danby: agency foster care worker.
Mr. and Mrs. Palowski: Jason and Sara's initial foster family.
Mr. Naylor: the children's law guardian (attorney; guardian ad
    litem).

Any child, including Mary, Jason, and Sara, is subject to the laws and policies that dictate the structure and process of administering family services. These include the Adoption and Safe Families Act (ASFA), "conditional surrenders," and the numerous local family court interpretations of child welfare law that have resulted in a multitude of policy changes over the last decade (Hardin 2005). This chapter provides practitioners and foster parents with an introduction to legal terms and the Family Court process. This knowledge, it is anticipated, will result in their having greater confidence and increased ability to skillfully advocate with both the court judge and attorneys who represent the agency, the children, the biological parents, and the court-appointed special advocate (CASA). These processes relate to kinship care as well, depending on the type of permanency goal (long-term placement option) to which the involved parties agree. Sometimes relatives serve as temporary caregivers while reunification remains the goal while at other times they are considered to be permanent legal guardians. A discussion of how policy results from the interpretation of law is highlighted in this chapter as well.

Advocacy Checklist

- Collect information accurately and efficiently.
- Understand the court process.
- Consider conditional surrenders and other open adoption options.

Collect Information Accurately and Efficiently

Identifying the Need

Foster parents, relative caregivers, and new practitioners need accurate information when it comes to court proceedings. Juvenile, tribal, and family courts "have jurisdiction over cases involving child abuse and neglect" (Hardin 2005:687). What this means for foster parents and practitioners is that they will have to answer to a judge when it comes time to report their progress on the goals set by the court and social services for a family. If the goals are met, the case moves forward and the children achieve permanency as soon as possible. However, if goals have not been met, the children may not be able to return to their family for several more months. Thus the court has the power to speed up the process or slow it down.

Ms. Danby wished she were familiar with every aspect of the court proceedings. She spoke to her supervisor, who gave her advice on how to work with Mrs. Randolf to observe the court-imposed deadlines on taking parenting classes. She also wanted to be clear on the visitation schedule as well as any latitude regarding changes in that schedule.

Analyze the Context

Courtroom proceedings often take place very quickly, making it challenging to keep up with the decisions. Sometimes people leave the courtroom and create plans based on what they *think* they heard instead of what actually transpired. Some proceedings move especially quickly if children's cases form only a small percentage of the docket heard by a larger court system and if the judge is less familiar with child welfare issues. A family has only a few minutes (or less) for the lawyers to present on their behalf each topic of each case. It is not uncommon for new workers and foster parents to leave wondering exactly what outcome they just heard because they may not have understood how it was expressed. Kinship caregivers may be in court because they are serving as guardian for the child on a temporary basis while the parents work toward reunification.

It is imperative that practitioners and caregivers understand key concepts involved in court proceedings as well as the court process itself (discussed in the next section). Understanding the context and organizing principles of Family Court can make the process appear less daunting.

To begin, we need to review why the cases are in front of the court in the first place. Children typically enter foster care because they have experienced child maltreatment such as child abuse and child neglect. This is also a large reason that youth enter kinship care. Each state has slightly different definitions of child abuse and neglect. An excellent Web site listing information by state about policies on this topic is the Child Welfare Information Gateway: http://www.childwelfare.gov/systemwide/laws_policies/state/.

For example, in California, physical abuse and neglect are defined as follows:

[Physical abuse is] [p]hysical injury inflicted by other than accidental means upon a child by another person. Willful harming or injury of the child or the endangering of the person or health of the child. Unlawful corporal punishment or injury.

[Neglect includes] the negligent treatment or the maltreatment of a child by a person responsible for the child's welfare under circumstances indicating harm or threatened harm to the child's health or welfare. The term includes both acts of commission and omissions on the part of the responsible person.

Severe neglect means the negligent failure of a person having the care or custody of a child to protect the child from severe malnutrition or medically diagnosed nonorganic failure to thrive. *Severe neglect* also means those situations of neglect where any person having the care or custody of a child willfully causes or permits the person or health of the child to be placed in a situation such that his or her person or health is endangered, including the intentional failure to provide adequate food, clothing, shelter, or medical care.

General neglect means the negligent failure of a person having the care or custody of a child to provide adequate food, clothing, shelter, medical care, or supervision where no physical injury to the child has occurred.

"Neglect" often typically encompasses the situation of youth witnessing domestic violence because the parent(s) are failing to supervise and therefore prevent the youth from observing it.

Sexual abuse means sexual assault or sexual exploitation, as defined below:

Sexual assault includes rape, statutory rape, rape in concert, incest, sodomy, lewd or lascivious acts upon a child, oral copulation, sexual penetration, or child molestation.

Sexual exploitation: Depicting a minor engaged in obscene acts; preparing, selling, or distributing obscene matter that depicts minors; employing a minor to perform obscene acts

Knowingly permitting or encouraging a child to engage in, or assisting others to engage in, prostitution or a live performance involving obscene sexual conduct, or to either pose or model alone or with others for purposes of preparing a film, photograph, negative, slide, drawing, painting, or other pictorial depiction, involving obscene sexual conduct

Depicting a child in, or knowingly developing, duplicating, printing, or exchanging any film, photograph, videotape, negative, or slide in which a child is engaged in an act of obscene sexual conduct. (Retrieved on 10/27/08 from http://www.childwelfare.gov/systemwide/laws_policies/ state/index.cfm?event=stateStatutes.processSearch)

When birth parents are found to be guilty of abusing or neglecting their children, the Adoption and Safe Families Act (ASFA) comes into play for these children, who now reside in foster care (this act is discussed further in chapter 9). A few of ASFA's mandates are briefly discussed below; the full list appears in table 4.1. ASFA is a good example of well-intended legislation that unfortunately does not include additional funding for the courts to assist in making the changes outlined in table 4.1.

TABLE 4.1 Mandates in the Adoptions and Safe Families Act (1997)

Broader federal funding for innovative practices.

Focus on child and family well-being.

Clarification of reasonable efforts.

Expanded court-related responsibilities, including permanency hearings and determining what reunification interventions are required.

Fast track for children of egregious [severe maltreatment] situations.

Funding for reunification, adoption, and postadoption services.

Interjurisdictional adoption rule.

Emphasis on accountability (Bass, Shields et al. 2004), including outcome reporting.

Permanency planning for children from the first day they enter foster care.

Recognition of kinship care as a permanency option.

Return to birth family while concurrently planning for "another planned permanent living arrangement" (APPLA).

The 15 out of 22 month rule.

Sources: Compiled from McGowan 2005:39–41 and www.childwelfare.gov.

When procedures change but resources stay the same, it can be especially difficult to know how and where to make changes in our advocacy.
Additionally, when the changes take place, the process may initially stay
the same, but then it becomes challenging to renavigate the system. In
our example, advocating for changes to the visitation plan that Ms. Danby
planned to make can occur early in the process—even as early as the intake.
Ms. Danby knew she had to quickly ensure that the visitation schedule
complied with ASFA.

After the children come into foster care, a "15 out of 22" month rule
comes into play, which means that parents whose children have remained
in foster care 15 out of the last 22 months are subject, with few exceptions,
to having their parental rights terminated (TPR). Practitioners facilitate
concurrent planning, which means planning at the same time for two
potential outcomes of the court case. That would include planning for the
children's return to family (reunification) and at the same time planning
for the possibility that they may need to be adopted if returning to family
is not possible (where parental rights would be terminated).

An alternative to the "15 out of 22" rule is the "fast track" option, which
"allows states to bypass efforts to reunify families in certain egregious situations" (GAO-02-585, 2002). The "fast track" provision means courts are
not mandated to put effort into keeping a child at home with their family of origin if a parent a) lost their rights in a sibling case, b) committed
certain types of felonies, such as murder or voluntary manslaughter of a
sibling, or c) subjected the child to situations like abandonment, torture,
chronic abuse, or sexual abuse. In these "egregious situations," the court
may determine that reasonable efforts are not required. Between the time
ASFA was enacted (1997) and 2002, the rate of adoption had increased 54
percent (http://www.gao.gov/new.items/d02585.pdf).

Another component of context applies to children who immigrated to
the United States and do not yet have the proper legal documentation to
reside here. These youth are also known as unaccompanied minors, refu-
gees, "separated" from their families, asylees, and immigrant children. If
they have a history of maltreatment, they can given "special immigrant juvenile Status." They are legally entitled to receive an education, short-term
emergency medical care (but not Medicaid), and "shelter or other services
necessary to address an emergency . . . this includes placement in foster
care" (http://immigrantchildren.org/Reports%20and%20Studies/united-
states/umsininscustody/view?searchterm=medical). The Center for Human

Rights and Constitutional Law also tells us that "Special Immigrant Juvenile Status (SIJS) is a federal law that assists certain undocumented children in obtaining legal permanent residency" and "(SIJS) is a way for a dependent of juvenile court to become a permanent resident of the United States (i.e., get a "green card")" (http://immigrantchildren.org/SIJS/). Undocumented children who are neglected or abused are thus eligible for long-term foster care if they are granted special immigrant juvenile status (Lincroft and Resner 2006). Some issues of concern in working with this population are language barriers (where English is a second or third language or unknown by the child), mixed status families (families who have some members in this country legally and others illegally), preservation of the child's culture, and poverty (Child Protection Best Practices Bulletin 2008).

As in a well-oiled machine, most cases properly go through the checks and balances of the professional care, scrutiny, and ethical review provided by the court process. However, like most ill-equipped systems, courts do not always operate as they should. Sometimes attorneys are not prepared and informed about their cases, especially when they are first assigned as law guardians (guardian ad litem) for children recently brought into foster care and this can also be true for public defenders assigned to birth parents who cannot afford private attorneys. Hardin (2005) articulates another challenge:

> State and local juvenile and family courts have the ability to hasten or delay children's movement in and out of foster care. Most courts that oversee the cases of children in foster care struggle to balance the competing needs of
>
> (1) protecting children from further harm,
>
> (2) making timely decisions about their futures and
>
> (3) respecting their parents' due process rights.
>
> In meeting these needs, the courts, judges, and attorneys rely on more non-legal professionals than do their counterparts in other court systems. (Hardin 2005:688)

The professionals that Hardin refers to include professional parents (i.e., foster parents), agency workers, court-appointed special advocates (CASAs), mental health workers, other health care professionals, and educators.

As mentioned, practitioners (and CASAs separately) need to collect accurate information as efficiently as possible because the court mandates certain orders and the practitioner, as well as the child's parents, must comply in providing information about the particular case. Providing this information is paramount during the entire duration that a child is in care, from the onset of the initial investigation of child abuse or neglect all the way to the visitation schedule and provisions of permanency planning.

Because practitioners will facilitate permanency planning, write reports, and attend court, and caregivers will assist in some of these tasks, definitions of some key legal terms are provided in table 4.2. These terms will help practitioners and foster parents prepare themselves for those times when a basic familiarity with terms is paramount. Such familiarity will also help the advocates feel more confident when appearing in court. Practitioners might

---

TABLE 4.2 Legal Terminology Relevant to the Child Welfare Court Process

Agency attorney: the attorney who typically represents the caseworkers/social workers in court, including presenting their plans for the case. The title can refer to either the attorney for the contract agency or the attorney for the Department of Social Services.

Adjudication: the decision or determination to either dismiss the case or request further action.

Appeal: a request to have a higher court review the case and its evidence.

Conditional surrender: document that states an agreement that the parent(s) will surrender their rights if certain conditions are met.

Court report: document that summarizes important information needed to prove the case.

Duces tecum: the process of producing documents.

Family Court: also known as Domestic Relations Courts. The portion of the court system that hears cases pertaining to matters related to families.

Guardian ad litem: an individual appointed by the court to serve as the representative of the best interests of the child or children. She or he is usually an attorney or a CASA-certified volunteer.

Jurisdiction: the power of the court to adjudicate cases and issue orders. Pertains to particular geographical locations of court coverage.

Least restrictive environment: the home setting that provides the lowest level of care while still providing for the child's safety. The term is taken from education law.

(continued)

TABLE 4.2 Legal Terminology Relevant to the Child Welfare Court Process
(*continued*)

Orphans' Court: the Orphans' Court hears all matters involving the deceased's estates that are contested and supervises all of those estates that are probated judicially. It approves accounts, awards of personal representative's commissions, and attorney's fees in all estates. The Court also has concurrent jurisdiction with the circuit court in the guardianships of minors and their property. In some states, all matters involving the validity of wills and the transfer of property in which legal questions and disputes occur are resolved by the Orphans' Court.

Parens patriae: the state or its agents (i.e., social workers) when they become the guardian of dependants such as children.

Parent's attorney: this attorney represents the best interests of the parent(s). The attorney is sometimes appointed by the court and other times hired by the parent.

Permanency plan: the plan outlining the process of finding a permanent living situation for the child(ren).

Petition: request to an authority identifying a certain need and making a request.

Petitioner: the person or persons who present a petition to the court.

Postadoption contact agreements: "cooperative adoption," or "open adoption agreements," are arrangements that allow some kind of contact between a child's adoptive family and members of the child's birth family after the child's adoption has been finalized.

Protective ally: an individual who has the ability to responsibly supervise and care for a child.

Respondent: the person or persons against whom the petition has been filed.

Shelter order: document that is used to take a child immediately into state custody overnight because of safety reasons. The practitioner has to be in court the next business day to provide the rationale.

Subpoena: an order that compels a person to give testimony. Foster parents are sometimes subpoenaed to testify in court.

Termination of parental rights (TPR): legal provision that is enacted when reuniting the child(ren) with the parent(s) is not possible; in such a case ASFA requires the state to end the parents' rights.

Testify: to give evidence, usually by serving as a witness.

also want to consult Legal Advocates for Permanent Parenting at http://www
.lapponline.org, and read Deihl and Fiermonte's (n.d.) *Legal Resource Manual
for Foster Parents* for detailed information on foster care and the law.

Develop the Plan

Developing a plan begins with ensuring that everyone's interpretation
of the court proceedings is clear and consistent. Several options exist to
determine if the proceedings were not clear. One option is to ask someone
involved in the case; typically the attorneys for the custody agent have the
list of outcomes. Another way to get clear information is to get a copy of
the court report from the custody agent. The court report will list a number
of items, including the findings (outcomes), visitation plan, permanency
goals, and court-ordered activities; unfortunately, it may take a few weeks
before the court report is mailed out. Do not wait for that to arrive—find
out the plan and the specifics about implementing it that will lead to the
goals as soon as possible.

After initial clarity was achieved, Ms. Danby needed to develop a plan for
visitation. She first had to schedule the visits with all the children together,
but then she observed how difficult it was for Mrs. Randolf to handle, bond
with, and discipline the children. Mrs. Randolf would sometimes engage
one of the children at the expense of ignoring the other two. The negative
impact of this was illustrated once when Mrs. Randolf, while talking with
Mary, did not notice that Sara had wandered away. If Ms. Danby had not
been paying attention, Sara would have wandered right out of the building. By this time the visitation plan had already been set by the attorneys.
Therefore, Ms. Danby had to help Mrs. Randolf quickly gain the skills to
nurture the children and keep them safe during the visits.

Practitioners must advocate for and plan for the process of changing
interventions. They also need to plan for the process of gathering all the
information necessary for the court proceedings, because they are the
ones who provide the majority of information to the attorneys for their
court preparation. This is a powerful position and should not be taken
lightly—their advocacy has a great impact on the case. In this instance,
Ms. Danby needed to gather information about how Mrs. Randolf handled
visits and then propose a plan for any changes that would help her hold
successful visits where she could be a protective ally. She also needed

to plan for court by practicing her facts so she could be ready if she was called to speak or testify.

In our vignette, the court order for the Randolfs stated that having visits together was an important goal for the children. The children's law guardian (the attorney appointed to advocate on behalf of the children), Mr. Naylor, knew the judge well enough to know the judge would ultimately demand joint visits because this is usually best for the children; Mr. Naylor advocated for this and the court granted joint visitation. Before court, the practitioners and foster parents can advocate for the children by speaking with the law guardian and the other attorneys involved. Moreover, they may be given the opportunity to advocate directly to the judge in the courtroom; however, this is not guaranteed.

Ms. Danby, the O'Donnells, and the Palowskis all needed to understand why the children had come into care. Some agencies share the court order(s) with the foster parents to make them completely aware of the child(ren)'s background as well as to help them understand their (the foster parents') role in whatever interventions they need to do to assist the children. For this reason, Ms. Danby made copies of the court order for the O'Donnells and the Palowskis. The court order is especially valuable to practitioners since they are ultimately responsible for carrying out the court order.

While the focus so far has been on practitioners, foster parents, too, have the right to be heard in proceedings held about their foster children, thanks to the Safe and Timely Placement of Foster Children Act of 2006. Caregivers have other legal status options in many states. Although they do not have appointed counsel in any state, and there are not many resources available to provide them with legal information or advice, foster and kinship parents are increasingly looking for ways to access the court (www.nationalcasa.org/JudgesPage/Article/new_fedora_law.htm).

Implement the Plan

Ms. Danby now needed to complete a recommendation to the Family Court about the visitation. The actual steps involved with implementing the plan to collect accurate and objective information for such a court report are included in table 4.3.

It looked to Ms. Danby as though Mrs. Randolf's rights would eventually be terminated—Mrs. Randolph was doing her best but she did not

---

TABLE 4.3 Steps in Producing a Court Report

1. Observe the child(ren) and parent(s) in visitation.
2. Collect data from the parties involved with the children and other family members; this includes social and medical data.
3. Put that information into a document/report to be submitted to the attorney representing the agency.
4. Submit the document to the supervisor for approval.
5. Send the document to the attorney.

---

appear to be bonding that well with her children. Again, the O'Donnells expressed interest in adopting all three children. The Palowskis continued to advocate for adopting just Jason and Sara. Therefore, Ms. Danby and her supervisor faced a dilemma—should they unite the children and allow the O'Donnells to adopt all three children while disrupting the bond the younger two had with the Palowskis, or allow the Palowskis to adopt Jason and Sara and hope they would schedule and hold visits with Mary. After many long meetings with the foster care agencies, foster parents, Mrs. Randolf, Ms. Danby, and the administrator for social services, the decision was made that Jason and Sara would join Mary with the O'Donnell's family because of the importance of keeping the entire sibling group intact. The deciding factor was this: Mrs. Randolf said she would surrender her parental rights if the O'Donnells would adopt all three children. The O'Donnells and the administrative teams of all agencies involved came to an agreement, which the court accepted. The Palowskis were heartbroken, yet understood that keeping the sibling unit intact was in the best interest of all the children.

Understand the Court Process

Identify the Need

Ms. Danby did not understand the court process; it was not part of her education or a component of her agency's job training once she had secured a position with her bachelor's degree in human services. The O'Donnells had some experience with and understanding of the court system but were not completely sure of the process either.

Such learning about a legal process may be particularly intimidating for practitioners and foster parents, who seldom have a legal background. While lawyers are the primary advocates in the family court system, having a basic understanding of the process can help the nonlegal advocates identify opportunities for advocacy. Therefore, all need to be oriented to the court process as to when, where, and how to advocate for the children.

Analyzing the Context

All child welfare cases that are taken to court are heard through the local family court system, which may or may not be a separate court. We need to mention that in many of the more severe physical abuse cases (such as when a child is burned or severely beaten), sexual abuse cases, and some neglect cases (such as child abandonment), criminal charges are filed and then the circuit court is involved with a criminal investigation. In these cases, it is the police (sometimes special advocacy units staffed by police detectives partner with child protective services to conduct the investigations) who bring the charges to court. Although exact procedures vary based on jurisdiction, the typical child welfare case in which a child is placed in foster care goes through the general stages shown in table 4.4.

Develop the Plan

The steps to follow for foster parents and workers to understand the court process include but may not be limited to

1. studying the procedures and language of the courtroom;
2. talking with others who have been in the court room with the judge assigned to the case;
3. practicing for the courtroom experience.

Ms. Danby decided that best way to understand the court process (step 1 above) was for her to review the Legal Advocates for Permanent Parenting Web site to enable herself to further understand the legal process and then

TABLE 4.4 Stages of a Child Welfare Case

1. *Intake:* Cases are screened to eliminate those that do not require court action and determine those that do (Duquette 1990).
2. *Fact-finding and adjudication:* This phase begins with a filing of a complaint/ petition about the allegations. The facts are put into the court report. A decision is then made to either dismiss the case or request further action (this is adjudication). When further action is required, it will most likely include a "social study," which is an evaluation of facts to be considered by the court. Practitioners are usually assigned to administer this fact-finding mission. The final phase of adjudication is having the disposition scheduled (Crosson-Tower 2004).
3. *Disposition:* Information from the social study is presented, and then a treatment plan for the child(ren) is determined. The plan must always follow the federal mandate that the best interests of the child be met in the least restrictive environment (Stein 1991; http://www.childwelfare.gov/ systemwide/service/soc/history/history.cfm). This phase may be reevaluated many times over, typically at six-month intervals.
4. *Hearings:* The court review hearing(s) review the progress of the case. Permanency hearings are held for children for whom the permanency goal has been determined; the welfare of the child is reviewed in respect to the permanency goal. If the child is old enough—deemed by the practitioner and attorney to be mature enough to appropriately be in court— they are to attend these sessions. Before the child appears in court, the practitioner, foster parents, and perhaps a counselor should work out a plan to help the child prepare for such a stressful formality. Foster parents must receive notice of these hearings and should attend along with the social worker.
5. *Decision:* At this final stage, there are two options: termination of parental rights (TPR) or return of the children to their birth family. This is very likely the most important decision in the child's life thus far.

to convey the relevant information to the foster parents and the children's birth mother, Mrs. Randolph. Ms. Danby knew that she herself could not give legal advice to anyone and planned to contact the agency attorney to help her prepare.

A good strategy for practitioners to practice for the courtroom is to role-play the situation with the attorney in charge (step 2). The attorney will know what sorts of issues may arise and what is expected of everyone who will be in attendance in the courtroom. Then, for step 3, Ms. Danby planned to practice. The agency attorney would pretend to both represent her (as the agency attorney) to cross-examine her regarding Mrs. Randolph's progress on reunification with her children. This rehearsal was also essential to allowing Ms. Danby to become more comfortable with appearing in court if she is requested to testify by an attorney or judge. It can be extremely helpful for practitioners, kinship caregivers, and foster parents to practice presenting information in the formidable setting of the courtroom.

Implement the Plan

It was time to implement the plan. Ms. Danby and the O'Donnells (the foster parents) prepared to practice for the courtroom experience and consulted with other foster parents on the breadth of laws governing their lives. The test came when it was time to advocate. While the laws do not specifically tell practitioners and caregivers *when* they can advocate, the rehearsal gave them a better understanding of what might and might not be negotiable. For example, Mrs. Randolf's cognitive challenge could be used as evidence for them to advocate for her to have an extended period of time to complete the court-ordered steps as long as she made enough progress for the attorneys to file extensions. This rehearsal paid off, for when the O'Donnells did testify, they felt more comfortable.

Consider Conditional Surrenders and Other Open Adoption Options

Identify the Need

According to the U.S. Department of Health and Human Services AFCARS (Adoption and Foster Care Reporting and Analysis System) site, approximately 51,323 children were adopted from foster care (including foster family care) in 2005. The most current data are available through reports found at: www.acf.hhs.gov/programs/cb/pubs/cw005/appendix/appendixe.htm.

Ms. Danby was working hard to see if Mrs. Randolf could raise her children but also kept in mind that the O'Donnells were available to adopt all three. A new worker, Ms. Danby had recently learned in her training that a variety of open adoption options, including a "conditional surrender," were available; her supervisor suggested that Ms. Danby consider whether a conditional surrender would be the preferred option in this case. She decided she had a need to learn even more about these options as part of working on the permanency plan.

Analyze the Context

Among the many options for adoption, one that could be publicized more is the conditional surrender. A conditional surrender is an agreement that the parent(s) will surrender their rights if certain conditions are met.

Often, one of the conditions is an agreement by the foster parents to adopt; sometimes the conditional surrender agreements include visitation plans for the postadoption period. Conditional surrenders of birth family's rights were quite controversial when introduced, especially in some counties in New York State. An administrative directive in that state (02 OCFS ADM-01) raised awareness of the need for clear directions in the surrender agreement if "there is a substantial failure of an important condition agreed to by the parties" prior to finalization of the adoption (New York State Office of Children and Family Services 2002). Yet many counties across the state did not honor the option of conditional surrenders as it was spelled out in the law. Conditional surrenders are a special form of open adoption because the birth parents, foster parents (who will likely adopt), and the practitioners are allowed to weigh in on the best type of relationship the birth parents should have in the child's life. Research shows that as children grow older, they will likely want to keep in touch with those people who were important in their lives when they were young (Quinton, Rushton et al. 1998). Therefore, in this situation, advocating for a youth in care is best exemplified by having a discussion with the birth family and helping them to understand that terminating their rights may be in the best interest of the child when the birth parents are not progressing on their court-mandated goals. Giving up legal parental rights, while likely traumatic, especially for the parent, does not necessarily mean that all contact between parent and child will be severed.

The specifics of a conditional surrender can vary among the number of options on the open adoption continuum. Open adoptions, a steadily increasing trend in adoption, are adoptions where some amount of agreed-upon contact between the child and the birth family can take place. Open adoptions require some level of communication between the parent (whose parental rights have been terminated) and the child. The degree of openness varies in accordance with what everyone involved (child, adoptive parent, birth parent, practitioner) believes is in the child's best interest. The continuum of potential open adoption options is displayed in figure 4.1. At the left end of the spectrum is the degree of openness that is facilitated by third parties. For example, information about the children might be sent from the adoptive family to a postadoption worker; then that worker would be responsible to send the information on to the birth family. This information might include notes about the child(ren)'s health, their grades in school, or school pictures. At the right end of the spectrum, the openness might involve full disclosure and frequent visitation, as in the case of Mary, Jason, and Sara.

Conditional surrenders can also be examples of the "postadoption contact agreements" (also known as "cooperative adoption agreements," or "open adoption agreements"), which "are arrangements that allow some kind of contact between a child's adoptive family and members of the child's birth family after the child's adoption has been finalized" (U.S. Department of

FIGURE 4.1 Continuum of Open Adoption Options

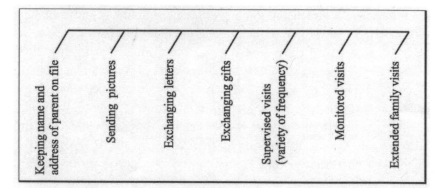

Health and Human Services 2005). These postadoption agreements can also help parents to feel more comfortable surrendering their children, thus avoiding a time-consuming court battle for custody.

Additionally, the Child Welfare Information Gateway (http://www .childwelfare.gov/systemwide/laws_policies/state) provides a state-by-state survey of where postadoption agreements are possible. It also notes some important reasons that postadoption agreements have become more common and accepted. The reasons they list include:

> Broader recognition of birth parents' rights to have decision making powers when it comes to their children. Of the more recent adoptions, many involve older children with attachments to birth parents such that continued contact is in the child's best interest. Birth parents and other relatives may be an excellent source of medical, social, and cultural history.

This increasing trend provides an important context for having these often-difficult conversations with birth parents, as well as for interactions with foster parents and the youth who are the reason everyone has gathered in the first place.

Develop the Plan

In the vignette, Ms. Danby came to believe that a conditional surrender was the best option, given Mrs. Randolf's minimal progress on the reunification goals. Ms. Danby informed Mrs. Randolf and Mrs. Randolf's attorney that her parental rights would likely be involuntary terminated by the Family Court due to the minimal progress she had made on her parenting. Ms. Danby discussed conditional surrenders with her, and with a mixture of sadness and relief, Mrs. Randolf stated she would surrender her parental rights, knowing the children would have the continuity of staying together and in the care of the O'Donnell family. She was especially pleased that she might be able to visit the children on a regular basis after the adoption. As the O'Donnells made plans to adopt, Mrs. Randolf made plans to surrender. Part of the plan was for the social worker to present the idea to her supervisor, the custody agent, the family treatment conference (an interdisciplinary team), and all attorneys involved—who would ultimately draw up the agreement and hope to have the court approve it.

It would not be fair to represent a positive outcome of a conditional sur-render without acknowledging the other court possibilities. In many cases, if the treatment team recommends a postadoptive agreement as being in the best interest of the child(ren), then the court will approve the agreement. The only way for agreements to be enforceable is if they are court-ordered. If the court opposes the agreement, it will likely send the team back to make changes or have the attorneys propose the change and make the judgment right then and there. Table 4.5 is an adaptation of an example of what one foster family took to their treatment team and attorneys as a starting point for a conditional surrender agreement. (The agency was required to attempt to contact Mr. Randolph, through newspapers' public hearing notices, but never heard from him; the court had previously terminated his rights.)

TABLE 4.5

Sample Conditional Agreement

First. Mary, Jason, and Sara, (hereafter known as the Children) will be surrendered for adoption by Mrs. Randolf (hereafter known as their birth mother). The children will be adopted by Mr. and Mrs. O'Donnell (here-after known as their foster parents). If the agency becomes aware that the foster parents cannot or will not adopt the children, the agency will immediately notify the parent and the agency shall follow all procedures designated under SSL 383-c and FCA 1055a (New York State Legislation).

Second. Subject to modification based upon the children's best interests, the birth parent of the children will have visitation with the children 12 times per year—at intervals of approximately once per month. These visits will occur on dates and times mutually agreed upon by the two parties. At each visit, the parties will consult their schedules and agree upon the date and time of the next visit. The parties will endeavor to agree to dates that are convenient for both of them and for the children. The parent may request that his/her visit coincide with a special or fam-ily occasion and the foster parents will endeavor to cooperate with such activity. All visits will occur under the following conditions:

a. The visits will be minimally three hours in length, but may be longer if the parties mutually agree.

(continued)

TABLE 4.5 Sample Conditional Agreement (*continued*)

b. The visits will be at a location the parties mutually agree upon.

c. The visits will be supervised by the foster parent(s) or someone they have approved of as a supervisor until such time as both parties agree that the foster parent and the child(ren) is comfortable with an unsupervised setting.

d. If the parent cannot or does not make a visit that had already been arranged for, for whatever reason, the foster parent is under no obligation to "make up" or offer an alternative visit. If the foster parent cannot or does not make a visit that had already been arranged for, the visit will be "made up" within a month's time at a time the parties mutually agreed upon. The parties will show as much consideration as possible to advise each other of visits which cannot be made.

e. If the parent misses 3 visits within any twelve month time period, excluding a provable crisis beyond their control, such as a serious illness, the foster parent is no longer obligated to provide any further visitation whatsoever.

f. The parties shall exchange telephone numbers and addresses but such information shall only be used to communicate regarding visits.

g. All visits will be discontinued if that is the recommendation of any therapist treating the child. Visits would only then recommence upon a therapist's recommendation and under terms recommended.

h. A visit will discontinue if the parent engages in any offensive conduct toward the children, the foster parent or anyone supervising the visit. A visit will terminate immediately if the parent appears to be under the influence of drugs or alcohol or uses same during a visit.

i. Visits will be discontinued if at any time after the child(ren) turns 12 years of age and the child states that he/she does not wish to visit the parent.

Third. Pictures and report cards are to be provided by the foster parent to the birth parent four times per year.

Fourth. This agreement shall survive the adoption of the children and shall be governed by the laws of the state.

Fifth. Upon finalization of the children's adoption with the foster parents, no court proceedings involving this agreement shall not, in any manner, impair the foster parents' adoption of the children.

(*continued*)

TABLE 4.5 Sample Conditional Agreement (*continued*)

Sixth. Unless commenced by (the custody agency), the foster parent and biological mother fully understand and agree that upon finalization of the children's adoption, any issues, including disputes involving this agreement, shall be between foster parents and biological mother and shall not involve (the custody agency) or the county of _____ (hereinafter 'county'). The foster parents and biological mother agree that should they commence any legal proceedings involving this agreement which names (the custody agency) or the county, they will be obligated in any such proceedings to compensate (the custody agency) or the county for any legal fees, including attorney fees, that the custody agency or the county may incur in defending any such actions. Any court proceedings involving this agreement shall be before the Family Court of the state of _____, county of _____. Unless commenced by (the custody agency), court proceedings seeking enforcement, modification, alleging violations, or in any manner referencing this agreement, shall not name or include (the custody agency), the county, or any employee of either (the custody agency) or the county, either officially or individually.

Seventh. Foster parents fully intend to follow through and finalize adoption of the children. However, should adoption of the children with the foster parents not occur, the biological mother agrees that (the custody agency) may place children in such other adoptive home and finalize adoption. In such event, the terms of this agreement involving any contact or visitation or any ongoing relation by biological mother with the children is null and void.

Eighth. This constitutes the entire agreement between the birth parent, foster and adoptive parents and (the custody agency).

If you are concerned that the options available for the child(ren) in your own situation do not fit the child's needs, speak with the treatment team or at least one of the members of the treatment team. It may be possible that another solution can be found. Remember: "Two heads are better than one" and "a whole team of people may create a plan that one person cannot conceive on their own."

Implement the Plan

Remember, part of the plan was for the social worker to present the idea regarding the permanency placement to her supervisor, the custody agent, the family treatment conference, and the attorneys involved. In the beginning, not everyone agreed that a conditional surrender was in the best interests of Mary, Jason, and Sara. It took the team a few meetings to agree on a plan that would fit the needs of all three children. The team had to balance the higher degree of bonding Mary had with her mother and the lesser degree of bonding that Jason and Sara had with her. After much thought, the treatment team finally came to the agreement that the conditional surrender was in the best interests of all three children. Ms. Danby asked the O'Donnells to supervise visits between Mrs. Randolf and the children after the adoption, and they agreed. Mrs. Randolph was happy with this scenario as well. Two weeks later, the court approved the plan and the O'Donnells began the formal process of adoption. After the open adoption was finalized, Mrs. Randolf visited Mary, Jason, and Sara on a monthly basis. The children were happy to be in a safe home and benefited from the love of one father and two mothers.

Summary

In the case of Mary, Jason, and Sara, not everyone agreed on the best outcome for the children. In this chapter we have examined foster care in the context of the family court system, which is one place where the adults must agree or else the judge will make a separate determination.

It is important to remember (1) that children rely on the adults in their life to advocate for them with attorneys, with CASA workers, and especially with judges; and (2) that the time spent in the courtroom is short, and information on a case must be presented succinctly and accurately (i.e., based on observation with objectivity, and not feelings with subjectivity). Cases come to the attention of the court system because of either abuse or neglect. Try to find consensus among the attorneys and their clients before going into the courtroom. This may take many months of negotiating, but it can also help avoid a painful delay in the short life of a child, a delay in returning home or in moving on to another permanent situation; thus Gladstone's quote "Justice delayed is justice denied." Understanding why the children are in care is as important as understanding what needs to happen for a child to leave foster care.

Another area to with which to familiarize yourself is the court process, which involves court-related vocabulary and laws surrounding court proceedings. This chapter also summarizes one of the creative options for children needing permanency when they cannot return to family—conditional surrenders. Conditional surrenders, while not appropriate for every child, can allow a compromise for the adults when visitation for children and their birth parents is warranted beyond termination of rights.

What needs to be remembered most through the entire court process is what is most appropriate and helpful for the child.

Discussion Questions

1. As a practitioner, how would you have decided where to place the children, and with whom to place them?
2. Why is it important for a nonattorney such as a practitioner or foster parent to become familiar with court procedure?
3. In your opinion, was it better for Jason and Sara to be adopted by the O'Donnells with or without a conditional surrender? Why?
4. What are the pros and cons of practitioners giving copies of the court orders to the foster parents and/or relative caregivers?

Web Sites

- Adoption and Foster Care Reporting System data: www.acf.hhs .gov/programs/cb/stats_research/
- Child Welfare Information Gateway: http://www.childwelfare.gov/
- Kinship Care Legal Research Center: http://www.abanet.org/child/ kinshipcare.shtml
- Legal Advocates for Permanent Parenting: http://www.lapponline .org/AboutUs/
- National Child Advocacy Center: http://www.nationalcac.org/
- National Court Appointed Special Advocates: http://www.nationalcasa .org/
- State and local government directory of government Web sites: http:// www.statelocalgov.net/index.cfm

5

Advocating Within the School System

Action is the catalyst that creates accomplishments. It is the path that takes us from uncrafted hopes to realized dreams.

—Thomas Huxley

Vignette

One week ago, in the month of February, the Family Court ordered that nine-year-old Juan Rodriguez be placed in the temporary custody of a kinship caregiver—his great-aunt, Mrs. Maria Lopez. Juan's mother, Ms. Rodriguez, lost temporary custody because she had abandoned him several times overnight while she used cocaine with friends. Ms. Rodriguez was ordered to complete inpatient treatment for cocaine dependency and depression; subsequent outpatient treatment; and parenting classes. Additionally, the Family Court ordered supervised visitation pending her discharge from outpatient treatment and would review the case in six months. Mrs. Lopez and her niece have a somewhat distant relationship.

Mrs. Lopez lives forty-five minutes away from the Rodriguez home. Currently Juan is attending the same school as he had before placement. She knows it is important for him to have stability at school. For the past three days, however, she has driven him to the school, which is very inconvenient for her and her work schedule. Mrs. Lopez does not know how she can continue this schedule for the remainder of the school year, nor is she acquainted with his academic record at school. All that she remembers is that he enjoys math and music classes.

Today, Mrs. Lopez received a call from the teacher. Juan had begun crying in class and walked out, despite being asked to stay. He ended up going to the principal's office and later sat with the guidance counselor. The guidance counselor called Mrs. Lopez to pick Juan up from school because he did not want to go back to class. When she picked him up from school, Juan hugged her forcefully and said he did not know want to go back there. When she asked him why, he said only, "School is too hard," and did not want to discuss it anymore.

Mrs. Lopez desperately wants to assist Juan and advocate for his welfare in school but is unsure what to do or how to proceed. She contacted her foster care worker, Mr. Robson, for assistance. Mr. Robson had just received the case from the child protective services worker. He also wanted to create a plan incorporating the most important considerations and tasks he can do to help Juan.

Key

Juan Rodriguez: child in kinship care.
Mrs. Maria Lopez: Juan's great aunt and kinship caregiver.
Ms. Rodriguez: Juan's mother.
Mr. Robson: foster care worker.

Alongside family and peers, the school serves as an important anchor in the lives of children. For children in care whose lives have been disrupted, the school as an institution provides particular support with respect to promoting stability and healthy child and adolescent development. Practitioners and caregivers can take steps to facilitate the role of the school in helping the children in their care.

Advocacy Checklist

• Maintain stable school placement.
• Ensure efficient school enrollment.
• Arrange for assessment and intervention·for youth with special needs.
• Learn about the school culture.
• Promote privacy.

Maintain Stable School Placement

Identify the Need

When a child comes into foster care and has to change residence, it is essential to preserve the stability of as many aspects of that youth's life as possible. It is a sad but common reality that the youth's primary relationships have likely become either strained or severed through the maltreatment they have experienced (Dore 2005). For these youth, remaining in their original school should be a priority, because they are familiar with the school environment and typically have developed relationships with their teachers and their peers. They know the routine. They are familiar with the school building and the layout of the classrooms. They have their peer group, whom they sit with in the lunchroom. They understand the rituals particular to the school culture, and they know which school events are most popular. Reducing multiple school placements—that is, reducing school mobility—is essential.

When a child is placed in family foster care or kinship care and the new family is located within the district served by the school, then changing schools is not an issue. Looking at the vignette, we see that keeping Juan at his familiar school presents a challenge to the family, because Mrs. Lopez lives forty-five minutes away, in another school district. She has neither the financial resources nor the inclination to move closer, yet she knows it would be beneficial for him to stay with the same teachers and friends. She is uncertain of what to do.

Analyze the Context

Statistics suggest that the need for school placement stability is of the utmost importance. One three-state study (Courtney, Terao, and Bost 2004) found that foster care children change schools twice as often as other children, while another study in New York discovered that 75 percent of youth changed to a different school once in placement (Advocates for Children of New York, Inc., 2000). A third study, directed by Casey Family Programs, discovered that more than two-thirds of former foster care youth had attended at least three elementary schools and one-third had attended at least five high schools (Pecora, Williams et al. 2006). These findings indicate that moving between schools (school mobility) is a dynamic that counters the need for stable attachment. In the light of these statistics, then, what can help Mrs. Lopez and Juan to reduce the possibility of multiple school placements?

Fortunately, this need has been centrally addressed in relatively recent federal law. The McKinney-Vento Homeless Education Assistance Improvements Act of 2001 (42 U.S.C. §11431 et seq.) provides a legal framework for advocating for youth when it comes to helping them remain in their home school. "Under the McKinney-Vento Act, youth who qualify as 'awaiting foster care placement' in your state generally have this right" (School Stability, Legal Center for Foster Care and Education, p.1). Specifically, the act states:

> (1) If the homeless child or youth continues to live in the area served by the local educational agency in which the school of origin is located, the child's or youth's transportation to and from the school of origin shall be provided or arranged by the local educational agency in which the school of origin is located.
>
> (2) If the homeless child's or youth's living arrangements in the area served by the local educational agency of origin terminate and the child or youth, though continuing his or her education in the school of origin, begins living in an area served by another local educational agency, the local educational agency of origin and the local educational agency in which the homeless child or youth is living shall agree upon a method to apportion the responsibility and costs for providing the child with transportation to and from the school of origin. If the local educational agencies are unable to agree upon such method, the responsibility and costs for transportation shall be shared equally. (http://www.ed.gov/policy/elsec/leg/esea02/pg116.html)

Although the McKinney-Vento Act is landmark legislation in addressing this need and providing parameters for intervention, the term "awaiting foster care placement" is defined differently from state to state, and so the application of the act varies. Some states interpret the law to include all youth awaiting care, while other states do not (although exceptions may be made) (School Stability, Legal Center for Foster Care and Education, p. 1). Additionally, some states may have their own provisions for youth in foster care when it comes to minimizing school placement disruption

(School Stability, Legal Center for Foster Care and Education, p. 1). Relative caregivers who are in the process of obtaining permanent guardianship and the practitioners who are assisting them should inquire as well about eligibility. In this vignette, Mrs. Lopez is serving as a temporary provider of care to Juan.

The McKinney-Vento Act does establish a federal guide for minimizing multiple school placements for youth like Juan. Moreover, it establishes the designation of a state coordinator and local liaisons who can answer foster parents' questions with respect to how their individual states implement the McKinney-Vento Act. This liaison can also assist foster parents and practitioners on state interpretations of "awaiting foster care placement" and how transportation may be coordinated. As the act requires, transportation is to be coordinated between the jurisdictions of the original school (that the child attends) and the new, geographically closer, school. The key again is whether the state defines youth *in* foster care as "awaiting foster care placement" and what additional state laws they have to guide their intervention.

Develop the Plan

According to the Legal Center for Foster Care and Education (School Stability, 2008), "the easiest and most effective way to keep a child's education stable is to minimize living placement changes" (p. 1). With this philosophy in mind, what factors are important in developing a plan in advocating to minimize the school mobility of youth in care?

Practitioners considering foster care placements should seek family foster or kinship care families that are located within the child's current school district. They should find potential foster parents and identify relative caregivers to see if a placement can be made that allows the child to remain in the original school. Practitioners can also increase the likelihood of this outcome by reminding their supervisors of the need to have foster families available in as many geographic areas as possible, rather than having foster homes clustered around a few school districts.

When a child comes into their care and supervision, foster parents need to remember the importance of his psychological link to his school. If the foster parent is in the same school district, any plans to move from the school district may need to include an assessment of the child's relationship with the school—that is, to what extent is the child flourishing, and can she draw upon relationships with both school staff and peers? It is also important to consider the school's curriculum —if a teenager in care is attending a high school that offers a particular "magnet" program of study that is of interest to him (e.g., culinary arts), and no other high school offers culinary arts in a 60-mile radius, then the importance of keeping the youth in that particular school remains paramount.

Practitioners and foster parents can consider and coordinate several steps in developing their plan (School Stability, Legal Center for Foster Care and Education, pp. 1–2). They can coordinate with each other on who will both look up and contact the McKinney-Vento liaison, who will provide more information. In addition, they can determine how "awaiting placement" is determined by each state or municipality. Further, foster parents and practitioners can become familiar with any state legal entitlements, including the rights for transportation to the home school. Finally, they can discuss placement options with kinship care providers (if available) and the youth themselves.

Implement the Plan

Mrs. Lopez and the practitioner want what is best for Juan. They now know the importance of keeping Juan at his school, the context of both the McKinney-Vento Act, and the importance of learning what additional state laws exist. Now it is time to implement the plan.

First, the practitioner should consider the importance of school stability when considering Juan's home placement *prior to placement*. Here an ethical dilemma might occur for the practitioner, because in all cases it is preferable that a child be placed with a caring relative if available rather than with kind-hearted strangers (family foster parents). However, what happens if the relative lives outside of the school district while four foster families are available in the same district as Juan's school? An ethical dilemma presents itself as the practitioner weighs the value of the child staying with a relative versus the value of the child remaining in the same school. Typically the former outweighs the latter, but this decision can be determined by the practitioner after consultation with her or his supervisor.

The practitioner should also talk with the child about his wishes as well. Often, we forget to ask what the child (who is at the center of this situation) wants; therefore, asking Juan questions like, "How important it is for you to live with your great-aunt (Mrs. Lopez)?" and "How important is it for you to stay at your school?" is critical for understanding his perspective.

Typically, the practitioner would then talk to the relative caregiver (if available) and assess the feasibility of Juan staying at his school. Recall that the McKinney-Vento Act makes school stability a goal when "feasible" (Blueprint for Change). Very likely, it will fall to the practitioner to bring up the issue of school placement with Mrs. Lopez because the practitioner should be much more familiar with this issue. However, in the event that the practitioner does not initiate this issue, Mrs. Lopez should ask the caseworker about maintaining Juan's school placement.

In making a decision on residence with a major emphasis on school placement, the practitioner and foster parent can decide who will contact the McKinney-Vento liaison for assistance and learn about state rights, including transportation. Mrs. Lopez and the practitioner decided that it is feasible for Juan to stay in his home school and decided that he will be picked up one hour earlier and get home one hour later than before his placement in foster care. While this is not ideal for Mrs. Lopez or for Juan, she believes that because Juan trusts his third grade teacher very much and has a few friends at school, she does not wish to interrupt his school year. She is glad that her state allows for him to remain in his home school and provides transportation for him to do so. Mrs. Lopez contacted the elementary school near her home; after she explained the situation, the local McKinney-Vento liaison worked out the transportation from Mrs. Lopez's home to Juan's original school.

Ensure Efficient School Enrollment

Identify the Need

This earlier outcome with Juan represents the best-case scenario—when it is feasible for the child to remain in her/his school. However this is not always the case; there are times when it is impossible for the child to remain in school because the foster parent or relative caregiver currently lives in or has imminent plans to move to a home in another school district that is just too far away. Let's amend the vignette a bit and state that Mrs. Lopez resides *two* hours away from Juan's original school. Although the

McKinney-Vento Act provides a mandate for transportation to the home school, the time Juan would have to spend on a bus makes it infeasible for him to continue at school. Therefore, Juan will have to enroll in another school during the middle of the school year.

School enrollment and record transfers must be as straightforward as possible (Blueprint for Change). Mrs. Lopez and Mr. Robson's shared need is to make Juan's transition to his new school as efficient as possible. Mrs. Lopez has no paperwork on Juan. Even though she is his great-aunt, she does not know her niece (Juan's mother) well at all. She does not have immunization or other medical records, Juan's birth certificate, past report cards, attendance records, or any record of past behavior incidents. Mr. Robson also knows it is a necessity to have comprehensive and accurate paperwork on Juan but does not know where to begin.

Analyze the Context

This situation emerges in a context where the need to enroll students quickly is very important. One study from New York found that "42% of the children and youth did not begin school immediately upon entering foster care"; almost half of these delays were due to "lost or misplaced records" (Advocates for Children of New York 2000:4). Another study discovered that in San Francisco, foster parents believed that home schools' failure to provide sufficient information made it an average of 6.5 times more likely that the youth's school enrollment would be delayed (Choice, D'Andrade et al. 2001:79).

Fortunately, the McKinney-Vento Act also makes provisions in the event that a child needs to enroll in a different school during an existing school year. The act discusses enrollment in the following manner:

(i) The school selected in accordance with this paragraph shall immediately enroll the homeless child or youth, even if the child or youth is unable to produce records normally required for enrollment, such as previous academic records, medical records, proof of residency, or other documentation.

(ii) The enrolling school shall immediately contact the school last attended by the child or youth to obtain relevant academic and other records.

(iii) If the child or youth needs to obtain immunizations, or immunization or medical records, the enrolling school shall immediately refer the parent or guardian of the child or youth to the local educational agency liaison designated under paragraph (1)(J)(ii), who shall assist in obtaining necessary immunizations, or immunization or medical records, in accordance with subparagraph (D).

(D) RECORDS: Any record ordinarily kept by the school, including immunization or medical records, academic records, birth certificates, guardianship records, and evaluations for special services or programs, regarding each homeless child or youth shall be maintained —(i) so that the records are available, in a timely fashion, when a child or youth enters a new school or school district; and (ii) in a manner consistent with section 444 of the General Education Provisions Act (20 U.S.C. 1232g).

As you can see, built-in advocacy is included in this legislation so that a child can be enrolled in school as quickly as possible even if key records, such as immunization records, proof of residency, birth certificates, and academic records, are not available or if the foster parent is not yet able to purchase a school uniform (Blueprint for Change).

Both the practitioner and the foster parent should be informed that this legislation exists, so that they can effectively advocate for the child in foster care. In addition, states have varying laws regarding school enrollment. For example, each state has a law on how soon a child needs to be enrolled in school, who has the appropriate custody to enroll the child (e.g., child welfare agency, foster parent), and particulars relating to the timetable of receiving records. As with the stable school placement advocacy plan, the same McKinney-Vento liaison is available to facilitate this process with Mr. Robson and Mrs. Lopez. The McKinney-Vento Act also provides a process for handling disputes relating to enrollment; once again, the liaison is the contact person who facilitates the investigation and resolution of the enrollment dispute. Again, relative caregivers who are seeking permanent custody should investigate the applicability of the McKinney-Vento Act with the liaison.

It is important to note that the school that Juan is transferred should conform to the concept of the "least restrictive environment"—that is, youth are enrolled in a school environment with as minimal distraction as possible. Sometimes schools place children where it is practically expedient, even if the school is not the most academically appropriate. For example, youth who do not need a residential school could be enrolled in one because it is the quickest way to enroll the child. Advocates should be aware of this and ensure that only appropriate placement occurs.

One other issue that could affect efficient school enrollment relates to diversity. Although this does not apply to Juan, there will be times when the child is not up to date on immunizations, likely because the parent has been neglectful in taking the child to the pediatrician. A different interpretation of being "neglectful" can be viewed through the lens of religious organizations (such as Scientology) that do not permit immunizations and do not believe this is child neglect. Though unlikely, if this ethical issue emerges, it is vital that the practitioner consult with the McKinney-Vento local liaison as soon as possible.

Develop the Plan

Under the new scenario, in which Mrs. Lopez lives two hours away from Juan's original school, Mr. Robson and Mrs. Lopez need to develop a plan that will ensure that Juan is enrolled as quickly as possible and with all supporting paperwork (immunization records, birth certificate, and academic records such as grade level, report card, attendance records, and information on any special needs).

A useful way to obtain this information is to contact the home school. "Many states require the prompt transfer of records between schools" (School Transitions, Legal Center for Foster Care and Education, p. 1). As many of us know, however, requirements stated in the law can vary when actually enacted; "promptness" on paper might look different from "promptness" in reality. One example of a school district that strongly advocates for foster children in terms of quick and efficient enrollment is the Broward County Public School System in Florida. One of the largest school districts in the United States, this system employs a "dependency coordinator" who regularly goes to court to coordinate the paperwork necessary to enroll the youth in the new school (D. Winters, pers. comm., June 3, 2008; see also Zetlin, Weinberg, and Shea 2006 on the use of an education liaison for youth in care), thereby improving educational prospects for youth in care.

Obtaining this information also requires the cooperation of the birth family. Success in this matter often depends on the practitioners' (and at times, the foster parents') relationships with the birth parent(s). The nature of the child's removal from the birth parent's physical custody (that is, how agreeable the birth parents were) and the actual school records the birth parent has in her possession determine the ease in which the practitioner can obtain them. Sometimes children's removal from a family is accepted willingly by the birth parents because they realize that they do need help in providing a safe and nurturing home to their children. In these cases, the practitioner can plan on simply asking the birth parent for this information and see what records the birth parent indeed has at her home. If an antagonistic relationship exists, where the birth parent is hostile toward the child and the process, the caseworker may not receive all necessary paperwork. Additionally, if the foster parent is a relative, the nature of the relationship between the foster parent and the birth parent might be better (that is, positive, or at least less adversarial) than the practitioner's relationship with the birth parent, and therefore, the foster parent might have an easier time in securing the information.

Mr. Robson, the caseworker, needs to be familiar with the state and local laws regarding enrollment and can ask school officials such as the principal or assistant principals for this information. Proper enrollment involves a number of additional factors, including ensuring that: (1) youth are able to receive credit/partial credit for past classes, (2) there is flexibility with timelines in participating in school activities and (3) provisions are made to award a diploma even if prior school(s) differed in relation to graduation requirements in comparison to the current school (Blueprint for Change). Mr. Robson also needs to find if positions such as a dependency coordinator (school staff that works with enrolling youth in care) exist in the school system. Finally, in developing the plan, it is important for either the practitioner or the foster parent to contact the McKinney-Vento local liaison for assistance in this process, which includes help with record transfers.

Implement the Plan

Making assessments on strategies of advocacy on a case by case basis is the foundation for implementing the plan. The cooperation of the practitioner and the foster parent is fundamental to initiating the process of making an efficient transition from one school to the other.

Based on information in the scenario provided, Mr. Robson, the caseworker, would first have to find out how much information he can obtain from Juan's mother, Mrs. Rodriguez. In the scenario, Mrs. Rodriguez was upset with Mr. Robson for removing Juan but wanted to ensure that Juan stayed in the family. Therefore, she gave Mr. Robson the phone number of Mrs. Lopez. Mr. Robson waited with Juan at his mother's house for one hour, until Mrs. Lopez arrived. After she was approved by his agency to take temporary physical custody of Juan, Mrs. Lopez and Mr. Robson strategized on getting the necessary paperwork for Juan. Mrs. Rodriguez did find and give his birth certificate to Mrs. Lopez, who, as Mr. Robson learned from the McKinney-Vento liaison, had the authority to enroll Juan in his new school. Mrs. Lopez said she would enroll him in school tomorrow (which was a Monday). Mr. Robson said he would take care of obtaining the remaining records.

On Monday, Mrs. Lopez came to school with only Juan's birth certificate and was able to enroll him. On Wednesday of that week, Mr. Robson personally picked up Juan's immunization and academic records from the original school and brought them to the new one. He had realized that although the original school would eventually send the records, he should try to speed up the process, and so he took the records directly to the new school. The process of coordination between Mr. Robson and Mrs. Lopez, along with the assistance of the school and Juan's mother, provided a fairly smooth transition for Juan.

Arrange for Assessment and Intervention for Youth with Special Needs

Identify the Need

Turning to another issue in our vignette, Mrs. Lopez was not surprised to hear that Juan had walked out of class; she knew that it was very stressful for Juan to move away from his mother, whom he dearly loved, have no contact with her (while the mother, Mrs. Rodriguez, was in inpatient treatment), and move in with his great-aunt, whom he did not know too well. The next morning, he stayed in bed despite Mrs. Lopez offering to talk to him and stating that it was very important that he go to school.

She felt bad for Juan but also was frustrated that she did not know what to do for him.

While we can anticipate that all children, whether in foster care or not, will have challenges in their transitions throughout childhood and adolescence, youth in foster care are particularly vulnerable, because of the traumatic experience of being temporarily (or perhaps permanently) removed from their family of origin. This vulnerability can manifest in cognitive, emotional, and behavioral issues that affect them at school. (A broader and more detailed analysis of these issues is discussed in the next chapter.) Additionally, because youth in foster care may not have had as much oversight by their families as those children who are still with their biological families, learning challenges that would qualify as "special needs" might not have been determined and therefore youth arrive in foster care without any assessment history. As advocates for Juan, both Mrs. Lopez and Mr. Robson need to be aware of any special needs that hinder Juan's learning process and ultimately his academic success.

Analyze the Context

It is invaluable for practitioners and foster parents to be aware that potential behavioral, cognitive, emotional, and medical needs can occur in children in care; caregiver knowledge about how these challenges can best be addressed will contribute to the children's success in school. Certainly, some children in care do very well in school and do not have any major academic challenges. However, some children in foster care may face challenges that can make learning difficult. It is perfectly reasonable to expect that children in care will have to make an adjustment in their new family and to the situation that can make school responsibilities very difficult for them. A number of "indicators" can suggest that a youth is having difficulty at school and might have a need that should be addressed.

For instance, from a behavioral standpoint, children in foster care might not want to attend school, have difficulty focusing in class or completing homework, disruptively interact with peers or teachers, achieve poor grades, and/or skip school (truancy). Cognitively, youth may have difficulty verbally expressing their thoughts or processing written information. They may not be fluent in English and therefore have a need for English as a Second Language (ESL) skill-building. (Advocates should take special note of any language barrier and work with school officials and interpreters provided by the school or social service systems for assistance.) Finally, children in care may experience the emotional toll of trauma from their own abuse or neglect within their birth family.

It is important to note that although some youth in care may already have a diagnosis of a learning or emotional challenge (e.g., reading disorder, dyslexia, attention deficit hyperactivity disorder [ADHD]), other youth who struggle in the classroom *have not* undergone an assessment. For these youth, an assessment is the first step in assisting them toward success in the classroom.

Assessing for special needs among children in foster care is critically important. A number of studies suggest that these youth face educational challenges (Barth 1990; Buehler, Orme et al. 2000; McMillen, Auslander et al. 2003). For example, some studies suggest that 24 to 37 percent of youth in care perform under grade level (English, Kouidou-Giles, and Plocke 1994; Iglehart 1994); in one study, 36 percent of youth had had to repeat a grade (Pecora, Williams et al. 2006). Although youth who reside in care longer have better outcomes in terms of receiving a high school diploma or GED (Casey Family Services 2001; Mallon 1998), youth in foster care do face a large challenge in obtaining the GED—with studies suggesting a high school or GED completion rate ranging from 45 to 65 percent (Barth 1990; Festinger 1983). A few studies suggest that youth in care have larger behavioral issues in school, and are at greater risk of being suspended (McMillen, Auslander et al. 2003; Seyfried, Pecora et al. 2000). Finally, with respect to special education:

> Numerous studies indicate anywhere between one-quarter and nearly one half (23%–47%) of children and youth in out-of-home care in the U.S. receive special education services at some point in their schooling. The national average of school-aged children and youth served in special education each year is close to 12%.   (National Working Group on Foster Care and Education 2007:3)

What is equally concerning is the finding from several studies that advocacy efforts should be greatly improved (National Working Group on Foster Care and Education 2007:3). For example, in a New York study, "60% of caseworkers/social workers surveyed 'were not aware of existing laws when referring children to special education' and over 50% said 'that their

clients did not receive appropriate services very often while in foster care' "
(Advocates for Children of New York, Inc. 2000:6).

These statistics document the needs that translate into challenging
outcomes for youth in care with respect to high school/GED completion,
grade repetition, behavior issues, and special education. Therefore, the
need to promote success in the classroom warrants the foster parents and
practitioners' attunement to any special needs the youth may have. Clearly,
a role for advocacy exists here.

Children in care such as Juan (as well as many youth not in foster care)
could qualify for a special accommodation called the individualized education plan (IEP). The provision concerning the IEP is contained in the 1974
federal law entitled the Individuals with Disabilities Education Act (IDEA),
which is intended to "protect the educational rights of children with disabilities and assures that they receive a free and appropriate public education" (O'Connor and Barbell 2001:3). In this case, "appropriate" refers to
educational services to be granted to all youth (not just those in foster care)
who have a recognized cognitive, mental, or physical challenge that inter-
feres with their ability to receive education. The IEP exists in the context
of the "least restrictive environment" (O'Connor and Barbell 2001), which
means that this accommodation should be incorporated into the youth's
education in as minimally distracting a way as possible. Such an accommodation ranges from allowing the child extra time for assignments and
offering him different ways to take an exam (taking an exam verbally versus written), to his receiving some instruction in a specialized classroom,
and from sending her to see a speech therapist or school social worker to
having her live in a facility that provides instruction and care (the school
district picks up the bill) (O'Connor and Barbell 2001).

All involved professionals can make a referral for a student to be evaluated for special needs (O'Connor and Barbell 2001). Parents are empowered with the right to request services; "adoptive parents fit this category,
as do relatives and even non-relatives who have assumed guardianship of
children in their care (this category includes caretakers participating in
subsidized or assisted guardianship programs)." IDEA establishes a provision for a "a special 'educational surrogate parent' for children or youth in
care" (O'Connor and Barbell 2001:7). It is up to the state education agency
to designate who the educational surrogates are; in some states foster parents are automatically appointed while in other states volunteers (such as
court-appointed special advocates [CASA] volunteers) are appointed (Elze,

Auslander et al. 2005). Relatives who are providing temporary supervision for youth in foster care should contact the school to see if, because they are kinship care providers, they are automatically educational surrogates (D. Winters, pers. comm., June 3, 2008). Relatives who are in the process of becoming permanent legal guardians or adopting the youth should contact the school as well.

Educational surrogates need to be aware of both the context in which they are authorized to act and their specific responsibilities. Elze, Auslander et al. (2005) remind us that:

> Unless parental rights are terminated, biological parents retain the right to make educational decisions for their children. Surrogate parents possess all the rights of a parent in the special education process, including requesting testing and evaluation, signing consent forms, participating in IEP meetings, approving special education services, and requesting due process proceedings. However, states vary in the eligibility criteria and appointment process for surrogate parents. It is not uncommon for children in foster care to slip through the cracks and experience delays in the assignment of a surrogate parent.   (Powers and Stotland 2002:201)

In Juan's case, Mrs. Lopez learned from the principal that because she was his great-aunt, she was also his educational surrogate. Knowing this, she now understood that she was responsible for helping develop a plan of action to help Juan in school.

Develop the Plan

The basis of a good plan of intervention is an initial assessment. How do foster parents, relative caregivers, and practitioners obtain the initial information that can provide the basis for a referral for IEP eligibility and potential intervention? Potential sources of data indicating that a youth might be having a challenging time in school include the child him/herself; school staff (e.g., teacher, nurse, school social worker, administrator); the educational surrogate; the caregiver (unless the caregiver is the educational surrogate); the practitioner; and the CASA volunteer.

For the first source, children who find it hard to concentrate in class might let the foster parent know about this difficulty when they go home from school. Statements such as "I don't understand the material," "School is too hard," and "I am mad, and I can't keep up" are all signs of potential special needs. Additionally, the professionals involved should be vigilant to any behavioral, learning, or emotional patterns that are repeated. Some of the patterns they can look for are detailed in table 5.1. Again, while none of these behaviors, in and of itself, is always a definite sign of a special need, they should be brought to the attention of the educational surrogate. Although formal assessment can be conducted only by a qualified educational, mental health, or medical professional, the foster parent and practitioner should be very aware of any possible indicators outside of the norm of child development, keeping in mind the likely additional challenges that children in foster care face.

For Mrs. Lopez, as the educational surrogate, her concern related to Juan leaving class and his statement that school was too difficult. Mrs. Lopez talked to both Mr. Robson and Juan's favorite teacher for their advice on whether her concerns were sufficient to warrant her requesting a special needs evaluation under IDEA (O'Connor and Barbell 2001). They both encouraged her to make such a request via a meeting at Juan's school.

TABLE 5.1 Patterns Indicating Potential Difficulty in School	
TYPE OF PATTERN	INDICATOR
Disciplinary	Visits to the principal Detentions Suspensions/expulsions Truancy
Academic	Difficulty with reading, math, writing, and speaking comprehension Incomplete homework Poor grades Running out of time to take tests
Emotional	Anxiety Crying Rage Social withdrawal

Implement the Plan

Implementing the plan involves requesting services for special education (under the IDEA) as well as having, once the request for services is approved, a professional assessment completed to determine if the child is eligible for an IEP. With the support of Mr. Robson and the teacher, Mrs. Lopez formally requested an evaluation with the special education coordinator at Juan's school (the school administration will inform you of the appropriate person to whom you should make the request). The assessments are commonly conducted by school psychologists and special education staff (although other staff, ranging from speech therapists to pediatric orthopedists, could be consulted based on need). Eligibility is determined by three factors:

> 1) Whether the student has a disability; 2) How the disability affects the student's progress in school; and 3) What services are recommended to address the student's individual needs. (O'Connor and Barbell 2001:9)

Fortunately, Mrs. Lopez's request for an IEP meeting for Juan was approved. (There are appeal processes that can be initiated if either the request for an IEP meeting is denied or, once an IEP meeting occurs, the eligibility for an IEP is denied [O'Connor and Barbell 2001]). A school psychologist and a special education consultant professionally assessed Juan and brought their findings to the IEP meeting. Aside from Mrs. Lopez, the following individuals were in attendance for the two-hour meeting: Mr. Robson, Juan's homeroom teacher, the guidance counselor, the assistant principal, the school psychologist, the special education consultant, and Juan's mother, Mrs. Rodriguez. Mrs. Lopez had asked Mr. Robson if Juan's mother should or could attend the meeting because she could contribute information about Juan's feelings about school that she (Mrs. Lopez) did not have access to. Mr. Robson stated that it would be appropriate for the mother to attend, and Mrs. Rodriguez was in outpatient treatment at the time and was interested in attending the meeting. Juan also attended for five minutes, so that he could see that everyone wanted to help him (he later had a short visit with his mother).

At the meeting, Juan's challenges and strengths were discussed and everyone in the room participated. The team that assessed Juan came up with a diagnosis of "reading disorder," which explained why school was somewhat difficult for him, as well as "separation-anxiety disorder," which explained why he did not want to return to school. The combination of these two challenges explained Juan's difficulty with school; an intervention plan based on addressing the two issues was approved. Specifically, Juan was provided, at the school's expense, with one-on-one tutoring, continued assessment for his reading challenges, and individual and family counseling with the school social worker to address the separation-anxiety issues. The IEP set out the specific action plan, with clearly stated goals to be addressed, how they would be addressed (with the tutoring, reading assessment, and individual and family counseling), and a timetable with review dates. Mrs. Lopez, Mr. Robson, and the others were all pleased with this plan. By months later, Juan's challenges had gradually diminished and he looked forward to going to school more. This is the hallmark of the value of an IEP in helping youth with special needs.

Learn About the School Culture

Identify the Need

Juan came home from his new school one Wednesday and complained to Mrs. Lopez that he had not had extra money that day. Apparently, Wednesday was school spirit day, and he was embarrassed that he did not have money to buy things. Mrs. Lopez was not aware of this special day, and wished she could have avoided his embarrassment. In another possible example, Juan could be in a new high school where participating in school sports or activities was considered the norm. As his foster parent, Mrs. Lopez might find it useful to explore with Juan what sports or activities he might wish to participate in—of course, this participation should be voluntary rather than mandatory.

While not part of formal policy, as the earlier needs were, the concerns in these examples highlight the need to assist youth with their (continued) adjustment to school by learning about the school culture. Just like helping them with their homework, taking part in parent-teacher conferences, and addressing any special needs, becoming familiar with the school's culture and acting on that knowledge is an act of advocacy.

Analyze the Context

When a youth comes into care, it is incumbent upon the foster parent to learn and understand as much as possible about the school culture (D. Winters, pers. comm., June 3, 2008). By school culture, we mean the particular norms and activities that embody the values of the school. With respect to norms, for example, if he knows that cell phones are allowed in high school for emergency purposes, then the foster parent is aware that it is his choice on whether to allow the child to have one. Some schools, however, may ban cell phones; awareness of a norm like this would prevent the child from "getting in trouble" by having to have the cell phone taken away.

Here is another example: Say Juan will move to a new private school at the beginning of the next school year, and is currently in a public school. Identifying the differences in attending public school versus private will be important in minimizing any adjustment challenges for the child.

A last norm could be, say, that students in the school are typically native English speakers. If a student's first language is Chinese and she is still learning English, then arrangements should be made for language instruction to reduce the stigma that a nonnative speaker might encounter in that school (see next section for a further discussion of stigma).

Such explorations, intended to assist in the adjustment process, are relevant for both when the child is remaining in his/her original school yet the school is new to the foster parent or kinship caregiver, and when the school is new to the child as well.

Develop the Plan

Once they are aware of this need, foster parents can think about which school staff would be best suited to introduce them to the norms of the school culture. Planning to ask the guidance counselor, school social worker, teacher, or principal is an effective strategy. Additionally, as the foster parent comes to know other parents of children who attend the school, these parents can assist them in discovering what norms, expectations, and activities are considered the most important.

Implement the Plan

Once foster parents have found out about the particular events, activities, and norms that represent the school culture, they can implement the plan by having discussions with the children about what to anticipate in school.

A high school–aged Juan would know that attending pep rallies is very important for school unity.

By no means is understanding school culture a reason to require youth to conform to all norms and attend all activities; rather, it is simply a strategy to enable you to identify the norms that exist and then share these with the child so that, together, the foster parent and the child have sufficient information to make decisions on how to participate in school culture. Implementing this plan grants the foster parent the opportunity to assist youth in their school adjustment by proactively identifying norms of school culture. For youth already managing many other changes in their lives, foster parents' knowledge of the culture serves as one less hurdle and promises to help with the youths' continued adjustment to school.

Promote Privacy

Identify the Need

Though this need might be considered to be at the forefront of advocacy, the need to maintain privacy can easily be forgotten among other concerns, and therefore should be explicitly addressed throughout.

Juan quickly began attending his new school and was officially enrolled. He was adjusting to the school process fairly well when, in the lunchroom, two of the students started to tease him, taunting that he was not "wanted" and claiming that that was why he was in foster care. They said that "they heard his Mom did not want him and that he is poor." Juan told them to shut up—all three started to argue. A cafeteria monitor came over and sent everyone to the office, where the principal intervened. When he asked where the two students had heard these things, they said they overheard their homeroom teacher talking to another teacher about Juan. Juan, along with the cafeteria monitor, told Mrs. Lopez that he had been teased at school, and he wondered aloud if the things that the others had said were true. Mrs. Lopez, understandably shaken, reassured him that he was loved by her and that his mother loved him as well; his mother (Mrs. Rodriguez), she told him, needed to take care of some things for a while and consequently Juan was living with Mrs. Lopez.

This scenario points to the sensitivity that must be exercised to promote privacy for children in care. When children have already experienced home and possibly school changes, the last thing they need is to be stigmatized and embarrassed over their status as a "foster child."

Analyze the Context

Operating within a large system, schools administration, teachers, and students are constantly exchanging information. One piece of information that *should never be shared except when absolutely necessary* is the child's status as a "foster" child. The stigma of being in foster care remains. In fact, the McKinney-Vento Act underscores the importance of professionals being attentive and sensitive to this issue by stating that homeless children (and "homeless children" can be interpreted to mean those in foster care) should not be stigmatized.

Develop the Plan

In pursuing the plan of guarding privacy, foster parents and practitioners advocating for youth need to play more of a monitoring role and to understand how privacy is handled at schools. Schools, of course, should have a policy to keep the child's foster care status, along with all records, private and inform staff only on a need-to-know basis. Staff, once they know, should be aware of the sensitivity of this information and be very respectful of Juan's privacy in the sharing of it. Although schools vary regarding what required documents are necessary, at the least a few staff people at school would have likely received (from the practitioner or educational surrogate) a copy of the state custody papers, documentation identifying the educational surrogate, and paperwork stating who has authority to sign permission slips and to pick the youth up from school. Certainly, schools cannot provide a hermetic seal to prevent the child's foster care status from becoming known in the community. Fellow students might know the child outside of the school environment (perhaps one student's mother is friends with Mrs. Lopez and they have talked). However, it is vital for practitioners and foster parents to ask the appropriate personnel at school about which staff members have knowledge of the child's foster care status and what their policy is on any sharing of this confidential information.

Implement the Plan

With this understanding, the practitioner or foster parent should ask the administrative staff about which staff members have access to this paperwork. Then the advocate should inquire about when and how this information would be shared. For example, it is important to find out if teachers ask specific information about who signed the permission slips. Of course, Juan's status in care will emerge in parent-teacher conferences, particularly if there is a problem with academics or school behaviors that leads to the development of an IEP. At this point, as part of the overall assessment, the foster parent would have to decide whether to reveal that the youth is in foster care.

The foster parent should also periodically ask the youth if he or she is feeling comfortable in school, as a foray into asking if she or he is being teased at school. Keep in mind that the youth might be embarrassed and therefore not forthcoming about any teasing. But remaining somewhat vigilant to this need is an important component of advocating for the youth and helping with their school adjustment.

Summary

Education and training regarding the aforementioned issues are essential for practitioners and care providers. These areas include: maintaining original school placements when feasible, efficiently enrolling youth in new schools, assessing and intervening for special needs, learning about the school culture, and upholding privacy. Federal laws such as the McKinney-Vento Act and the Individuals with Disabilities Education Act, combined with state laws, provide a legal foundation to assist with these advocacy efforts.

The topics explored in the classroom are important elements in the education of practitioners and foster parents. The following words can be applied to foster parents as well to practitioners: "Child welfare caseworkers are often confused about their responsibilities related to the educational progress of their clients, and should receive training that clearly delineates their obligations" (Elze, Auslander et al. 2005:199). What is important for foster parents and practitioners to know is to familiarize themselves with these issues and know that support in the school system is available though the extent to which it is accessible varies from school to school. It was the intent of this chapter to provide an understanding of some of the most important issues in educational advocacy for youth in care. While the advocacy process certainly takes time, coordination, and communication, the end result is that the child is placed in the appropriate grade and skill level with appropriate supports and is thriving in the school environment, both in and out of the classroom. This is the hallmark of advocating for the child in the school system.

Discussion Questions

1. What aspects of educational advocacy seem to be the easiest? Most challenging? Why?
2. How might your advocacy for Juan change or stay the same if he was a sixteen-year-old high school student?
3. Juan is staying in kinship care with his great-aunt. What, if anything, would change if he was placed in care with foster parents whom he did not previously know?
4. Successful advocacy depends on professional foster parents and practitioners collaborating together. What do you see as areas of advocacy at which both groups may be equally effective in advocating for children like Juan in the school system? What areas might the foster parent have more success? What areas might the practitioner have more success?

Web Sites

- Court-Appointed Special Advocates for Children (CASA) of Humboldt County: http://www.humboldtcasa.org/advocacy_handbook.html
- Legal Center for Foster Care and Education: http://www.abanet.org/child/education/home.shtml
- National Association for the Education of Homeless Children and Youth (NAEHCY): www.naehcy.org
- The National Center for Homeless Education (NCHE): www.serve.org/nche
- National Foster Parent Association (NFPA): www.nfpainc.org/uploads/EDUCATIONAL_ADVOCACY.pdf

6

Advocating Within the Health and Mental Health Systems

The greatest wealth is health.

—Virgil

Vignette

Thirteen-year-old Brooke came into care after witnessing domestic violence between her parents and receiving bruises from multiple beatings by her father. She was extremely attached to her mother, but because of her mother's inability to shield Brooke from the domestic violence and protect her from her father, Brooke was brought into care, with the Williams family.

The Williams family lived about 10 minutes from Brooke's home, and Brooke was able to stay at her school as well as visit with her mother twice a week at the local Department of Human Services agency. Her grades were average (mostly B's with a few A's and C's).

Brooke was underweight. Although she had her last annual medical checkup 10 months ago, her pediatrician, Dr. Zaslow, made another examination and stated that her weight was in the low end of the acceptable range. Since coming into care, Brooke had been polite with the Williams but spent much of her time in her room. When eating dinner, she would eat large portions of food but often would secretly go into the bathroom and vomit her dinner. She loved to swim daily at the local swimming center.

Visiting her mother was crucial for Brooke. She longed to see her mother and was tearful when the Williams drove her home after her twice-a-week visits. She was angry that she could not see her mother more and was very worried for her mother's safety. Brooke stated she hated her father and did not want to see him. Her father did express remorse and was ordered to go to therapy and anger management classes.

Once or twice a week, Mrs. Williams would be awakened by Brooke crying out in the middle of the night. When Mrs. Williams went to see what was wrong, Brooke would be drenched in sweat. Brooke said she was recalling her father hitting her mother and herself. Mrs. Williams would hold her until Brooke fell back asleep. The nightmares had been going on for two weeks. They did affect Brooke's sleep schedule, and she sometimes complained that she was too tired to focus on schoolwork.

Mrs. and Mr. Williams were quite concerned about Brooke's welfare. They knew that something might not be right but didn't know if her eating issues and nightmares were just part of her adjustment to foster care. They asked Ms. Chao, the caseworker, to advise them on their questions.

Key

Brooke: the youth in care.
Ms. Olsen: Brooke's mother.
Mr. and Mrs. Williams: the foster parents.
Dr. Zaslow: Brooke's pediatrician.
Ms. Chao: the caseworker.

Because the foster care system has recently cast increased attention on the physical and mental health needs of youth in care, foster parents and practitioners find themselves in key positions to see this focus carried through (McCarthy and Woolverton 2005). This vignette suggests several potential issues that could affect both Brooke's mental health and her medical health. Although they are not physicians or mental health professionals, the Williams and Mrs. Chao need to be aware of important points of advocacy they can act on when advocating for Brooke in the healthcare arena. What follows are some of the central areas of advocacy in which human service practitioners and foster parents should become conversant in order to support the mental and medical health of children and adolescents like Brooke.

> ## Advocacy Checklist
>
> - Assess for medical health needs.
> - Assess for mental health needs.
> - Assess for developmental needs.
> - Develop a strengths perspective.
> - Clarify authority to consent.

Assess for Medical Health Needs

Identify the Need

When youth like Brooke come into care, they receive their required annual medical checkup with a pediatrician who takes Medical Assistance. All youth in care qualify for Medical Assistance and therefore must go to pediatricians, dentists, and other health and mental health professionals who take this insurance. Brooke's medical checkup showed that her health was good overall, although she was a little underweight (but still within normal ranges for her gender and age). Additionally, Brooke's blood work revealed that her sugar level was a little high; the pediatrician told Mrs. Williams and Brooke that they should monitor this as well.

Analyze the Context

While it is fortunate that youth in foster care are required to have annual checkups, studies show that "85% of youth in foster care receive medical services for their needs vs. 78% who stay in their homes" (McCarthy and Woolverton 2005:130). The statistic for youth in care should be 100 percent, because foster parents and practitioners must ensure the youth receive medical evaluations for proper care. Although all youth, regardless of their foster care status, have a right to health care, children in foster care are particularly vulnerable to certain medical conditions, as statistics unfortunately bear out. For example, almost half of youth in care experience some chronic health challenge (Simms, Dubowitz, and Szilagyi 2000).

> Out-of-home placement and adoption history were associated with higher rates of chronic health conditions and special needs. Children who had been placed out of home at least once during the 3-year study period (32%) were significantly more likely to be reported as having ever had a chronic health condition (CWS) than those without a placement history (27%). (NSCAW 2007:3).

Shedding additional light on these statistics, the American Academy of Pediatrics found that youth in care have elevated rates of chronic physical disabilities and birth defects (McCarthy and Woolverton 2005:131–132). Some of these health issues (and their incidences) include:

> The most commonly reported condition was asthma (13% of all children over the course of 3 years). Other conditions less frequently reported over the course of 3 years included repeated ear infections (5%), other respiratory problems (5%), severe allergies (5%), epilepsy (2%), and eczema or other skin disease (2%). There were no differences in the report of these chronic health conditions by child gender or race/ethnicity. (NSCAW 2007:2)

Medical needs are not always evident or even occur when youth enter care. Regarding medical conditions (as well as special needs), 36 percent of youth (compared to 35 percent at the baseline) had these challenges at an eighteen-month follow-up and 28 percent had such challenges at the thirty-six-month follow up (both statistics use the incident of alleged maltreatment as the baseline) (NSCAW 2007). Little relationship existed between the type of maltreatment (e.g., physical abuse, sexual abuse, neglect, multiple types) and the child having a long-term medical condition or special need (NSCAW 2007).

Develop the Plan

The Williams were glad that Brooke had had her initial health checkup. They made a plan to continue to monitor her diet to make sure her weight did not dip into the underweight range. They also planned to search online for information on juvenile diabetes to learn exactly what they could do to prevent Brooke from getting juvenile diabetes.

Examples like this showcase foster parents' continued advocacy via developing a plan to monitor the health needs of youth in care. Practitioners can serve in a supportive role by providing foster parents with information and referral regarding a range of health issues, for instance, by directing them to the American Academy of Pediatrics (AAP) Web site for information on their standards of practice and other written material for children and youth in foster care (aap.org). Advocates can also plan to research Web sites focusing on particular medical issues (in Brooke's case, juvenile diabetes), which can provide lists of important indicators. Pediatricians vary in their knowledge of the issues of foster care, but practitioners and foster parents can proactively review forms developed by the AAP that address particular issues that might be overlooked (http://www .aap.org/healthpics/fostercare.cfm). Finally, developing a plan requires that foster parents be particularly attentive to daily observations of children in foster care to see if any aspect of their physical health appears out of the ordinary. Just a few of the host of "symptoms" to which foster parents should be attentive are loss of breath, visual, auditory, or other concerns, and difficulty with mobility.

Although they are not pediatricians or other child medical specialists, it is important that foster parents be willing to monitor youth, including asking about any concerns that relate to the body's systems (e.g., gastro-intestinal, pulmonary). If a child complains of an upset stomach or difficulty with vision, for instance, foster parents should be particularly mindful that these could—although certainly not always—indicate a more serious medical concern. It is not possible to know everything that can possibly occur, but foster parents and practitioners with general knowledge of what symptoms might be cause for greater concern are in a position to be better advocates. Of course, all youth should have extensive medical records ("healthcare passports") available; some children have major medical issues that foster parents should see documented in the records when the children come into care. For example, youth who are on a feeding tube, in a wheelchair, or dependent on leg braces, or who are visually or auditory challenged, require an elaborate plan of coordination with the pediatrician, medical specialists, and other medical professions, including physical therapists, occupational therapists, and nutritionists.

Implement the Plan

Having identified Web sites to research and developed a plan to monitor Brooke's diet, the Williams were in a good position to promote Brooke's health. They developed a diet in which she would eat less sugar and carbohydrates; they knew Brooke was at risk for developing juvenile diabetes even if her diet was good, however, because Mrs. Chao informed them that Brooke's father had had juvenile diabetes as well. Brooke began to eat healthier at mealtime but was still secretly purging some of her food. They knew that the adjustment had not been easy as she missed her mother very much and had occasional nightmares. Despite their best efforts, they knew that something was still bothering Brooke and that they needed to return to their plan to consider other factors.

Another key factor in plan development—considering *mental health* needs—is now addressed.

Assess for Mental Health Needs

Identify the Need

The Williams, Mrs. Chao, and the pediatrician were understandably concerned about Brooke's diet and continued to monitor her for both a "normal range" of weight and sugar level. However, in reviewing their assessment, they realized that they needed to expand their notion of Brooke's health to include her *mental health*, that is, her emotional and psychological health. When the Williams and Mrs. Chao thought about their concerns for Brooke in this light, they began to consider the psychological reasons for why Brooke was losing weight and took more seriously her recurrent nightmares.

While medical health remains a top priority for youth in care, assessing for mental health is often a lower priority. "Despite research documenting the pervasive mental health needs of children and adolescents in the child welfare system, there is evidence that these needs are seldom adequately met" (Dore 2005:150). In addition, a national study of youth in care discovered that only 23 percent of those who had been in care for at least twelve months were able to access mental health services (NSCAW 2003a). Reasons that mental health is not always addressed include lack of provider awareness and sensitivity, as well as the stigma that still continues to be associated with mental illness.

Analyze the Context

Framing Brooke's eating issues and nightmares from a mental health perspective—instead of maintaining a strict medical perspective on her weight and a more casual perspective on her nightmares—would greatly help in achieving a different assessment and consequent understanding for Brooke's behaviors. Again, only mental health professionals (e.g., licensed social workers, psychologists, psychiatrists, psychiatric nurses, counselors), along with qualified pediatricians and physician assistants, can make diagnoses and develop treatment plans. However, foster parents, relative caregivers, and human service practitioners can make use of general information available from the American Psychological Association's Web site (apa.org).

Certainly, not all youth in care have mental health needs. Indeed, all children are resilient. But statistics suggest that the mental health needs of children in foster care should not be ignored.

> Recent studies suggest that up to 80 percent of children entering foster care have moderate to significant mental health problems (Clausen, Landsverk et al. 1998; Simms, Dubowitz, and Szilagyi 2000). This contrasts with 18% to 22% of children in the general population (Costello, Angold et al. 1996; Roberts, Atkisson, and Roenblatt 1998). . . . Even compared with children from similar socioeconomic and demographic background, those in foster care are at greatly increased risk or psychopathology (Halfon, Berkowitz, and Klee 1992; Landsverk and Garland 1999).   (Dore 2005:150)

Additionally, youth in care utilize mental health services (for both mental health and other developmental challenges) more than youth who are receiving other public assistance programs (dosReis, Zito et al. 2001). As we can see, mental health concerns and their treatment are a serious concern for youth in care.

What lies behind the statistics specific to the mental health needs of those youth in care who *have* experienced maltreatment? Sadly, experiencing child maltreatment is an additional risk factor in developing a mental health concern. While youth in care may develop a mental health need in spite of their maltreatment, the maltreatment *itself* is a risk factor. What is revealed by these statistics is the importance of attachment and how it is affected when maltreatment occurs (Bowlby 1980; Herman 1997).

> According to attachment theory, the nurturing relationships that an infant experiences with its earliest caregivers set the stage for the child's ability to relate to others throughout life. Attachment is constructed through day-to-day interactions between caregiver and child, the product of a process of mutuality driven by qualities in both the infant and caregiver. The security children feel in these caregiving relationships allows them to venture forth to explore their environment, expanding their understanding and awareness of the world, and thereby promoting cognitive and social development. (Dore 2005:153)

Child abuse and neglect, in infants for example, disrupts the healthy attachment process and contributes to the development of mental health issues such as trauma (Herman 1997). In fact, the idea of "permanency" in child welfare—that is, ensuring that youth in care have a stable, nurturing permanent family as soon as possible— supports emotional health, among other aspects of well-being (see Frey, Greenblatt, and Brown 2005).

Therefore, understanding the importance of attachment as well as the impact of being separated from the *familiar* environment of the parents, regardless of whether the relationships were healthy or unhealthy, can help the Williams and Mrs. Chao place Brooke's missing her mother and her nightmares in context.

Develop the Plan

Developing a plan for addressing Brooke's mental health needs is similar to addressing her medical needs—advocates should plan to become as educated as they can on a variety of mental health issues and to monitor the child in their care. They should also plan to find good referrals to mental health professionals who can diagnose and offer counseling (individual and group as well [as family counseling as long as this is appropriate for the child]).

The number of mental health challenges that a child in care (like children in general) can face is overwhelming. Table 6.1 provides a list of mental health issues that foster parents and practitioners may want to research and familiarize themselves with. Again, this list is provided not to alarm advocates but to provide them with information on some of the mental health diagnoses that the youth in their care may have; the "disorder" may or may not be related to the maltreatment that led to their placement in foster care. It is also very important to stress that because a child is having a difficult time at home or at school does not *automatically* mean that he will receive a mental health diagnosis. Do not worry—the process of assessing and formally diagnosing is left to the mental health/medical professional, and you are always welcome to seek another professional opinion.

TABLE 6.1 Potential Mental Health Disorders in Children and/or Adolescents

Adjustment disorders (responses to stress)
Attention-deficit disorder and attention deficit/hyperactivity disorder
Depression, bipolarism, and other mood disorders
Eating disorders (anorexia nervosa and bulimia nervosa)
Elimination disorders (encopresis=involuntary defecation [diagnosis at minimum four years of age] and enuresis=involuntary urination [diagnosis at minimum five years of age])
Oppositional defiant disorder and conduct disorder (a more extreme form of oppositional defiant disorder)
Post-traumatic stress disorder and other anxiety disorders
Reactive attachment disorder of infancy or early childhood (resulting from neglect)
Schizophrenia with childhood onset (hallucinations and delusional thinking)
Separation-anxiety disorder
Substance dependency and substance abuse

Source: American Psychiatric Association 2000.

Implement the Plan

Treatment for mental health challenges should be made in consultation with the mental health professional, the child, the foster parents, and the caseworker. The range of treatment options includes providing therapy and/ or prescribing psychotropic medications. A wide range of therapies exist, including "talk" therapies (e.g., cognitive-behavioral, dialectical-behavioral, solution-focused, narrative, client-centered) and other professionally organized therapies (e.g., play, art, music, journaling, guided imagery, dance, sand, eye movement desensitization and reprocessing [EMDR], hypnosis). Specific clinical treatments formulated for working with abused children and their families include abuse-focused cognitive behavioral therapy (AF-CBT), for dealing with physical abuse; assessment-based treatment for traumatized children (trauma assessment pathway [TAP]); and group treatment for children affected by domestic violence (National Child Traumatic Stress Network 2008). These treatments may involve individual, group, and/or family counseling as well as psychotropic medication. The mental health professional will consult on treatment options with the all parties involved. Foster parents and professionals should monitor the children for any side effects of medication as well as anything unusual between counseling sessions. In rare instances, youth might become suicidal or homicidal; in such cases, it is mandatory that the foster parents or practitioners contact the police or take the child to the closest hospital to ensure the child's safety.

In Brooke's case, the Williams continued to be concerned about her lack of appetite and the nightmares; they scheduled an appointment with a licensed clinical social worker to evaluate Brooke. When making mental health diagnoses, mental health professionals consider "differential diagnoses," which includes ruling out medical causes of the behaviors. The licensed clinical social worker consulted with Dr. Zaslow (Brooke's pediatrician) and talked with Brooke and the Williams about her feelings toward, and behaviors relating to, eating and exercising (recall that Brooke went swimming every day). After this consultation and discussion with the parties, the social worker diagnosed Brooke with the eating disorder bulimia nervosa. As with the many other potential mental health diagnoses, "children in out-of-home care may experience eating disorders that place them at serious health risk . . . [and] typically signal problems related to self-concept and self-esteem and problems associated with separation from the family" (cited in Child Welfare League of America 2008:18). Although nightmares are a symptom of post-traumatic stress disorder, the social worker found that Brooke did not meet the qualifications for that diagnosis. The social worker recommended weekly counseling and continued diet monitoring in consultation with Brooke's pediatrician. The purpose of the counseling would be to address Brooke's feelings of self-esteem, as well as her thoughts and behaviors. The Williams were relieved that Brooke was finally getting help.

Assess for Developmental Needs

Identify the Need

Assessing medical and mental health is critically important. The third component of a general health assessment is identifying any developmental delays that a child may be experiencing. It is important to distinguish between mental health and developmental delays, as they are separate components of health. "Mental health" refers to an individual's psychological functioning while "developmental delays" reference delayed functioning in regard to an individual's cognitive, emotional, or physical growth. Developmental delays may affect mental and physical health issues, but they are a distinctly different issue.

The specific definition of developmental delay (as it used to be called, a "developmental disability"), as defined in the American with Disabilities Act, states that

> a developmental disability is a condition or disorder—physical, cognitive, or emotional— that has the potential to significantly affect the typical progress of a child's growth and development or substantially limit three or more major life activities, including self-care, language, learning, mobility, self-direction, capacity for independent living, and/or economic self-sufficiency (Developmental Disabilities Act, 1984). A developmental disability may be congenital, or identified or acquired prior to the age of 22.   (Weaver, Keller, and Loyek 2005:175)

A number of developmental delays that occur in children can result in a formal diagnosis by a medical or mental health professional. They include: mental retardation (IQ is 70 or below), borderline intellectual functioning (range of IQ is 71–84), reading disorder, mathematics disorder, expressive language disorder, disorder of written expression, developmental coordination disorder (motor skills), autism, and Asperger syndrome (a milder form of autism) (American Psychiatric Association 2000).

Additionally, the term "developmental delays" refers to slower progress in achieving the typical childhood milestones, based on age and gender; these may or may not result in a medical diagnosis. These milestones refer to the expected time frame in which children can be reasonably expected to achieve certain developmental tasks as they relate to speech, toilet training, feeding and dressing, mobility (moving head, following objects with eyes, sitting up, crawling, speech, and walking), and social interaction.

Although in the original vignette, Brooke does not have a developmental delay, for the purposes of discussion, let's imagine that Brooke had difficulty in school expressing herself in her writing and the teacher initially interpreted Brooke's academic progress as indicating poor commitment to her work. Brooke told her foster parents that her teacher was unfairly grading Brooke lower; Brooke insisted that it was not that she did not *want* to be successful in her writing but rather that it was very difficult for her to express herself in this mode. The Williams had also noticed when they reviewed Brooke's written homework that it appeared challenging for her to be clear, focused, and organized. This issue even manifested itself when Brooke tried to take an elaborate phone message for the foster parents, and they could not understand its full content. They had a strong sense that an assessment for Brooke regarding her writing abilities was an important component in advocating for her well-being.

Analyze the Context

Although we have found no studies that determined the incidence of specifically developmental delays (disabilities) among youth in care, a recent national study provides broad insight on this issue, surveying learning challenges, developmental delays, and special needs (some of them were considered "emotional disturbances," which relate more to the previous mental health section).

During the 3 years after a CWS [Child Welfare System] investigation for alleged maltreatment, 33% of children were reported by caregivers as having had a learning problem, special need, or developmental disability. At any given time, between 19% and 28% of children were reported to have such a need. Most commonly, children were reported as having a learning disability (21% of the total sample), emotional disturbance (14%), or speech impairment (12%). Although less commonly reported, a noteworthy proportion of children were reported to have mental retardation (2%), hearing impairment (2%), vision impairment (1%), or autism (1%). There were no differences in the report of these special needs by a child's race or ethnicity. As in the general child population, reports of special needs did differ by gender. Boys (19.8%) were significantly more likely than girls (13.3%) to be reported over the study period as having a special need. (NSCAW 2007:2).

While certainly youth have developmental delays independent of any maltreatment, a correlation exists between child maltreatment and developmental delays. Youth who have a developmental disability may cause frustration in the parents because the parents' expectation of how their child should "typically" act is not being met in reality. The consequent frustration on some parents' part can lead to child maltreatment. Consider the following conclusion:

All children depend on their caregivers for safety, emotional support, education, and physical care. Because of their physical and/or cognitive needs, children with disabilities often require more intense care than do children without disabilities . . . , placing them at greater risk for maltreatment. (Weaver, Keller, and Loyek 2005:176)

In a national study, Crosse, Kaye, and Ratnofsky (1993) learned that the maltreatment risk was 1.7 times greater for children with disabilities than those without disabilities.

This tragic correlation is reciprocal as well—that is, not only does the presence of a developmental delay have an impact on maltreatment, but maltreatment can certainly lead to a developmental delay (Weaver, Keller, and Loyek 2005). Infants born addicted to alcohol and other drugs can experience developmental delays. Fetal alcohol syndrome, for example, can lead to mental retardation and developmental delay.

According to Dore, "A child's psychosocial development represents a series of adaptations or, occasionally, maladaptations to new experiences or changing situations, determined by biological capacity, previous life experiences, and current environmental demands" (2005:152). When maltreatment occurs, it can damage the child's natural foundation of growth and adaptation. For example, "neglect in the form of inadequate supervision, nutrition, nurturing, or enrichment during the early years also can affect a child's development" (Weaver, Keller, and Loyek 2005:176). These negative effects may be temporary or could lead to permanent delays that manifest as mental retardation and learning challenges.

Develop the Plan

Foster parents and practitioners face a challenge that they can meet by addressing a youth's developmental needs, such as Brooke with her writing delay. Practitioners in particular have a central role to play in advocating for the youth. "If a child with a disability is abused or neglected and enters the child welfare system, this safety net is stretched and sometimes torn beyond repair" (Weaver, Keller, and Loyek 2005:173), so it is of utmost importance for the advocates to develop a plan to avoid placement disruption. One of the most important components is to become educated on the nature of the specific delay.

The pediatrician's office is typically the first stop in learning about "normal developmental milestones" for youth and the signs that development may be constricted; next is consulting with the pediatrician on a treatment plan. Advocates such as practitioners and foster parents should be sensitive to, and informed and prepared for, the reality that some delays occur as a result of maltreatment while other delays result independently of, and may indeed contribute to, the maltreatment itself (see Weaver, Keller, and Loyek 2005). Foster parents can also look for different support groups (in-person, telephone, online) that offer education, guidance, and support for them in raising children with developmental delays. Finally, delays can impact a child's schooling. Drawing on the youth's rights under the Individuals with Disabilities Education Act, and collaborating with the educational surrogate (if not the foster parent), the creation of an individualized education plan (as discussed in the last chapter) can be requested. School personnel will assess and diagnose the youth, and the IEP will address how to meet the youth's educational needs in as "typical" a school environment as possible. In these cases, children could qualify as "other health impaired" (Dore 2005).

Implement the Plan

Following the plan they developed, Mrs. Williams accompanied Brooke on a visit to her pediatrician, who evaluated Brooke for any physical problems that might be responsible for her writing challenges. He did not discover any and concurred with Mrs. Williams (who was Brooke's educational surrogate) to follow up with a special needs assessment of Brooke through her school psychologist. Mrs. Williams' request for the creation of an IEP was later granted, after the psychologist gave Brooke a diagnosis of "written language expression disorder." The psychologist told the team that Brooke's writing problems might stem from the years that Brooke witnessed the domestic violence between her parents as well as from the physical abuse from her father. The hypothesis was that because Brooke had felt so disempowered by the maltreatment, this led to her difficulty in feeling confident enough to express herself, in this case, in written language.

As a result, the assembled team that was helping Brooke (Brooke's reading teacher, her special education teacher, her psychologist, Mrs. Williams, and the school social worker) recommended that the following supportive components be put in place for: extra time on written assignments, tutoring, and counseling. Additionally, Mrs. Williams was trained by the special education teacher on strategies to help children with this particular delay in written expression ability. Mrs. Williams also joined an online support group for families working with children with developmental delays.

Although this was a satisfactory implementation of the plan, the Williams and Mrs. Chao knew that they needed to continue to be vigilant and monitor Brooke's progress on this front while watching for any new changes in behavior, as reported by Brooke or observed by them. They also needed to continue to consult with the pediatrician and the school team. Such collaboration, combined with increased educational and subsequent advocacy, increases the likelihood of identification of youth with such delays and the prompt referral of youth to the appropriate services. This advocacy process will then counter Sullivan and Knutson's (1998) conclusion (as cited in Weaver, Keller, and Loyek 2005:176) "that child protective workers [and foster parents – *added by authors*] fail to identify or document disabilities in the many children under their care," giving inadequate attention to this critical issue.

Develop a Strengths Perspective

Identify the Need

For the Williams and Mrs. Chao to help Brooke, she ultimately needed a diagnosis of bulimia nervosa disorder or written expression disorder (or perhaps juvenile diabetes at some point), which provided insight into how a certain amount of symptoms can represent a problem that was causing her physical, psychological, and cognitive distress. The Williams and Mrs. Chao were appreciative that Brooke's diagnoses had shed light on what was wrong and that treatment plans were put in place that sought to remedy her problems. They also felt very sorry for Brooke and focused on how tragic Brooke's life had been, being physically abused and witnessing domestic violence between her parents. All of these hardships added up, from their perspective, to tremendous problems that this young woman had to face; they decided that the best way to help her was to treat her very carefully, like she was a fragile doll.

The difficulty with this perspective is that it tends to overemphasize what is wrong with the child in care and to underestimate what is right. Children who are raised in this manner —where so many things are framed as "problematic and wrong with them," coupled with the belief that adults and society will "fix" them—develop a bleak perspective of themselves because their problems and diagnoses are always prominently featured. They can develop as well an overreliance on the help of others. This negative perspective leads to children developing a pessimistic view of themselves as they grow, seeing themselves merely as a series of problems that need to be fixed; they can feel disempowered to do anything about the issues on their own.

The remedy to this is to adopt a "strengths perspective," which acknowledges that the child faces a variety of challenges but also emphasizes all the wonderful qualities that the child does possess; it works to demonstrate to the child that her own particular qualities can lead her into optimistically addressing any needs she has (Saleeby 2006). This need to employ such a perspective is unique in that foster parents and practitioners may never have any "clear evidence" that it is necessary. It requires them to initiate self-examinations into how they think about, talk about, and otherwise respond to the problems of the child or children in their care.

Analyze the Context

The strengths perspective emerged as a counterresponse to the prevailing "medical model." The philosophy behind the medical model, which of course stems from the discipline of medicine and has been similarly influential in the mental health field, is that individuals need to be diagnosed and treated by experts who have sole control over the knowledge of diagnosis and treatments. The focus of the medical model is on pathology, and this pathology is emphasized; therefore, a person with alcoholism is seen as an "alcoholic" or a person with schizophrenia is seen as a "schizophrenic." In this model, the diagnosis or disease becomes the person, rather than one issue that the individual is managing, and the merger of disorder with the individual himself becomes indissoluble. In our vignette, Brooke suffers from bulimia nervosa and written language expression disorder, and is in danger of developing juvenile diabetes. These maladies exist against the backdrop of Brooke's history of child maltreatment.

The strengths perspective challenges this medical model. Simply put, a strengths perspective frames working with clients by focusing on their strengths, which are those resources, both internal (personality characteristics, psychological resources, hobbies) and external (social supports, physical and financial resources), that help empower clients and lead to their resiliency in tough times (Saleeby 2006). The strengths perspective recognizes that assessment and consequent comfort should be provided, but it focuses on what is right with the individual rather than what is wrong.

While alleviating a problem can certainly bring relief and comfort to the child, it also unfortunately can reinforce that something is "wrong" with them, and place an unhealthy focus on how medicine or therapy "fixes" them. It leaves the notion in many children that they are somewhat damaged and need to be fixed. Again, it is important to give comfort but a strengths perspective is helpful because it concentrates on the person's strengths and how they are good humans who face an *aspect* or *issue* that needs improvement, rather than inculcating the belief that *they* themselves need improvement (Saleeby 2006). He acknowledges that the necessity for naming a diagnosis is a reality in healthcare but cautions against placing too much emphasis on it:

> [Writing to a social work audience, he states] "Assess; but do not get caught up in labels. Diagnosis is incongruent with a strengths perspective as it is understood in the context of pathology, deviance, and deficits. . . . While diagnosis is associated with a medical model of labeling that assumes unpopular and unacceptable behavior as symptoms of an underlying pathological condition, it is often required to access services. . . . A diagnosis should not be viewed as the central feature of help seekers' identities or life experiences or the only outcome of an assessment." (2006:105)

Focusing on individuals' strengths involves attention to a variety of factors—from the personality characteristics, say, of resilience, intelligence, and sense of humor, to the psychological characteristics of maturity and adaptability, and from the hobbies of drawing and exercising to the social supports of family and friends, caring professionals, and other resources such as having a comfortable home and pets. An individual with an illness is then viewed in this complete context and the focus is on mobilizing his strengths to address the disease.

Develop the Plan

By drawing on the strengths perspective as well as being aware of the dominance of the medical model in their conversations with many healthcare professionals, foster parents and practitioners will provide an important service to the children in their care as they develop the plan to raise and nurture them. Aside from these two important components of developing a plan, the professionals involved should deliberately examine their own feelings toward a child with a "disease" or "disability." In the rush to have children treated for a host of medical, mental health, or developmental issues, advocates should learn to accept the child for who she is and remember that the child is not the disease. For example, say foster parents have taken a two-year-old child into their care and it is discovered when the child is three that he has autism. It is imperative that of course they examine and incorporate the latest treatment in working with children with autism but it is equally important that they accept that the child has autism and that the *child is a child first and not an autistic child first* (N. Moss, pers. comm., July 10, 2008). This acceptance and placing of the child in his or her entirety first, before the illness, is an example of strengths-based practice and will go a long way in determining both the philosophy by which the foster parents raise the child and how they intervene in treatment. In their self-examination, advocates should honestly reflect on what is brought up in their own feelings and what "helping" really means to them.

Additionally, professionals' attitude toward the disease or illness, in the context of the whole child, will also serve as an example to the child herself (as well as to any other children in the family) on how they should perceive the illness. Chapter 2 explores in fuller depth how to determine the types of children foster parents feel comfortable with and ready to parent. Applying Saleeby's advice to social workers to foster parents as well and thinking of the child as the client, we can see that "it is the *client's perceptions* of the worker that creates the quality of the relationship. This plays a part *if the client* experiences the worker as warm, understanding, accepting, and encouraging" (2006:37). It is argued here that greater acceptance of a child for who she or he is will result in fewer placement disruptions once diagnoses are made or when illnesses persist during placement with foster parents.

Implement the Plan

Implementing the plan in Brooke's case meant that the Williams had a discussion with each other after they learned of Brooke's bulimia nervosa; they reminded themselves that Brooke was still the wonderful young woman they had come to know and agreed that they would focus on her strengths in order to view her as a young woman with bulimia nervosa rather than as a "bulimic." This thinking applied as well to her other issues (note how "issues" suffices for "disabilities" from a strengths perspective). Ms. Chao, as a new worker, separately discussed the strengths perspective with her supervisor. These conversations served to help shift their thinking from a medical model to a strengths-based perspective. They realized how important this shift could be to the youth in their care:

> If therapists are to resist the pull to steer clients automatically toward diagnosis and medication, the belief in client capacity to conquer even extreme (and often dangerous) personal circumstances must go deep. Clients can use an ally in overcoming often dramatic obstacles to personal recovery. When professionals use their inevitable positions of power to hand power back to the clients rather than block client capacities, clients can even more readily reach their goals.   (Saleeby 2006:22)

The above quote offers important "food for thought" for all advocates for youth in care with respect to how they think about and perceive the youth's "problems."

Additionally, when the Williams and Ms. Chao attended Brooke's IEP meeting and several school personnel kept focusing on Brooke's diagnoses, they gently suggested that it was important to remember what Brooke did well and to incorporate her strengths as resources in the treatment plan. For example, one of the strengths Mrs. Williams identified was Brooke's enjoyment of drawing—therefore, one option was that Brooke could draw her response to literature while she was working on her written responses to stories.

Finally, implementing a strengths-based perspective means including a child in interventions; the child is often peculiarly absent from actual decision-making in her healthcare treatment. After advocates consider what is appropriate for their age and abilities and within the parameters of the law, children in care should be included as one of the decision makers as often as possible. By virtue of the fact that they are in care, they have likely had tumultuous experiences that were neither empowering nor nurturing. Therefore, advocates' remembering to value and consult with the youth, again in a developmentally appropriate manner, is key to operating within a strengths perspective. This following account showcases the need for this:

[A fifteen-year-old young woman in care stated that she had not been consulted in her medical treatment plan. She continued:] "Near the end, my social worker presented the plan for me to sign. I looked at it and discovered that in the health section, it said, 'Begin taking birth control pills.' I was astonished. At that point in my life, I had never had sex, I had no boyfriend, and I did not need birth control pills. I asked why this was part of the plan. My worker said that they wanted to be sure that I didn't get pregnant. It really upset me that everyone at the table assumed that I was sexually active, and that no one knew me well enough to know how I felt about my own sexuality. I refused to sign the plan." (McCarthy and Woolverton 2005:132)

Examples like this strongly suggest the need to include the youth in the treatment plan as well as bring up potential ethical issues for practitioners. For example, what if a practitioner knows a fourteen-year-old child is sexually active and is not using birth control but the child states he does not want his foster parents to know. Then the caseworker needs to balance the client's right to privacy and self-determination with educating the client and informing the foster parents. (In these scenarios, the practitioner should consult with his supervisor for further direction.)

Returning to Brooke's vignette, during her initial counseling session, Mrs. Williams attended as well. The clinical social worker (who provided the counseling) included Brooke by asking her (as well as Mrs. Williams) to brainstorm on Brooke's strengths. They made a list that included that she was "tough," "very loving," "friendly," a "good artist," a "fantastic swimmer," and "excellent with caring for the Williams' dog." Then they talked about her concerns around her eating and Brooke said that she felt that she needed to control her eating because she could not control the abuse. The treatment plan centered around Brooke exploring her feelings of loss of control through drawing, swimming when she felt stressed, and finding other avenues to show control—including increased responsibility for caring for the Williams' dog.

This process, and the resulting plan, is the embodiment of the strengths perspective. It does not ignore Brooke's maltreatment history and neither does it minimize the challenges she faces. However, it reorients her management of them by empowering Brooke as part of her own treatment, drawing on her strengths, and linking her to caring professionals who think of her in a similar way. It is the strength perspective's hallmark to convey optimism and hope, rare gems in a foster care system, yet treasures that can become increasingly common as this approach is adopted.

Clarify Authority to Consent for Health Care

Identify the Need

This last need is both substantive and logistic. The need to understand who has the right to give consent for any and all treatment for medical, mental health, and developmental needs for children in care might be considered very small, but yet it is significant, particularly in instances when time is of the essence. Generally, "consent" in health care covers consent for treatment and consent to receiving HIPAA (Health Insurance Portability and Accountability Act) forms (federal laws governing confidentiality of healthcare treatment and records) and specific providers' forms relating to confidentiality and record release. "Treatment," though, is vast and covers routine care like healthcare screenings and dentist appointments, and can range from mental health visits to major surgery and perhaps the creation of advance directives (such as a "do not resuscitate order").

It is critical both to achieve clarity on who has authorization for medical decision-making in regard to treatment and to convey that information to all healthcare professionals involved.

Analyze the Context

Confusion often exists with respect to who has the authority to consent to what particular type and level of treatment.

> Child welfare workers and healthcare providers are frequently frustrated by delays in procuring assessments and treatment for children. Such delays are often caused by confusion over who has the authority to consent for these services. In developing strategies to expedite issues of consent, it is important to involve birth parents in the process and educate them about the need for certain types of consent as it relates to their children's healthcare, as well as their rights to provide or deny consent. Youth in care who are over the age of eighteen may consent to their own treatment. (McCarthy and Woolverton 2005:144)

Additionally, this confusion relates to "the roles of foster and birth parents, as well as about issues regarding consent for treatment and the role of the court in ordering and monitoring healthcare services" (McCarthy and Woolverton 2005:133). Relative caregivers also need to understand any court order and to consult with attorneys about their authority. Clarity about who can consent is important to consider in developing a plan, as is a consideration of the role of the court.

Develop the Plan

The plan should include a review of the court order and a consultation with the judge, if further clarification is necessary to delineate the parameters of the authority of this healthcare consent (routine medical, dental, mental health, and development needs assessment and treatment, surgery, advanced directives). Then, it is important for practitioners to have a conversation with the child's birth parents, if available, to inform them that because the court has awarded temporary custody to the agency, part of this custody includes the consent authority given to the agency. Which agency staff member is required to give consent to certain medical treatment can vary from agency to agency. Additionally, if a subcontracted agency is involved as well, authority in various health-related concerns can be split between the custody agent (the primary agency recognized by the court) and the contract agency (subcontracted agency). For example, a subcontractor may be allowed to authorize "routine" medical care while only the custody agent can authorize surgery. The worker should clarify and provide in writing for the caregivers which components of healthcare are authorized by which agency.

Practitioners should inform the foster parents in a conversation that the agency awarded temporary custody retains the full authority to consent. The practitioners can then work out who will provide a copy of the court order to the range of healthcare providers involved in the youth's care and the process by which the worker will gather the information to update the court on the youth's healthcare needs and any treatment.

Implement the Plan

Drawing on these considerations, Ms. Chao reviewed the court order, which stated that all medical care was the responsibility of the public agency and its "designee"—the contract agency. Upon discussion with her supervisor, Ms. Chao realized that, while her agency was authorized to consent to routine assessment and treatment for Brooke, in the unfortunate event that Brooke needed surgery, only the custody agent could grant authority. Ms. Chao also learned that in the event of an emergency for Brooke, all reasonable efforts should be made to contact Ms. Olsen to include her in the medical decision-making as a show of good faith and attempt to build rapport with her if reunification continued to be a goal. Ms. Chao informed Ms. Olsen, as well as Mrs. and Mr. Williams, of this protocol as well. Additionally, Ms. Chao told the Williams that she would provide Brooke's pediatrician and clinical social worker with a copy of the court order and that both providers were required to report Brooke's progress to Ms. Chao, who in turn would include Brooke's healthcare updates in her regular reports to the court.

The strategizing and communication described in this vignette provides clarity for the consent process. This simple component of healthcare management is a form of advocacy, for it provides efficiency to the process of helping Brooke with her healthcare needs.

Summary

This chapter outlines the variety of issues that practitioners and foster parents should be attentive to when helping children in care with their healthcare needs. Because of research that suggests children in care have particular vulnerabilities to their medical, mental health, and developmental needs, it is vital that their advocates have them initially assessed and monitored in these respects. They should make sure they expand their notion of healthcare to include attentiveness to mental health and developmental needs—this expansion is a critical part of a comprehensive, culturally appropriate assessment (McCarthy and Woolverton 2005).

Throughout the healthcare process, it is equally important for all advocates to adopt a strengths-based perspective in thinking about and talking with the child in foster care about her health. Such a perspective may be particularly challenging because it is often requires a reprogramming of how one thinks about health and illness; also, many providers will continue to think and operate from a medical model. This thus becomes an added opportunity for advocacy, as foster parents and practitioners educate themselves and others and work to change the language from a focus on disease and illness to one on health and well-being. Finally, it is important to have clarity on which the agency can consent to which type of healthcare procedure.

By keeping in mind all these varied areas of healthcare advocacy, foster parents and practitioners will play a major role in improving health among children in foster care. As this occurs, children like Brooke will have an increasingly joyful and healthier childhood and adolescence.

Discussion Questions

1. What factors can help kinship caregivers, foster parents, and practitioners in advocating for a foster child's health needs?
2. In the vignette, Brooke was a teenager. Assume now that she is a one-year-old girl. How might the advocacy process be different? How would it remain the same?
3. Assume a child does not wish to follow a course of treatment that a provider thinks is very important. What suggestions would you have in resolving this issue?
4. The strengths-based perspective is a powerful approach to viewing with and working with people. How do you think it could be applied to Brooke's parents in the vignette?

Web Sites

- American Academy of Pediatrics (AAP): http://www.aap.org/health-topics/fostercare.cfm
- American Psychological Association: apa.org
- Child Welfare League of America, "Standards of Excellence": http://www.cwla.org/programs/standards/standardsintrohealthcare.pdf
- U.S. Department of Health and Human Services, Survey of Child and Adolescent Well-Being (NSCAW): http://www.acf.hhs.gov/programs/opre/abuse_neglect/nscaw/
- U.S. Government Accountability Office: http://www.gao.gov/new.items/d0926.pdf

[7]

Advocacy in Interdisciplinary Teams

The whole is greater than the sum of its parts.

—Aristotle

Vignette

Ms. Penna worked at the front desk of a small motel. She loved her children but found she just could not handle Zand, age 9, who had been diagnosed with attention deficit hyperactivity disorder (ADHD), and Leesha, age 8, who had been "acting up" since she was four years old. Ms. Penna began to drink more and more to cope with the stresses of being a single parent with two active children. After a time, the children were removed because of physical abuse. Their father had abandoned the family long ago.

Mr. Taylor was a new foster dad. He enthusiastically participated in all the steps of the certification process. His paperwork was always handed in on time or ahead of time. Now that his children were grown and out of the apartment and his divorce was a few years behind him, Mr. Taylor looked forward to becoming a father figure for one child or two siblings in foster care. There was just one thing that bothered him. He knew he would be expected to participate on a multidisciplinary team of professionals (called a family team conference [FTC]), and that intimidated him. While he knew he had the skills to raise children with vulnerabilities, he was not so sure he would be a valuable team member. It was his understanding that the team included people with degrees and maybe the birth parents of the children. He thought that meant that all these people would have more knowledge about the children than he would. Mr. Taylor discussed his concerns with his homefinder, Mr. James, who tried to reassure Mr. Taylor that the FTC was a meeting where he could advocate for the children and that the participants would also be advocating to help him with the children.

Zand and Leesha were placed with Mr. Taylor, and Ms. Anaston was assigned to the case. Fortunately, she was a talented social worker, well-versed in the workings of FTCs. She talked to Mr. Taylor about FTCs and helped him to feel more optimistic about them. She also encouraged the children's mother and their new foster father to work together. Although they had a cordial relationship, friction soon arose between Mr. Taylor and Ms. Anaston. Mr. Taylor found Ms. Anaston condescending, while Ms. Anaston thought Mr. Taylor should be more organized in how he communicated about the children's progress. This conflict at times manifested during the FTCs when they were working on their goals for Zand and Leesha. At the first FTC meeting, it was apparent that Mr. Taylor and Ms. Anaston were not getting along. The conflict was affecting the rest of the team, and the other team members began to think that this FTC was a waste of time.

Key

Ms. Penna: the birth mother.
Zand and Leesha: siblings in care.
Mr. Taylor: the foster parent.
Mr. James: homefinder.
Ms. Anaston: the social worker.

Promoting a stable and successful placement experience is the goal for Ms. Penna, Mr. Taylor, and Ms. Anaston as they advocate for the children in their realm of responsibility. This chapter discusses how the multidisciplinary team (also known as the interdisciplinary team) can help the parents with the complex challenges of advocating for youth in foster and kinship care. It explores how foster parents, kinship parents, and practitioners can effectively advocate for children by being members of interdisciplinary teams, and it addresses potential obstacles to maximum team functioning.

Additionally, it examines the important skill of collaboratively evaluating children's progress as a vital aspect of teamwork.

Advocacy Checklist

- Focus on collaboration.
- Form a trusting, communicative team.
- Collaborate on evaluation.

Focus on Collaboration

Identify the Need

There were two needs that Ms. Anaston had to address with the team. One related to Ms. Penna, the children's mother. Although Ms. Penna was improving in her job performance as well as reducing her alcohol dependency (both goals she was working on for reunification with Zand and Leesha), she was having difficulty getting to visits to see them. The visits often fell during work hours, or they were so close to the end of the workday that Ms. Penna couldn't finish her shift and get to the visits on time. She was continually late to visits and even missed some. She asked her boss to adjust her work hours, but unfortunately the boss refused. Feeling torn between her job and her children, Ms. Penna, crying, called her social worker, Ms. Anaston. Ms. Anaston quickly changed the visit schedule to accommodate Ms. Penna; however, Ms. Penna's previous inconsistency in attending visits left lasting memories with the children—who felt they never knew when, or even if, they would see their mother again. Both Ms. Anaston and Mr. Taylor provided support to the children.

Another need emerged in this vignette. The reading abilities of both Zand and Leesha were below their age levels. They had just been evaluated by a reading specialist provided by the school system, and the specialist had stated that their reading needed to be supported in their home environment. Ms. Anaston wanted the two parents involved to address this because she believed that these delays, coupled with Ms. Penna's inconsistent visitation, would contribute to the children losing their sense of security, which had already been compromised by their removal from home and entry into foster care.

Ms. Anaston took both of these needs to the FTC to express her concerns and for help in working on these goals.

Analyze the Context

Why work together in a collaborative fashion? In citing the merits of working together over working solo, Gummer (1991) wrote, "A group approach, as compared with an individual effort, has advantages in helping individuals, organizations, and communities accomplish tasks." He also advises us that "democratic participation is highly desirable" (Gummer 1995:85).

One of the merits of working collaboratively with the birth parents was cited by the Surgeon General in a 1999 report: "Research has shown that when parents are actively engaged in their children's mental health service planning and treatment, their children have better outcomes" (cited in Jensen and Hoagwood 2008: 23). This collaboration between parents and service providers, and among service providers with each other, results in an integrative approach to treatment that is based in the "systems of care" movement (see Jensen and Hoagwood 2008), which helped lay the groundwork for the use of the multidisciplinary family treatment conference (FTC).

Such collaboration, specifically in FTCs, is essential. The FTC is a meeting in which team members formally exchange information, observations, and knowledge about the clients; the specific goals of the FTC are listed in table 7.1.

TABLE 7.1 Goals of the FTC

Envision the goals for the children.

Plan for permanency in accordance with the Adoption and Safe Families Act (ASFA) by planning their return home while simultaneously planning for another permanent option (i.e., adoption, return to a grandparent, etc.).

Document the plan.

Distribute a copy of the plan to all parties involved.

Determine a plan for evaluating progress of the plan's goals.

According to the Family Violence Prevention Fund's *Family Team Conferences* (Mitchell-Clark 2003), the FTC "brings together people whom the families trust and who can respond to the issues the families face" (2003:4). This may include: (1) the child(ren) (if appropriate); (2) birth parent(s) and advocate; (3) other caregivers, who may care for the children upon their return to family; (4) foster parent(s); (5) custody agent/CPS worker; (6) social worker; (7) education professionals (e.g., teacher[s], aides, specialists); (8) healthcare professionals; (9) child's attorney/law guardian; (10) court-appointed special advocate (CASA worker); and (11) facilitator (who plays a neutral role and facilitates collaboration). It is crucial to be sensitive to the fact that one parent or other caregiver may have perpetrated both the maltreatment and some form of domestic violence; separate conference sessions, one for each of these individuals, may be necessary. When interdisciplinary practitioners (one or more professionals from different disciplines, such as social work, education, medicine) and residential caregivers (e.g., the foster parents) come together to work on a team to devise a family plan, they engage in an important work-related activity, collaboration. The process of collaboration consists of five core components: (1) interdependence, (2) newly created professional activities (for team members), (3) flexibility, (4) collective ownership of goals, and (5) reflection on the process. Bronstein's model (2003) for this collaboration appears in figure 7.1.

FIGURE 7.1 Components of an Interdisciplinary Collaboration Model

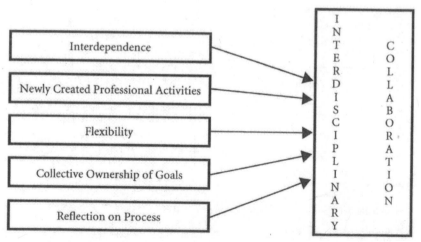

In this case, *interdependence* means "reliance on interactions among professionals" (Bronstein 2003:299). As the team interacts, they will build trust among themselves as each person completes assigned tasks successfully. For example, if the teacher says she will get a reading list to Mr. Taylor, she needs to follow through. *Newly created professional activities* refers to the synergy that can be created when the group members "achieve more" as a group than they would if they had acted "independently" (2003:300). "Behavior that characterizes *flexibility* includes reaching productive compromises in the face of disagreement" (2003:301). Fortunately for the team in our vignette, Ms. Anaston was highly skilled at negotiating goals, which involved making some compromises.

Collective ownership of goals is the epitome of family team conference outcomes. It entails "shared responsibility" throughout the "entire process of reaching goals, including joint design, definition, development and achievement of goals" (Bronstein 2003:301). The overall process would be incomplete, however, without *reflection on the process*. This includes processing and "incorporating feedback to strengthen collaborative relationships and effectiveness" (2003:302). Sands (1993) describes three major components of the team meeting discussion that can be applied to the goals of a FTC. They are:

- Identification of the clients'/consumers' major problems;
- Identification of members' objectives to be achieved in their evaluations of the client/consumer; and
- The formation of a plan for achieving each objective (that is, the plan would define which discipline was responsible for each part of the assessment).   (Sands 1993:551)

A number of skills essential for interdisciplinary collaboration are listed in table 7.2; the presence of these skills is essential to the success of the team meeting. Social workers' and foster parents' skills in group dynamics could serve as preparation for their work on interdisciplinary teams.

As an added benefit of collaborating in the FTC, because all the service providers are assembled in the same room, the possibility of duplicating services is eliminated or at least reduced. As the plan is developed and each member takes responsibility for her own part, the responsibilities are clearly divided and differentiated. This is important because the duplication of even small tasks means that time is wasted. For example, if the foster father is made responsible for contacting the school or serving as the

TABLE 7.2 Skills for Interdisciplinary Collaboration

Adaptability
Being articulate
Efficiency
Establishment of good relationships with medical providers
Flexibility
Good sportsmanship
Humility
Resourcefulness
Sense of humor
Utilization of group work knowledge and roles

liaison with the school practitioners, then the other providers can use their time and energy for other tasks. Foster parents, relative caregivers, birth parents, practitioners, and other professionals have only so much time and energy to devote to each area. Therefore, collaboration can lead to a vastly more efficient and effective process.

Develop the Plan

Returning to the vignette, Ms. Anaston saw her role in the meeting, as well as that of Ms. Penna and Mr. Taylor, as an opportunity to advocate for Zand and Leesha regarding the needs she had identified. She planned to prepare in advance her evidence of these needs and was ready to share them in the FTC as well as to facilitate the strategizing about addressing them.

Separately, Mr. Taylor and Ms. Penna were doing their own preparation. In developing their plan for the meeting, Mr. Taylor suggested to Ms. Penna that they generate questions about structure and process of the FTC; the answers to these questions would help them feel comfortable at the team meeting. Mr. Taylor suggested this because neither had ever attended an FTC. Together, Mr. Taylor and Ms. Penna came up with a question list to ask Ms. Anaston before the meeting, so that Mr. Taylor and Ms. Penna could be effective and informed meeting participants; these questions appear in table 7.3.

TABLE 7.3 Questions About the Structure and Process of Family Treatment Conferences

Where and when is the meeting?

When will the meeting begin and end?

How often will the team meet?

Who will be at the FTC?

What are the priorities of each player at the meeting?

What are the credentials of the meeting attendees?

What is the goal of the meeting?

How do the goals fit into the court mandates?

What needs to be accomplished at the meeting?

If I have a concern, when is the right time to bring it up?

They then jointly came up with some questions to ask during the FTC itself. Ms. Penna and Mr. Taylor made a list of their questions: (1) How could the children be reassured that their mother would be at visits?; (2) Who would reassure them?; and (3) How could the children's reading needs be addressed in a holistic manner? They received the answers to their earlier questions about the FTC from Ms. Anaston and now felt more comfortable going into the meeting.

Implement the Plan

The day of the first FTC arrived. Once all the FTC participants arrived (including their teachers and psychiatrist), Ms. Anaston led the meeting and shared the goals for the FTC. Then Mr. Taylor and Ms. Penna asked the questions specific to the children. Regarding the visitation, Ms. Anaston replied that the most effective way to reassure the children about visits was for their mother to be prompt for each visit and that Ms. Penna should take the lead in reassuring them. Ms. Penna stated that she would do a better job with this. As for addressing the youth's reading challenges, several ideas were exchanged in the meeting and a plan was put in place. The strategy included Ms. Penna reading with Zand and Leesha for twenty minutes at visits and Mr. Taylor reading nightly for thirty minutes with Zand and Leesha in the foster home.

Recall that there was an underlying tension between Ms. Anaston and Mr. Taylor; for this first meeting, it did not rise to the surface. They were able to effectively collaborate to help Ms. Penna with her responsibilities.

After the first meeting of an FTC, a very useful instrument can be used to gauge the foster parent's involvement; this is the "measure of 'quality of involvement' of the foster parent in the development of the foster care plan" (it can be adapted for use by all participating team members) (Mac-Clean 1992:48). Foster parents, like all team members, will likely participate

---

TABLE 7.4 Measure of Quality of Involvement of the Foster Parent in the Development of the Foster Care Plan

1. Were you given opportunity in the planning conference to ask questions and express your views?   Yes   No

2. Did you feel your presence and participation was important?   Yes   No

3. Was adequate time allotted to cover all the issues?   Yes   No

4. Were your issues seen as important and addressed with concern?   Yes   No

5. From the foster care plan, are you clear as to your roles, the agency's expectations of you and your responsibilities with this child as well as the agency's role and responsibilities?   Yes   No

6. Is the foster care plan a useful tool in caring for this child?   Yes   No

7. Do you feel you are accepted as a valued partner in the parenting of this child?   Yes   No

8. Are you in full agreement with the content of the foster care plan?   Yes   No

9. Do you feel you could differ strongly with the agency in presenting the best interests of the child to the point of going through the service complaint procedure?   Yes   No

10. Was the time shared by you and the worker informative and useful?   Yes   No

Low Quality of Involvement   High Quality of Involvement

1	2	3	4	5	6	7	8	9	10

Low (0–4)   Medium (5–7)   High (8–10)

Example: Answering yes to eight out of ten questions would classify the foster parent input as "high quality of involvement."
Source: MacLean 1992:48.

to the extent they feel valued. And because advocacy for children like Zand and Leesha requires active participation in FTCs, such involvement is critical. The measure appears in table 7.4.

Form a Trusting, Communicative Team

Identifying the Need

One month had passed and it was time for another FTC. At this meeting, the psychiatrist and Zand's teacher attended as well as the three members from last month. While the first FTC had gone relatively smoothly, this meeting was different. Ms. Anaston raised her voice twice at Mr. Taylor because she thought he was discussing the goals in a disorganized manner. Mr. Taylor became defensive, shut down, and refused to participate. The psychiatrist reminded them why they were in the room—to focus on the children, who relied on the adults to work together in their advocacy. The teacher was wondering if this meeting would be useful. Although this was a new team with great potential, the members still needed to learn to trust each other and become a cohesive group.

Analyze the Context

Many of us have all heard the old adage, "The letter 'I' does not appear in the word 'team.'" In this case, the team represents the interests of the child(ren), not "I" as a foster parent or "I" as a practitioner. An FTC works just like any other team, in the sense that the individuals collaborate to make "something" happen. That "something" in the Penna case is reassuring the children and helping them to be on par academically.

Trust is one of the basic tenets of any relationship that requires collaboration. Building trust was one of the biggest responsibilities yet greatest challenges for the team players working for Zand and Leesha. Finding ways to build trust can also be seen as a way for team members to advocate for themselves. Trust is also one of the building blocks that forms the other components of collaboration. The "personal relationship between collaborators [is] characterized by . . . trust, feeling understood and liking each other . . . [and] define[s] a positive experience" (Bronstein 2001:121).

Individuals can "vary widely in their capacity to trust. . . . Those with higher self-esteem and solid interpersonal functioning may plunge into exploring their problems after only a few moments of checking out the practitioner" (Hepworth, Rooney, and Lawson 1997:561). Trust formation can be especially challenging in cases where the practitioners "appear" different from the client (e.g., different race, gender, socioeconomic status). This is where cultural competency (having the capacity to function effectively within the context of culturally integrated patterns of human behavior as defined by the group) is crucial (National Association of Social Workers 2007).

> In family-centered practice, the child welfare agency and its staff strive to be culturally competent and ensure that services provided to children and families are respectful of and compatible with their cultural strengths and needs.   (www.childwelfare.gov/famcentered/competence.cfm)

To build trust, practitioners and foster parents need to understand and respect the culture of the birth parents as well as each other's culture and that of other members of the team (Cohen 2003). For Ms. Anaston, that means she must be mindful of the fact that Ms. Penna may perceive her as coming from a different culture, whether that culture reflects a difference in class or in race. Ms. Anaston also needs to be respectful and find goals that are compatible with the children's needs as well as with Ms. Penna's culture; for example, Ms. Anaston might ask if "services [are] accessible, available, and culturally appropriate" (Cohen 2003:153).

In addition to requiring cultural awareness, building trust relies on effective communication. Effective communication flows in two directions between the sender and the recipient. It relies on genuine respect for the role and work of every team member of the FTC. Open communication, where people's nonverbal body language and facial expressions are congruent with their words, builds trust. If the recipient does not understand what the sender is communicating, then the communication is ineffective and incomplete; conflict can thus result, and team members might confront, avoid, or accommodate instead of striving to achieve effective collaboration.

FTCs have many benefits, arising largely from the increased communication that they provide; these benefits appear in table 7.5. It is important for team members to keep these benefits in mind so that they become invested in the process rather than perceiving it as a waste of time—as the characters from our vignette were beginning to think. The structure of the beginning of team meetings such as FTCs can set the tone for "cohesion,

TABLE 7.5 Benefits of Family Team Conferences

Increased parent engagement, and the development of a greater investment by families in service planning through partnership in decision making and strengths-focused plans.

Increased understanding by the family members of their situation, and the impact of their own efforts to cope with stressors.

Expedited stabilization of family crises through the swift development of a safety and permanency plan.

An opportunity for the family's support network to be involved in planning.

Facilitation of cooperation, communication, and teamwork among all stakeholders.

An increased sense of shared responsibility for protecting children through community involvement in the conference process.

A thorough assessment (including multidisciplinary information sharing) of family dynamics and underlying factors that threaten child safety;

Access to appropriate services in a timely manner that can result in accelerated safety, stability, and permanency.

An obviated or expedited Family Court process through the involvement of parents in a service plan early in the child protective process.

Source: Chahine and Higgins 2005:119.

reduced conflict, and higher member satisfaction (Stockton, Rhode, and Haughey 1992). Therefore, all practitioners and foster parents, among others, should approach these meetings with respect for each other and allow for all members to openly express themselves. This openness sets the stage for building trust and healthy communication.

Develop the Plan

The actual steps in developing the plan of trust and communication can be more successful if the issue of trust is addressed first. Some agencies have programs where someone facilitates trust-building exercises. This can be as simple as going around the table and having each person at the table share one of their goals for the meeting, or it can be as elaborate as having a facilitator come in and lead a retreat on trust-building through experiential activities. One of this book's authors worked on a team where the team's first meeting consisted of attending a wilderness adventure program together to share and learn from each other, form bonds, and begin to create trust. Not all teams have such an elaborate facility at their disposal, but with some creativity, effective bonds can still be born, and such bonds will promote stronger advocacy and better outcomes in working with youth in care. Planning to get to know team members and understand their motivations can occur even before the first FTC meeting.

Recognizing each person's responsibility as well as the perspective of the other, and committing to collaboratively resolving the conflict, will go a long way in building or in restoring trust after a breakdown in communication.

It is worth noting that particular care must be taken in developing a plan of fostering trust and communication in those instances where kinship caregivers are raising their relative's children. In kinship care situations (Pecora and Maluccio 2000), trust can be especially fragile between birth family members. Long-standing feelings of hurt, resentment, and inadequacy can exist between these relatives; practitioners would be wise to assess these dynamics and develop a plan that might suggest family counseling, as appropriate, for these relatives.

Implement the Plan

Returning to our vignette: after the second FTC meeting, both Ms. Anaston and Mr. Taylor reflected on their interaction and realized that their conflict had overshadowed the meeting for Zand and Leesha and prevented it from being fully useful. Ms. Anaston called Mr. Taylor and made an appointment to stop by his home. She apologized to Mr. Taylor for her attitude and stated how unprofessional she had been. In turn, Mr. Taylor admitted that he understood why Ms. Anaston had been frustrated, because he knew that he could do better in organizing his thoughts as he discussed the children's progress.

The lesson here is that, while retrospectively resolving conflict that has already occurred should be applauded, efforts should be made to proactively resolve conflict whenever possible. While conflict is natural and will always occur, establishing trusting and open relationships provides a springboard for more quickly and efficiently resolving conflicts in a collaborative way.

Collaborate on Evaluation

Identify the Need

Both Mr. Taylor and Ms. Penna had the children's best interests at heart. They were committed to their roles and knew they needed to report on the children's progress. Let's imagine that part of the plan established for the children was an evaluation of their social skills. Mr. Taylor had been well trained in evaluation methods by his homefinder and fellow foster parents. He used a quality measure, the parent daily report checklist, to gauge the children's social skills (Chamberlain, Price et al. 2006; this checklist can be obtained via www.oslc.org).

Ms. Penna, however, did not evaluate her children's progress on social skills during the visits because she did not understand the necessity. When Mr. Taylor reported on the youth's progress at an FTC meeting by means of the instrument he used, Ms. Penna was confused and felt inadequate. It was hard to accurately report on the children's progress when their perspective on measurement was vastly different.

Analyze the Context

Measuring progress can be challenging. In fact, tracking the data on the youth in care is an area in which caregivers, practitioners, and parents can feel the most uncomfortable, because evaluation of youths' progress on goals can be at least a partial reflection on the quality of the foster parents' and others' skills. If such data show, with specific numbers, how often a behavior is happening—and adults are the ones responsible for eliminating that behavior—many people feel shame or guilt for not being more successful in helping the children eliminate the behavior. Yet documenting progress on goals is required and strongly aids in identifying areas of growth and continued need. Indeed, evaluation can be among the most powerful forms of advocacy because unmet needs are clearly defined and resources can be shifted to addressing them. Royse, Thyer, Logan, and Padgett (2006) discuss a variety of measures, called "single system research designs," that can serve as examples of monitoring change on client goals.

It is important as well to "be on the same page" when conducting an evaluation. This means developing a "common language," which can be challenging for individuals who have been socialized differently (Abramson and Mizrahi 2003). Developing a common language can include various caregivers attending joint classes offered by agencies; for example, a parenting class could be offered to both foster parents and their birth parent partners (Linares, Montalto et al. 2006).

Develop the Plan

After discussing his ideas with Ms. Anaston, Mr. Taylor decided that he would meet with Ms. Penna and suggest that she also use the parent daily report checklist (Chamberlain, Price et al. 2006). Mr. Taylor would show her how to use it during her visits with the children. Additionally, Mr. Taylor would tell Ms. Penna that the FTC members would help interpret the data from the evaluation.

Implement the Plan

Mr. Taylor and Ms. Penna each used the parent daily report checklist to keep track of the children's behaviors (although admittedly Ms. Penna had far less opportunity to do this, as her only observations came during the visits). When they attended the next FTC, each had the same kind of data to report, which made for a stronger report. Because Mr. Taylor and Ms. Penna were now using the same tool, they had a common language in which to discuss the children's social skills data, both with each other and with the FTC.

Ms. Anaston was pleased and praised both of them for their work. They could compare their observations, especially in relation to both the strengths and the areas of growth for Zand and Leesha. This was part of their responsibility for advocating for the children in helping get their needs addressed. The FTC invited the children in as well so that they themselves could report on how they were doing with their social skills. All of this data helped the FTC in further collaborating on their goals for Zand and Leesha.

Summary

With increased expectations of foster parent and birth parent involvement in advocacy and planning in addition to the customary involvement of practitioners, teachers, and the like, "team work [has become] a desired and essential commodity in providing the safety net in which to care and treat the child" (MacClean 1992:11). This chapter has reviewed three areas of awareness for foster parents and practitioners who are working on an interdisciplinary team (family treatment conference). It has discussed the importance of collaboration, identified trust and communication as essential factors in creating such a collaborative environment, and focused on cooperating in order to optimize one aspect of the FTC, evaluating progress.

What makes interdisciplinary teams work is both ownership of goals and group work knowledge (pers. comm., Laura R. Bronstein, June 16, 2008). Every member needs to take responsibility for his or her part. In advocating for youth in care, it is comforting to realize, looking around the table at a team meeting like an FTC, that we are not working alone.

Discussion Questions

1. Why is collaboration so important in advocating for children in foster care?
2. How might Ms. Anaston and Mr. Taylor have begun their relationship in a more positive manner?
3. The discussion in this chapter focused on collaboration between adults. How would you collaborate with children on their progress?
4. Why is collaborating on evaluation important? In addition to using the instrument presented, how might you evaluate Zand and Leesha's progress regarding their social skills?

Web Site

- The Family Team Conferences in Domestic Violence Cases, Guidelines for Practice: http://fvpfstore.stores.yahoo.net/fatecoindovi.html

Part III

Advocacy for Change in Agency Policy, Law, and Communities

8

Advocating for Agency Policy Change

Those who expect moments of change to be comfortable and free of conflict have not learned their history.

—Joan Wallach Scott

Vignette

Mr. and Mrs. Alvarez had served as foster parents for Mytown Children Services, a subcontracted foster care agency of the Millville Department of Social Services, for seven years. Throughout their service, they had fostered twenty-five children. The Alvarezes were among the most competent, caring and reliable professional parents the agency employed.

Overall, their experience with working with the staff at the agency had been good. The couple principally worked with three foster care workers, and, fortunately, the supervisor had remained the same for the duration. However, there was one issue that constantly annoyed them: the lack of input they were given by the agency when a child was to be removed from their care. Specifically, of the twenty-five children they'd fostered, five were removed from their care with the agency having given them but a few hours' notice. Additionally, the Alvarezes were continually annoyed that they were not consulted on the children's status prior to their removal. This pattern occurred with all three foster care workers.

They had not said anything prior to taking in their most recent child, nine-year-old Juanita, but her removal—quickly and without consultation with them—was the "last straw." The worker, Ms. O'Brien, told them that Juanita had to move to a group home because her psychologist had stated that she needed more frequent supervision than the psychologist believed a family foster care setting could provide. One evening Ms. O'Brien came by the Alvarezes' home at 7 P.M. and quickly reported this decision to them. She allowed them to say goodbye to Juanita and then transported her to the group home. The Alvarezes did have time to take Ms. O'Brien aside to inform her of their frustration about the situation, but Ms. O'Brien replied that this was an agency procedure (to quickly remove children upon a psychologist's decision). Although Ms. O'Brien empathized with them, there was little she could do.

The Alvarezes were angry because they had not been told of this decision sooner and because they were not consulted about whether they could provide the additional structure for Juanita in their own home. In fact, Mrs. Alvarez had been considering switching from full-time to part-time work, and the couple was quite fond of the young girl. But they now had come to feel that their opinions didn't matter, and this rapid removal had occurred time after time. Though they were committed to fostering, they were now thinking about quitting the agency.

Ms. O'Brien too was not happy about how agency policy was enacted but was afraid to speak up for fear of losing her job.

Key

The Alvarezes: agency foster parents.
Juanita: child in foster care.
Ms. O'Brien: foster care worker.

Foster parents and practitioners do experience frustration with agency bureaucracy from time to time. Often such bureaucracy appears overwhelming, and agencies seem like enormous machines possessing little thought or care for foster parents' and practitioners' needs. That is, children are "processed" through the system in a set manner, and caregivers and practitioners may feel that they have little say or power in improving that procedure. This chapter responds to this perspective and presents a strategy for these professionals to advocate in agencies—such advocacy holds the potential to increase the satisfaction of individuals like the Alvarezes and Ms. O'Brien.

> Advocacy Checklist
>
> - Identify and assess policy effectiveness.
> - Prepare and document your case.
> - Present the suggested change through the appropriate channel of authority.

Identify and Assess Policy Effectiveness

Identify the Need

It is virtually impossible for all practitioners, foster parents, and kinship caregivers to be pleased about every policy—that is, the explicit and implicit rules that an agency sets forth for its operations—to which a foster care agency subscribes. Adding to this frustration is that these professionals at times need to navigate several agencies and their bureaucratic policies; these agencies include both the public department of social services, which typically serves as the "custody agent" of the child, and any number of sub-contracted agencies, which provide the actual domicile care—that is, the daily physical, social, emotional, and educational care that a child needs.

The professionals working in foster care may find a "mixed bag" when it comes to assessing how effective agency policies are. They encounter some policies that work exceedingly well, some policies that make sense even though they themselves may disagree with them at times, and some policies that simply run counter to best practices—by not serving the caregivers or practitioners well, and ultimately serving not to support but rather to stifle the child's progress and development.

In the above vignette, both the Alvarezes and Ms. O'Brien express dissatisfaction with the agency policy that strictly limits the amount of input foster parents can have with respect to a child's continuing placement. Foster parents can come to feel "frustrat[ed] about not being valued and trusted in their roles" because they are not considered "partners in decision-making" (Rosenwald and Bronstein 2008:293). Aggravating this concern in our vignette was the very quick turnaround time that historically has been employed by the agency. These concerns, time after time, and year after year, had served to disempower the Alvarezes to the extent that they were seriously considering quitting the agency.

In addition, Ms. O'Brien found that her own morale was affected, for she truly wanted to be an advocate for the clients. She made her own initial attempts at advocacy when she approached her supervisor about changing the policy, which solely relies upon a psychologist's opinion without taking the foster parents' perspectives (or the practitioners' opinions) into consideration. The sad irony is that rigid agency policies, typically put in place to serve the "best interest" of the child, at times do the opposite. In the vignette, for instance, we have foster parents who are thinking of quitting and a caseworker who is facing increasingly low morale (which can certainly lead to burnout and turnover).

Yet advocating within agencies is possible! Such a strategy must begin by identifying the particular policies that appear to the professionals involved to be the most ineffective.

Analyze the Context

In working as employees at an agency, practitioners and caregivers inherently have to consider the extent to which the agency's policies sufficiently address the physical, medical, psychological, social, cultural, and spiritual needs of children in care, as well as the core goals in foster care of safety and permanency. Once this review is completed, they are ready to advocate for policy change to assist the youth in care. Of course, the outcome of such influence can be policy succession (the policy is successfully altered), policy termination (the policy is successfully ended), or, sometimes unfortunately for the advocate, policy maintenance (the policy is unchanged) (Peters 1999:176–177). Table 8.1 provides a visual demonstration of both a traditional "top–down" flow in which policies dictate the experiences of foster parents, practitioners, and youth *and* an alternative flow of practitioners and foster parents advocating for policy change on behalf of youth in care and themselves.

There are many ways in which one can advocate for change in agency policy; these can be divided into the categories *direct* and *indirect*. Direct policy advocacy has a direct impact on the lives of the youth in foster care. One such area is the youth's placement itself—what is the policy on both placing and removing a child from a particular placement or a particular level of care (i.e., entry-level versus treatment)? A second area relates to

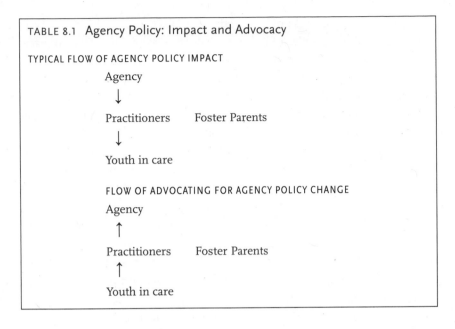

TABLE 8.1   Agency Policy: Impact and Advocacy

TYPICAL FLOW OF AGENCY POLICY IMPACT

Agency
↓
Practitioners   Foster Parents
↓
Youth in care

FLOW OF ADVOCATING FOR AGENCY POLICY CHANGE

Agency
↑
Practitioners   Foster Parents
↑
Youth in care

financial support—what is the policy on providing monies for youth for material needs and discretionary funds such as an allowance? A third refers to supervision—how often does a child in care need to be monitored—by both the foster parent and the practitioner? A fourth relates to decision-making—is there a policy on the extent and particular domains in which a youth in care must be consulted (e.g., selection of type of foster family/choice of kinship care placement; choice of school; decision to see birth family)?

Indirect policy advocacy focuses on improving the experiences of practitioners and foster parents; this can lead them to be more content in their roles and increase their retention (Brown and Calder 2002; Rhodes, Orme, and Buehler 2001; Schooler and Jorgenson 2000). Additionally, one of the findings from the National Foster Parent Association's (NFPA) membership survey in 2007 was that members wanted NFPA to provide more current information on child welfare news, developments, and trends (NFPA 2007). Knowledge of recent developments, including policies and best practices in response to these policies, enhances advocacy.

Satisfied foster care parents, for example, are more likely to continue in their role, which in turn provides more continuity and stable attachment for youth in care, who particularly need reliable caregivers.

Let's examine the areas of direct advocacy discussed in the above paragraph from the perspective of indirect advocacy. First, with respect to placement, what must practitioners and caregivers report on and implement with respect to placement change? Second, relating to financial support—what is the policy on stipend/salary and benefits, and any increases in these, for the caregivers/practitioner involved? Third, with respect to supervision—what are the requirements of supervision for the caregiver and the practitioner? Fourth, relating to decision-making, to what extent are the practitioner and caregiver consulted, and do they have the authority to decide important issues that affect the youth? A fifth area relates to professional education and training—what credentials does the agency require for these professionals? Finally, a sixth area concerns the very important issue of caseload and ensuring that both practitioners and foster parents are able to successfully assist the number of children in their care without feeling overwhelmed.

Table 8.2 provides a summary of areas for direct and indirect advocacy in working to improve agency policies.

Several considerations are also important for advocating for change in agency policy. In considering policies to be changed, practitioners and caregivers will need to determine which policies are explicitly written (typically provided in a policy manual that is given to each/made available upon hire) and which policies, though not written, are informal and "understood." Additionally, they will need to assess which policies are within the purview of the agency to change, and which policies are determined by federal, state, and local law (these would require legislative advocacy rather than agency policy advocacy; see chapter 9). For example, states vary in the number of hours of training they require for foster parents. Moreover, though practitioners and caregivers have been grouped together in this section, the policies relating to each will vary according to their particular role in the agency (and some agency policy differs for foster parents versus kinship caregivers). Therefore, it is essential to understand the particular policies that relate to a particular role, as this knowledge will be the foundation upon which to advocate for change.

Develop the Plan

What can be done to improve the outlook for the Alvarezes and Ms. O'Brien, in the vignette? Recall that the Alvarezes are on the verge of quit-

TABLE 8.2 Policy Areas in Which to Advocate for Change in Agencies		
POLICY AREA	SUBJECT TO DIRECT ADVOCACY (Affecting youth)	SUBJECT TO INDIRECT ADVOCACY (Affecting foster parents, kinship caregivers,* and practitioners)
Placement	Criteria to be placed/ removed from place-ment.	Criteria for reporting and implementing placement change.
Financial	Allocation funds for material needs and dis-cretionary funds such as allowance.	Increases to stipend/ salary and benefits.
Supervision	Required number of home visits.	Requirements for the foster parent and the practitioner.
Decision-making	Choices open to consul-tation (e.g., character-istics of foster family; choice of school; decision to see birth family).	Extent of input on important issues (i.e., visitation schedule) that affect youth.
Training	Not applicable.	Required credentials for these professionals.
Caseload	Not applicable.	Appropriate and man-ageable caseload.
*Note: Requirements for kinship caregivers may vary from those of foster parents.		

ting as foster parents; to be willing to continue in their role, they needed to feel empowered. A plan had to be developed that would identify the policy they needed to change. After settling on a particular policy and ensuring that it was within the agency's domain to change the policy (as opposed to the particular policy being mandated by law), they also need to con-sider a number of other issues regarding that policy. Table 8.3 offers some

TABLE 8.3 Questions to Help Identify Policies Upon Which to Advocate

Is the nature of the policy "formal and written" or "informal and unwritten?"

To what extent does the policy place the child at risk?

To what extent does it empower caregivers?

To what extent does it empower practitioners?

To what extent does it value caregivers' expertise?

To what extent does it value practitioners' expertise?

How regularly is the policy relied upon?

Are there sufficient resources (time, money, physical space, other professional expertise) available to support the policy?

questions that can guide caregivers and practitioners in working to identify policies to change.

The answers, of course, will vary based on the role of the individual, but the experiences of both caregivers and practitioners are useful nonetheless. Caregivers, for example, can brainstorm on the formal policies (usually found in the agency foster care handbook—ask for it to be produced!) as well as the "informal" policies of the agency. Similarly, practitioners will need to review the policies in the operations manual and can consult table 8.3 for some ideas for assessing which are working and which are not. Additionally, practitioners play a key role in assisting foster parents and relative caregivers in developing this plan; it is important that a collaborative, trusting relationship exist between the two.

In the example from the vignette, the intent of the agency policy was to respect and to follow the assessment of a credentialed mental health professional (the psychologist) concerning Juanita's placement. No one would argue about the need for professional assessment of children in care—but when the policy for acting on the professional recommendation is rigid and does not include a consultation with the foster parents, as in this case, a challenge arises. The Alvarezes, using the questions listed in table 8.3, found that the policy (they could not find it written anywhere) was both disempowering and devaluing of their expertise.

Implement the Plan

Now equipped with some ideas for identifying the policies to advocate on, foster parents like the Alvarezes would find it very useful to find support and to determine the extent to which others agree. Several avenues exist for this. One option is to share the concern with the practitioner. In the case of the vignette, does Ms. O'Brien agree that the Alvarezes have a legitimate complaint that their perspective is minimally considered, if at all? Does Ms. O'Brien believe that it is an isolated incident or a pattern in which a number of foster parents have been affected? The extent to which the Alavarezes will consult with Ms. O' Brien depends on their relationship. Despite the collaborative perspective that should be achieved and the obvious legal authority, the vast majority of agencies are structured so that the worker has more authority than the foster parent. For relative caregivers, the extent of agency involvement (and the services provided) depends on the court order's mandate regarding the formal role of the relative in respect to the child—for example, temporary care, permanent guardian, or seeking adoption/ serving as an adoptive parent. Practitioners should be very conscious of this fact and be very diligent regarding both their approachability and their availability to foster parents and relative caregivers.

From the practitioner perspective, Ms. O' Brien also has options for implementing a plan to assess and collect support for policy change. She can go to her supervisor—a step that depends very much on the relationship she has with her supervisor. Additionally, she can talk with colleagues, to see if they also have similar views on the issue. Depending on the parties involved, the next step for advocating for youth in care by means of policy change is to document and build the case.

Prepare and Document Your Case

Identify the Need

At times a review of documented examples will initiate the process of thinking about which policy to advocate on, and how. In other cases documentation will follow a "felt" need for change that has never been put in writing by a foster parent or practitioner. A mutual relationship can be said to exist between documentation and identifying the policy.

It is important to distinguish whether the policy that needs to be changed is written or unwritten. A written policy is more easily referenced than an unwritten policy, which is often harder, though not impossible, to challenge and change. However, in the case of the latter, it is particularly important to document the incidents that have occurred that conflict with the intent of the policy.

In the vignette, the Alvarezes, as mentioned, did not find a written policy on excluding foster parents from decision-making regarding a youth's placement. They felt that they wanted to do something about their continued frustration but were not sure where to start. Although they enjoyed a cordial relationship with Ms. O'Brien, the couple was not fully sure they could rely on Ms. O'Brien to be anything more than superficially supportive. Separately, Ms. O'Brien also felt her hands were tied and wondered what to do.

Analyze the Context

Documenting is an important strategy for building a case for advocacy, particularly when there is initial resistance to agency change. It is also consistent with evidence-based practice, which suggests that best practice should be linked to empirical findings (Royse, Thyer et al. 2006). Practitioners can take the lead in encouraging foster parents to record the occurrence of the action that represents the "need." Specifically, this record can include the date, the time, the duration, the parties involved, the description of the activity, the reasons for the activity occurring, the consequences of the activity, and the response (to the extent known) of all parties involved. Additionally, this record can be linked to the agency's mission as added support. For example, say the Mytown Children Services' mission (the subcontracted foster care agency that employs Ms. O'Brien and contracts with the Alvarezes) includes a reference to "helping foster children by providing foster parents who are fully involved in the youth's care." The Alvarezes could then write about how their real experience of repeated lack of consultation on removing the children in foster care from their home over the years stood in contrast to and thereby conflicted with the agency mission.

In the absence of a written mission or agency policy statement that can support the "need," one other consideration is to link the concerns to those identified by outside groups' perspectives. For example, linking this documentation of experience to written policy standards or recommendations from professional groups external to the agency can provide extra merit or support in the advocacy efforts. Drawing on the missions of the agency's accrediting agency (e.g., the Joint Commission on Accreditation of Healthcare Organizations [JCAHO]) (which can have particular import, considering it is approving the agency) or an outside organization, such as the Child Welfare League of America or the National Foster Parent Association, is a smart strategy that can be used as additional leverage. Sometimes these outside organizations serve as "checks" to what agencies should be doing. For example, in referencing healthcare standards for youth in care, "In a recent nationwide survey, only one-third of state child welfare agencies responding to the survey reported having adopted Child Welfare League of America/ American Academy of Pediatrics standards" (Halfon, Inkelas et al. 2005). (Chapter 10 provides further examination of the role of community non-profit organizations in advocacy efforts.) Therefore, if the area of advocacy was to lead an agency to increase its health care standards for youth, the Child Welfare League of America and the American Academy of Pediatrics could be used for support in preparing and documenting your case.

Develop the Plan

Developing the plan means drawing on these experiences and planning to present the case in a manner that can be positively received. Specifically, *how* the documentation is written and communicated is an art in and of itself; the goal is to be articulate, thorough, and collaborative (versus confrontational) in nature. Most individuals at agencies—indeed, most individuals in general—can receive a critique better if it is mentioned along with what is working successfully as well. This approach is helpful when documenting the "need." The Alvarezes were aware of this strategy but were still not sure if they felt comfortable enough to act.

Fortunately, Ms. O'Brien, believing that the Alvarezes were not alone in their concern, was bothered by their experiences and wondered if she should do something more, beyond talking to her supervisor, to advocate for the Alvarezes and perhaps other foster parents on the issue of increasing their decision-making input. In her reflection, she also faced an ethical challenge—should she encourage all of the foster parents to document when they felt disempowered or would this be too disruptive to her agency? On the one hand, she felt that initiating a process for foster parents to document their experiences would certainly be very empowering to the foster parents. On the other hand, she was concerned about what she was doing—she liked her supervisor and respected her supervisor's position that she (the supervisor) did not have the authority herself to do anything about this unwritten policy; Ms. O'Brien did not want to "rock the boat." She liked her job enough and did not want to develop a reputation as a "troublemaker," which could possibly place her job on the line. Ethical issues like this are challenging, because they can relate to conflicting ethical standards between advocating for clients (foster parents, and by extension, children in care) and supporting the agency. Ethical decision-making models can help practitioners with these dilemmas (see Dolgoff, Loewenberg, and Harrington 2008).

Implement the Plan

Confronted by this dilemma, Ms. O'Brien came up with a creative strategy. She decided to initiate a foster parent support group and determine how many foster parents had the concern that their input on children being removed from placement was not sufficiently valued. However, rather than solicit feedback on this specific concern, she decided she would ask about any general concerns that foster parents at Mytown Children Services had. Additionally, she thought it would be valuable to discover what the foster parents felt was going quite well in their tenure as foster parents. Framing her approach as initiating a support group to determine both what was going well and what was not provided a different vantage point to document the need, one that she believed she could "sell" to her supervisor. In fact, Ms. O'Brien did receive the support of her supervisor and organized the group.

Over the course of one month (and four support group meetings), Ms. O'Brien learned that 75 percent of the foster parents attending felt disempowered and wished they had more input in the decision-making process with respect to the removal of youth from their care. Additionally, the foster parents identified other policies they would like to see changed, including receiving an increase in the stipend they received for youth and having the agency assist them in getting a second opinion for medical care. The Alvarezes, among the others, were grateful to Ms. O' Brien for taking the lead in facilitating the group; they felt that Ms. O'Brien had more authority than they thought they themselves had. She advised the foster parents to document their concerns, including, specifically, the amount of time the foster parents had had to say goodbye to the child in their care, the lack of consultation they had experienced, and the frequency with which this had occurred. For balance, she also asked the foster parents to write down some of the positive experiences they had over the years, and they were willing to do this as well.

With respect to the specific policy issue that the Alvarezes had originally identified, Ms. O'Brien rewrote their concerns (she reported them in aggregate with names removed)—expressed as "It is not fair we are not included" and "We have no time to terminate with the children"—and positively reframed them to say "It would be helpful to have more decision-making input" and "We would like more time to terminate with the youth in our care." This positive perspective was part of the written documentation created in preparation for Ms. O'Brien's advocacy. Notice the use of the words "appreciate" and "it would be helpful" as strategic choices that will likely be more persuasive.

Adding a rationale extends the comment beyond an emotional component to explain how it will be helpful. Therefore, after confirming with the foster parents and documenting in her notes, Ms. O'Brien suggested, for example, that

"We would appreciate more decision-making input."

should become:

"We would appreciate more decision-making input prior to the youth's removal from our care because, while we recognize the importance of the psychologist's assessment, we would like to be consulted as well. This is because we have spent the most time with the children, and we believe we can offer a valuable perspective on their progress; also we wish to explore possible options in maintaining the children in our home for the sake of stability."

This tone—positive and recognizing a portion of the agency's stance—will go a long way in the presentation of the documentation. Additionally, recognizing any positive attribute of the agency policy (i.e., the importance of the psychologist's assessment) *prior* to the suggestion of a policy change is an important strategic step with respect to resolving this potential conflict. Indeed, recognition of the other party's needs, combined with stating your own needs, essential in successfully resolving conflicts (Bush and Folger 2005).

Therefore, effective and strategic documentation is an essential prerequisite to building a case and a crucial step in the advocacy process. The Alvarezes played a key role in bringing the matter to Ms. O'Brien's attention. However, they still felt afraid to become "activists" in the agency and instead were thinking of avoiding the conflict and quitting. Ms. O'Brien then took their initial idea and formulated a strategy whereby she had foster parents document their concerns as well as their positive experiences, and she "packaged" it in a positive way that she thought could be "heard" by her supervisor and her supervisor's boss in Mytown Children Services.

Present the Suggested Change Through the Appropriate Channel of Authority

Identify the Need

Once the documentation has been generated, it is important to understand the agency's chain of command to effectively know who is/are the appropriate individuals to present the documentation and the ideas on change regarding the identified policy. Additionally, it is critical to assess the actual process by which this presentation can and should be made. As mentioned, the policy changes that are being advocated for will vary depending on their nature (formal versus informal, etc.); additionally, the structure of the agency hierarchy of power, the personalities of those individuals who "occupy" the positions of power, and the agency's commitment to client-centered change will widely vary as well.

In our vignette, the Alvarezes and Ms. O'Brien need to understand both the levels of authority and the process(es) by which to present and advocate for a policy change. Particularly helpful to the foster parents in this case is that Ms. O'Brien occupies the first organizational level of authority, because of her position as a credentialed social worker (she has a Master's degree in social work and a social work license). In Ms. O'Brien, the Alvarezes have found a champion of their cause, and as a result of the skillful support group facilitation that Ms. O'Brien provided, a number of issues have been identified and documented. In her initial attempt to informally bring this issue to her supervisor, however, Ms. O'Brien was not successful. Now equipped with documentation, she was prepared to do something more but was not sure how to proceed. The Alvarezes were both thankful to Ms. O'Brien and patiently relying on her for her continued advocacy—in fact, her success in this matter would determine whether the Alvarezes continued as foster parents. While Ms. O'Brien felt some pressure, she also knew that this was a change for which she needed to advocate.

Analyze the Context

The type of advocacy-related change that Ms. O'Brien is engaged in is referred to as "staff-initiated organizational change" (Lewis, Lewis et al. 2001). It has the following five components:

1) the "change agent/action system," which consists of "employees with no prescribed authority or responsibility to initiate change,"
2) "primary sources of legitimacy," which are "professional ethics and values, employee or professional associations,"
3) "primary sources of power," which are "other workers, knowledge of the problem, professional expertise,"
4) "common tactics," including "participation on agency committees, fact finding, building internal support through education and persuasion," and
5) "major constraints and sources of resistance," including "superiors' disagreement, insufficient time or energy, uncertain legitimacy, fear of reprisal and disapproval, job insecurity. (Lewis, Lewis et al. 2001:282, 289)

Ms. O'Brien was not the agency director and therefore, was not obliged to initiate change simply by virtue of her position. However, spurred by the ideas, documentation, and support of the foster parents, she chose to serve as the *change agent/action system*. She did seek support from her peers on her same organizational level, and while several were privately supportive of her efforts, they did not want to publicly join her because of fear of agency reprisal and possible job termination. As a social worker, Ms. O'Brien drew her *primary source of legitimacy* from her professional code of ethics, which states "Social workers challenge social justice" (National Association of Social Workers 1999; see also Netting and O'Connor 2003). She drew on the *primary sources of power* by collecting information from the foster parents, receiving private confirmation from her peers, and following her own perspective of the issue. Through fact-finding and planning to gain the support of her supervisor and the agency director, she was employing *common tactics*. These were the ingredients that Ms. O'Brien needed to pursue her advocacy efforts.

Ms. O'Brien, however, was not naïve; the concerns of both the foster parents and her peers, and even her supervisor, made her aware that it would be challenging to advocate. She knew that *major constraints and sources of resistance* to changing policies in agencies should be anticipated and problem-solved beforehand. For example, it did not surprise her that the Alvarezes did not have the energy to become more actively involved with advocacy, nor did she find it strange that she herself was somewhat anxious about the security of her job based on this pursuit. As Lewis, Lewis et al. add, "Because substantive organizational change often confronts indifference or resistance and leads to discomfort or stress on the part of employees or larger units in the organization, it is not surprising that many change efforts fail" (1996:290).

In reviewing these "constraints and sources of resistance," it is particularly important to examine both the leadership structure and the attendant organizational culture arising from that leadership. An understanding of the "chain of command," provides important information regarding the amount of power given to different levels of authority. In essence, these dynamics illustrate how power "works" in an agency, hinting at how accepting or resistant the organization will be to the sort of policy change Ms. O'Brien, and the Alvarezes and other foster parents, are requesting.

The types of leadership that manifest in an agency play a large role in how receptive an agency is to the change process.

Leadership is the unifying factor for all management processes. Agency executives and, in fact, managers at all levels need to be leaders who help keep the organization and all staff focused on key organizational outcomes and processes necessary to get there; provide energy, confidence, and optimism regarding meeting the challenges facing human service organizations, and oversee the agency's constant evaluation and change so that it remains responsive to community needs and concerns. (Lewis, Lewis et al. 2001:20)

Lewis, Lewis et al. discuss the two types of leadership that can occur in organizations—"transactional leadership" and "transformational leadership." Transactional leadership is more common, but change in the agency occurs more incrementally; transformational leadership, though less common, is more effective in bringing out the potential of all agency staff (Lewis, Lewis et al. 2001). The slow pace of policy change under transactional leadership can at times directly clash with ideas of social justice; for example, Shulman perceptively writes, "Sadly, agency cultures can foster stereotypes of a whole class of clients—a process that at its worst can be racist, sexist, ageist, homophobic, and so forth" (2006:578).

Transactional leadership can be contrasted with transformational leadership, which "is often seen as more desirable, because it emphasizes important principles such as shared values, motivations, and higher purposes" (Lewis, Lewis et al.2001:269). Agencies guided by transformational leadership engage in "critical reflectivity," which is organizational self-examinations that are "essential in assessing not only personal beliefs and attitudes but also how the social/structural environment of the organization may be continuing or extending majority power and privilege to the detriment of the more vulnerable" (Netting and O'Connor 2003:57). Although from the perspective of practitioners and caregivers, transformational leadership would be ideal for advocacy, this is not always the leadership situation.

Complicating advocacy further is that sometimes several child welfare agencies—and therefore several leadership structures—are involved. Virtually all public child welfare agencies are the "custody agents," which means they are the agencies legally entrusted by the courts to provide for the complete care of the child while he or she is in foster care. However, a number of public child welfare agencies are now subcontracting their services to private foster care "contract" agencies, as a result of many factors, including a trend toward privatization, increased state oversight in response to publicized "failures" of public child welfare agencies, and layoffs in public staff. While the public child welfare agencies usually retain legal custody of the child (as discussed, for example, in chapter 6 with respect to issues of consent for healthcare), the private foster care agencies are charged with providing the foster parent training and supervision as well as all needs relevant to the physical custody of the children in their care.

Two agencies (and at times more) are often involved then, when advocacy for change is involved, each with its own set of organizational power structures and organizational climates that have their own respective views on change. Foster parents and practitioners, with practitioners likely taking the lead, can help sort out the chain of command both *within* the agencies and *between* the agencies. The public child welfare agency has the ultimate authority because it is the custody agent. However, the type of policy being changed will determine in which agency and at which level the advocacy process of case presentation should begin. For example, the authority to change the amount of allowance that foster parents can provide to youth may reside in the subcontracted agency while the authority to change how decision-making on a child's future occurs (as in the case of the Alvarezes) may rest with the public child welfare agency—in this case, the Millville Department of Social Services.

A final comment should be made on the relationship between the custody agent and the subcontracted private foster care agency, involving the different practitioners. While each child has a practitioner who presents that child's case in court and provides consent in healthcare and education decisions (in the case of the latter, if the caseworker is the educational surrogate), each child also has a worker employed by the private agency on his behalf. There are thus two sets of supervisors and two sets of "chains of commands" for each case. The private agency worker ultimately needs to defer to the public agency worker, but, as mentioned, instances exist in which the authority to make the policy change lies with the private agency. Ideally, discussion of these issues will occur collaboratively between practitioner and foster parent (chapter 7 discusses the importance of collaboration).

This seemingly dizzying array of components explains why advocacy in foster care by changing agency policy can often be a long and tiring process, yet it does take place. For example, documentation of the issue of youth in care who go missing led to changes in child welfare agencies (including increasing oversight and providing personal safety training for youth) to address and reduce this tragedy (Kaplan 2004). Therefore, recognizing and anticipating from the beginning the potential barriers to change, with particular emphasis on the leadership structure(s) involved, is immensely helpful in understanding and problem-solving the process of agency policy change.

Develop the Plan

Developing a plan of action can be guided by a number of questions that practitioners and foster parents can use to navigate the agencies involved. These questions, presented in table 8.4, can be used to help assess the structure of authority in an agency and the likelihood of organizational change being achieved.

A scenario like this is quite realistic and would be daunting in reality, as agency employees, whether practitioners and foster parents, may be unsure what to do when their experience does not match formal or informal policy. In developing the plan, Ms. O'Brien, in consultation with her supervisor, confirmed the Alvarez's suspicion that *not* consulting with foster parents was an informal policy of her employer, Mytown Children Services. Her agency, however, was subcontracted by Millville Social Services, and according to her supervisor, any change approved by Mytown Children Services would possibly need the approval of Millville Social Services. Additionally, Ms. O'Brien knew that change would not come easily at either of these agencies (they both subscribed to transactional leadership models that

---

TABLE 8.4 **Questions to Use in Developing a Plan of Action**

Is the policy formal (written) or informal (not written)?

Is a contract agency involved?

Does the authority to change the policy reside with the contract agency? The custody agent? Outside of the agency?*

What are the agency's (ies') views on organizational change? How compatible are these sets of views?

To what extent do collaborative relationships currently exist between the caregivers (foster parents, relative caregivers) and practitioners? Practitioners and supervisors? Supervisors and agency executives? Agency executives and boards of directors?

Note: If this is the case, the advocacy then turns to legislative or community advocacy discussed in the next two chapters. Perhaps the agency can serve as an ally in these advocacy efforts.

allowed only incremental policy change) and her supervisor confirmed this. However, Ms. O'Brien did learn that the respective directors and boards of directors of the agencies maintained good, collaborative relationships with each other; in fact, the executive director at Mytown Children Services had been employed as the deputy executive director at Millville Social Services.

In another type of collaborative relationship, advocates can engage in informal conversations with the person at the appropriate authority level to gauge if policy change can occur in that simple way or at least to determine the process by which change can occur. This is a good first step. Once this first step is tried and if it is unsuccessful, creating and strategically providing the documentation can then be tried. It is important to retain a collaborative attitude even when a more "formal" approach needs to be taken. Additionally, those who are interested in policy change should also learn through their agency manuals, what, if any, formal steps or even grievance procedures exist that would support at least the sharing of the need with someone in authority.

Drawing on and engaging in collaborative relationships, using written, positively framed documentation and supporting documents, and understanding the agencies' chain-of-command and views of change are all essential components in developing a plan.

Implement the Plan

Ms. O'Brien was now able to implement her plan for further advocacy. The current informal policy in Ms. O'Brien's agency was, as mentioned, that the psychologist's assessment had the highest credence in determining the child's placement. Ms. O'Brien asked her supervisor if this informal policy was the same as the custody agent's policy. Her supervisor thought this was an excellent question and stated that Millville Social Services almost always concurs with the decision of Mytown Children Services, but she (the supervisor) did not know if Millville Social Services actually had a written policy on the inclusion of foster parents in the decision-making surrounding a youth's removal from their care. The supervisor suggested Ms. O'Brien contact Mr. Hughes, who was a supervisor at Millville Social Services. She learned from Mr. Hughes that the written policy was that Millville Social Services "strongly considers the recommendation of any subcontracted agencies that are charged with the physical care of a child."

This additional information was helpful; recalling the collaborative relationship between the two agencies as well as between the two supervisors, Ms. O'Brien then came up with another strategy to provide the documentation of the policy change in the context of the findings from the support group. She requested a meeting with her supervisor and shared the findings, including, of course, the recommendation for the policy change to include more decision-making input from foster parents. The good rapport between Ms. O'Brien and her supervisor helped to persuade the supervisor that this was good evidence to request a meeting with the agency director (the supervisor's boss). Again the findings were presented, and because the policy requests had evidence to back them up and were included with the positive findings from the support group (recall the importance of the presentation of the documentation), the director was quite impressed with Ms. O'Brien's efforts. The director believed it was reasonable, and stated that she (the director) would contact the Millville Social Services executive director and have a conversation about whether it was feasible to formalize Ms. O'Brien's recommendation as Mytown Children Services policy.

After the discussion between the two agency directors, the Millville Social Services director stated that as long as Mytown Children Services continued to prioritize the assessment of the psychologist or other credential mental health professionals, formally including foster parents' (as well as practitioners') perspectives on the decision to remove a child from care was fine with him. In turn, the Mytown Children Services director received permission from her board of directors to institute the change. The policy was formally written and a memo of policy change was distributed throughout the agency. Ms. O'Brien was elated, and her supervisor and director were so impressed by her efforts that she received a promotion to assistant supervisor! Thrilled, Ms. O'Brien shared the great news with the foster parents, including the Alvarezes, who were also overjoyed—they felt truly empowered, as did Ms. O'Brien. The policy was then enacted and monitored over time. The Alvarezes decided to stay on as foster parents.

Summary

It cannot be sufficiently emphasized that this process of advocating within an agency can seem overwhelming, tedious, and certainly exhausting. Moreover, the fears that advocates may have about disrupting the agency status quo and having any change efforts labeled as subversive are real. Although this chapter's example concluded positively, unfortunately, there are no guarantees that advocating in agencies will always be successful (or at least occur quickly).

But the phrase "Keep your eyes on the prize" provides inspiration and the necessary reminder that hard work *can* pay off. While some foster care agency policies are certainly very relevant, helpful, and important, other policies do not produce a positive consequence and in fact run counter to, or at least diminish, advocating for youth in foster care. Working through the components of advocating in an agency—assessing policies to change, building the case through accurate and constructively framed documentation, and deciding how to present the suggested change via the agency hierarchical structure—provides strategies to maximize your success in advocating in agencies for policy change.

Discussion Questions

1. How would this scenario have turned out if the Alvarezes happened to have a practitioner who was not helpful as Ms. O'Brien? Assume they were still interested in serving as foster parents—what could they have done?

2. Brainstorm on other effective strategies that Ms. O'Brien could have tried, aside from facilitating the focus group?

3. The vignette focuses on an issue that primarily affects foster parents. What are some issues of agency advocacy for policy change that primarily affect kinship caregivers? Practitioners?

4. The chapter references the potential ethical dilemma between supporting clients and supporting the agency. What other ethical implications might exist in advocating for change in agencies? You can read the National Association of Social Workers Code of Ethics (see below) for ideas.

Web Sites

- National Association of Social Workers, Code of Ethics: http://www .socialworkers.org/pubs/code/default.asp
- Transformational Leadership: http://changingminds.org/disciplines/ leadership/styles/transformational_leadership.htm

9

Advocating Legislatively

I have come to the conclusion that the making of laws is like the making of sausages—the less you know about the process the more you
respect the result.

—Unknown

Vignette

Mr. Hanson is a social worker and former foster care worker who rose
up through the ranks to become the director of foster care for a private
foster care agency. Over the years he has noticed an increase in the
number of youth in foster care who identify as lesbian, gay, bisexual,
transgender, or questioning (LGBTQ). He believes this is because
society has slowly but increasingly become more accepting and therefore more youth have "come out," that is, they have disclosed a sexual
orientation or gender identity that is not the norm. Mr. Hanson also
thinks that the agency's diversity training for foster parents and practitioners, which he expanded two years ago to include issues of sexual
orientation and gender identity, has made all parties involved more
comfortable, accepting, and supportive of openly LGBTQ youth in
care. Specifically, he has ensured that the agency is consciously aware
of specific issues that youth who are LGBTQ may face. First, he was
successful with his board of directors in adding sexual orientation and
gender identify to his agency's nondiscrimination statement. Additionally, he had the agency conduct support groups for LGBTQ youth,

train workers on including sexual orientation and gender identity in their assessment and practice, and provide diversity training for staff, including practitioners and foster parents.

Although he feels optimistic about the learning curve that his agency has engaged in with this expansion of training, he knows that he has taken a "risk" in the eyes of other child welfare agencies in becoming a foster care agency with a reputation as the "gay foster care agency." Mr. Hanson knows that this prejudicial environment is wrong and believes that other agencies should provide similar nondiscrimination protections for youth. In fact, he became an advocate when, several years ago, several lesbian and gay youth requested to be transferred to his county's agency because the agencies that the youth were in were not as supportive of their lifestyles and these youth had caseworkers who knew of his agency's support for LGBT youth.

Ever since, Mr. Hanson has been a champion of these youth among all others, and has been disturbed by the prejudicial climate that still lingers within child welfare agencies across his relatively politically conservative state. So far the county social services agency that subcontracts with his agency has not stated anything one way or the other, although Mr. Hanson knows that, based on the political tide, his agency's contract with the county might not be renewed. He is afraid to "rock the boat" for fear of losing his contract. Therefore, he wants to know if another strategy—legislative advocacy—might be something more he could do to protect this segment of youth in care.

Key

Mr. Hanson: director of foster care for a private foster care agency.

Although the previous chapter discussed particular strategies to effect change in agencies, unfortunately no strategy's success is guaranteed. Sometimes advocating for youth in care must take the form of creating strategies to meet their needs outside of the agency itself. Although agency staff should take part in advocacy whenever possible, there are times when an environment external to the agency should be examined as an arena for advocacy. A community strategy of legislative advocacy, which seeks a change in the law, is presented in this chapter.

Advocacy Checklist

- Determine if current law exists.
- Identify legislative status of issue for advocacy.
- Understand the legislative process.
- Gain familiarity and use legislation.

Determine If Current Law Exists

Identify the Need

Mr. Hanson learned from an informal discussion with the director of the custody agency (the county agency that subcontracts with Mr. Hanson's agency) that he should not "rock the boat"—the County Commission was somewhat conservative and would not likely support adding "sexual orientation" and "gender identity" to the county's nondiscrimination statement. Such change might occur in another few years, when some of the commission members rotated off, but for now the timing was not right. Therefore, Mr. Hanson thought about advocating outside of the agencies and decided to see what laws currently existed on this topic. He recalled a section from the Code of Ethics for Social Workers that he had read in graduate school:

> Social workers should engage in social and political action. . . . Social workers should be aware of the impact of the political arena on practice and should advocate for changes in policy and legislation to improve social conditions in order to meet basic human needs and promote social justice. (National Association of Social Workers 1999)[1]

He believed pursuing this quest was ethically sound and even ethically necessary.

Before beginning an advocacy campaign on any specific issue, it is crucial that practitioners and caregivers identify and develop a basic understanding of the laws in place that govern the practices related to foster care in general. This need is the first stage of legislative advocacy—the effective legislative advocate is first knowledgeable about the law and then typically expands on, changes, or overturns existing legislation.

Analyze the Context

For purposes of this section, federal laws that have been enacted that relate both broadly and specifically to youth in foster care and the practices to help these youth are reviewed below. Historically, three needs have been identified that serve as the bedrock for federal legislation. These needs are child safety, permanency, and well-being (McCarthy and Woolverton 2005). "Child safety" includes ensuring that youth are protected from physical, sexual, and emotional abuse as well as neglect (ensuring youth have appropriate food, clothing, education, hygiene, medical care, supervision, and social interaction). "Permanency" references the need for youth to have a stable, long-term placement. "Well-being" refers to promoting the general emotional, physical, cognitive, social, and spiritual health of children and their families in a nurturing environment where they can flourish.

In 1874, advocates successfully fought to bring the case of "Mary Ellen," a nine-year-old girl who had suffered extreme physical abuse and neglect, in front of a court and argued that this young girl could be viewed as an "animal," and therefore should be granted the same legal protection from harm that laws protecting animals provide. While at first it may appear bizarre that animal protection laws were used to protect a child from maltreatment, it was a sad reality that no laws existed for child protection. Since that time, laws protecting youth have leapt forward. What follows are some of the most significant pieces of legislation relating to foster care.

In 1935 the ground-breaking Social Security Act "provided grants to rural communities that lacked privately funded children's services to establish public child welfare services, including child protection"; in 1956 its follow-up amendment, the Home Life Amendment to the Social Security Act, called for "federal funding . . . to establish public child protective services in all communities, rural and urban" (Dore and Feldman 2005:437).

The next ground-breaking piece of legislation came eighteen years later, in 1974—the Child Abuse Prevention and Treatment Act

> provided federal funds to states to treat families identified as abusive and neglectful toward their children. It was the first federal recognition of the pervasive national problem of child abuse. It grew directly out of

efforts by the American Humane Association [recall the case of Mary Ellen] and other advocates for maltreated children.   (Dore and Feldman 2005:437–438)

It is important to remember that laws do not emerge in a vacuum. We often forget that the laws on the books that we may enjoy and/or think are very important did not magically appear. In fact, their existence is typically based on years of tireless advocacy.

A few years later the Indian Child Welfare Act of 1978 was passed to promote Native American culture by shifting authority for child welfare placement decisions from the U.S. government to tribal authorities; "[t]he act represents an important recognition of the hegemony of a minority group over the welfare of its own members" (Dore and Feldman 2005:438). This was an important decision and can be perceived as providing a foundation for the recruitment of diverse foster (and adoptive) parents with the MultiEthnic Placement Act, which would come into being sixteen years later.

While safety had always been paramount in child welfare and child protective services, the idea of permanency, as discussed above, was explicitly placed into law with the seminal Adoption Assistance and Child Welfare Act of 1980. This act

called on state and local child welfare agencies to review the status of all children in out-of-home care every 18 months and to make reasonable plans for permanency for each child. Permanency options, in order of preference, included 1) Returning the child to his or her birth or extended family 2) Terminating parental rights and placing the child for adoption, 3) Establishing guardianship with relatives or others, [and] 4) Making a specific plan for long-term foster care. The law required the use of the least restrictive, most homelike setting possible for every child. It was an attempt to shift public policy away from breaking up families and placing children. Not only did it emphasize timely reunification or the development of alternative plans for permanency for the child, it also called on public child welfare agencies to prevent "the unnecessary separation of children from their families by identifying family problems, assisting families in resolving their problems, and preventing the breakup of the family where the prevention of child removal is desirable and possible."   (Dore and Feldman 2005:439)

The priorities of the Adoption Assistance and Child Welfare Act of 1980 showcased an emphasis on family preservation—a policy that focused on protecting children from harm while working to improve parenting skills to keep families together and keep children out of foster care. This act, and the funds that supported it, successfully reduced by 50 percent the amount of youth in foster care and led to the development of such family preservation models as the popular "home builders model" (Dore and Feldman 2005). A 1993 amendment to the Social Security Act called the Family Preservation and Support Services Program gave federal funds for such programs, as well as family support services (cited in Dore and Feldman 2005).

However, with the epidemic of crack cocaine, poor drug treatment, and difficulties in developing successful family preservation models, the number of youth in foster care began to steadily increase again (Dore and Feldman 2005). Therefore, a paradigm shift occurred that focused on the expediency of placing children in a permanent situation, whether in their own home (the family preservation model) or through legal adoption after their parents' termination of parental rights (TPR). In 1997 this shift was represented by the landmark child welfare legislation called the Adoption and Safe Families Act.

> This legislation requires timely review of foster care cases and severance of parental rights of parents who fail to actively move toward reunification with their children. It requires permanency-planning hearings for children within 12 months of entry into out-of-home care. It also gives states the right to require even shorter periods for case review for children under 3 years of age. (Dore and Feldman 2005:441)

Now specific timetables had to be followed and parents and caregivers had to accelerate positive changes in their family dynamics to ensure they did not run out of time and lose their parental rights.

Such a shift in the approach to working with families of youth who were maltreated was not without critique. Some critics stated that the act was racist and classist because institutionalized racism and low minimum wages were structural factors that made it harder for African-American and Latino families, as well as poor families (who were affected by the new timelines of the welfare reforms of 1996), to find, secure, and maintain a job (Dore and Feldman 2005). Other critiques included the lack of funds for adequate substance abuse and dependency treatment programs. Consider Dore and Feldman's summary:

> Parents struggling to rebuild their lives can leave their children in foster care for no longer than 15 months within a 22-month period before their parental rights are terminated. Given the limited resources devoted to supporting reunified families, there are grave concerns about the vulnerability of this particular group to termination of parental rights. (Dore and Feldman 2005:441–442; see also Wexler 2002).

Despite the critiques, the act has maintained its legal authority and has influenced child welfare practices around the country.

Other important laws include the establishment of a special immigrant juvenile status (part of the Immigration Act of 1990), which provides legal protections and services for undocumented children with a history of maltreatment (http://www.nationalcasa.org/JudgesPage/Article/special_immigrant_juvenile_status.htm); the Multiethnic Placement Act of 1994 and its subsequent amended version; and the Interethnic Placement Act of 1996, which, after complaints to the contrary, helped to ensure that "foster placements were not delayed or denied on the basis of race, color, or national origin" (McGowan 2005:38–39).

Several laws have focused on foster care that specifically supports youth who were facing a difficult time being adopted and therefore remained in foster care for years. Championed by Senator John Chafee of Rhode Island, the Foster Care Independence Act of 1999 provided monies and

> required that states prioritize permanency for older teens, increase youth participation in decision making, provide both participation and services to Native American tribes and tribal youth, and provide services to young people aged 18 to 21 who had already left foster care. (Nixon 2005:577)

Therefore, agencies had to place increased emphasis on older youth, who are not perceived as "adoptable" as younger children. Additionally, older youth who still were in foster care were enrolled in independent living programs to help make their transition to adulthood an easier process. Finally, adults who had recently left foster care were also provided monies and services to help them with transition issues that had not been completed when they were in care. These programs typically assisted youth by providing classes on maintaining a home, nutrition, healthy relationships, resume writing and finding employment, and budgeting, as well as providing funds for such expenses as college and items that support a college education (i.e., transportation and computers). This focus on helping older youth in care to be adopted was also a component of the Keeping Children and Families Safe Act of 2003 (Keeping Children and Families Safe Act of 2003). Further, a revision to the federal Adam Walsh Protection and Safety Act states that certain crimes committed by individuals who are currently or potential foster parents will preclude them from becoming or continuing in that role (Administrative Directive).

Most recently, in 2008, the Fostering Connections to Success and Increasing Adoptions Act of 2008 was passed; among other items, it provides (1) financial support for kinship care providers and the agencies and tribal governments that help them, (2) provides educational and other assistance to youth in care up to age 21, and (3) requires that siblings be placed together when at all possible (Children's Defense Fund 2008).

As one can see, child welfare legislation spans approximately a century, with an increased amount of legislation from the 1970s on, including the landmark Foster Care Independence Act for youth in foster care.

Develop the Plan

Examining what laws are on the books is relatively easy to do. Most child welfare texts – including Mallon and McCartt Hess 2005 and Crosson-Tower 2007—provide good information on the federal laws that exist. The Internet, of course, provides a seemingly endless resource regarding federal laws. The Child Welfare League of America's site provides a thorough review of federal laws as well. Although federal legislation provides the foundation on which state and local governments must operate with respect to foster care specifically and child welfare generally, it is equally important to review the state and local laws that exist as well. One Web site (it is a paysite) that provides information on all federal and state laws is www.loislaw.com.

Although it is beyond the scope of the book to attempt to provide information on the laws pertaining to child welfare and foster care in all of the U.S. states and territories, as well as their thousands of counties, parishes, and municipalities, finding out what state and local laws do exist can be determined fairly easily. The place to start is the Child Welfare Information Gateway, which provides some, but certainly not all, information on laws pertaining to child welfare in your state. The Web site, mentioned several times already throughout this book, is http://www.childwelfare.gov/systemwide/laws_policies/state/.

Foster parents and relative caregivers who need information should contact the caseworker for assistance; practitioners can ask their supervisors. For those not currently a part of the foster care system, it may be useful to know that the public agencies that address foster care may be called [Name of State or County] Department of Social Services or Department of Children Services—although the names do vary. Calling and asking to speak to a supervisor or examining Web pages are two strategies to find out what the laws are. Area schools of social work as well as local librarians could also assist you. Law libraries will have the full text of all laws. Finally, you could contact your local community college or a nearby college to see if there is a class that is taught on child welfare history and policy.

In our vignette, Mr. Hanson used these sources of information in working to find out about state and local law.

Implement the Plan

With his understanding of the laws that exist and upon a review of these laws, including an exploration of Web sites and making phone calls, Mr. Hanson's suspicion was confirmed—he found no laws at any of the three levels of government that addressed nondiscrimination protection for LGBT youth. He saw that the Multiethnic Placement Act, while important in focusing on issues of race and ethnicity and the overrepresentation of youth of color in care, did not focus on sexual orientation or gender identity. The current state nondiscrimination law on foster care that guides the operation of public social service agencies and its subcontractors (Mr. Hanson's agency is subcontracted) states that "agencies will not discriminate in their practices with youth regardless of gender, race, ethnicity, age, religion, national origin or ability." He found no nondiscrimination law at all at the county level.

Although it had taken a little time to do the research and review, Mr. Hanson now had a better understanding of the current language of the state nondiscrimination law as well as the knowledge that legal protection for LGBTQ youth was missing from both the local and county level. His actions were consistent with the recommendations of Weaver, Keller, and Loyek (2005), who discuss the importance of workers familiarizing themselves with legislation (p. 181). Mr. Hanson was hopeful that legislation could be enacted at some point to expand the state's nondiscrimination statement to help youth who already were vulnerable due to homophobia and/or transphobia in the child welfare system (Clements and Rosenwald 2007; Mallon 2001).

Identify Legislative Status of Issue for Advocacy

Identify the Need

Mr. Hanson knew that adding "gender identity" and "sexual orientation" to his state's nondiscrimination statement for serving youth in care would help ensure the protection of youth in care by legally protecting their rights. He had chosen the state as the appropriate level on which to advocate because he felt that advocating on the federal level was too daunting and would take too much time. In turn, he believed that advocating at the local level, county by county, would not be productive because the county foster care agencies were governed by state law.

Although he personally felt comfortable in his conviction regarding the need for the addition to the nondiscrimination policy, he wondered whether he was alone in this pursuit. Mr. Hanson wanted to know what organizations, and other individuals, were already (if at all) advocating for this addition to the nondiscrimination statute. Mr. Hanson would not be satisfied until a law existed that could be translated into policy to assist LGBTQ youth in care.

Analyze the Context

It is crucial for foster parents and practitioners to learn about the context in which legislative advocacy develops. There are two different routes individuals can take to determine the extent to which legislative advocacy is already occurring on a topic relevant to foster care (or any issue, for that matter). Specifically, if no law currently exists on a given issue, individuals can work to discover whether legislative advocacy is currently underway to get a bill introduced into the relevant committee of the federal, state, or local legislative branch; if a bill does exist, they can search out its current legislative status.

The first route for determining what the status of legislative advocacy on a foster care issue might be is to examine the Web sites of national, state, and local organizations that are devoted to issues concerning children, including child welfare and foster care/kinship care specifically. Two of the largest national child welfare advocacy organizations in the United States are the National Foster Parent Association (NFPA) and the Child Welfare League of America (CWLA). A third national advocacy organization, the National Association for Social Workers (NASW), promotes a number of issues important in child welfare/foster care as well. In addition to these three, the Foster Family–Based Treatment Association (http://www.ffta.org/) and the Children's Defense Fund (www.childrensdefense.org) are other national associations that address essential issues in foster care.

CWLA and NASW provide their legislative agenda—that is, a prioritized listing of different issues, ranked from most to least urgency—via their Web sites. Legislative agendas are useful because they help organizations

> prioritize [their] objectives by assessing them in context with [their] resources, . . . act as a control against overextending [their] legislative capabilities through numerous unplanned activities, . . . [serve as] a concise document to communicate [an organization's] legislative interests and objectives to the legislature and public, and help . . . [the organization] assess [its] legislative objectives and successes after the session. (NASW 2003:6)

Because of limited resources in time, staff, and money, as well as the important issue of the right timing to initiate a bill, the NASW manual recommends that priorities in legislative agendas can be conceptualized via a three-tier approach and that organizations work together cooperatively to achieve success. Table 9.1 presents this prioritization. As you can see, prioritizing issues on when and how they will be advocated in the legislative arena is an important way of managing a large number of issues that cannot all be addressed at once.

TABLE 9.1 Prioritizing a Legislative Agenda	
Level 1 Priority issues	"[The organization] will take the lead [on these issues] in coalition efforts and can have a unique impact."
Level 2 Priority issues	"[The organization] will work in coalition on issues important to the profession, while another organization identified with this issue leads the coalition."
Level 3 Back-burner issues	"[The organization] will recognize that these issues are important, but that the chapter is unable to devote the resources to work on them during this legislative session."
Source: Adapted from NASW 2003:6.	

The NFPA, the CWLA, and the NASW all give position statements on child welfare and foster care issues. On its Web site (http://www.nfpainc. org/content/page=POSITION%20STATEMENTS&nmenu=1&title=NFP A%20Position%20Statements), for instance, the NFPA includes statements on such various topics as secondhand smoke, taxation of foster care stipends, and foster parent recruitment and retention. The CWLA posts its legislative agenda, prioritized by topic; in 2008 (http://cwla .org/advocacy/2008legagenda.pdf) these priorities included increased funding to finalize adoptions and the reauthorization of the Child Abuse Prevention and Treatment Act. The NASW posts a similar document (http://www.socialworkers.org/advocacy/images/grmaterials/GRLEG-genda Rpt2007.pdf). These sites may also reference the status of active bills at the federal level; both the NASW and the NFPA have chapters that likely follow the relevant issues on child welfare and foster care at the local level.

There is also a second route by which you can find information on whether a current bill relating to foster care is under consideration: researching the activities and hierarchies of the legislative branches on the federal, state, and local levels. Fortunately, because of the Internet, this information is readily available. For example, on the federal level, bills relating to foster care and child welfare in general are often introduced in the United States House of Representatives' Committee on Education and Labor and in the United States Senate's Committee on Children and Families.

Although you can find the information on other Web sites, the quickest way to find pending legislation that relates to foster care is by going to http://thomas.loc.gov/, where the Library of Congress documents all activity on a bill. Simply typing "foster care" (or "kinship care") into the keyword search will bring up a voluminous list of bills and their activities relating to foster care; by clicking on "bill summary and status," you can easily see the bill number, title, text of the legislation, sponsor, cosponsors, related bills, latest major action, and other related information. State and local government Web sites provide information on bills at these levels. The committees in which such bills would be introduced at the state and county level vary by name and structure. Most bills are introduced into a committee or subcommittee focusing on children and families.

Develop the Plan

Mr. Hanson now knew that relevant organizations have statements and at times legislative agendas on issues relating to child welfare and foster care. He had also learned how to access legislative branch Web sites to identify the status of current bills. Therefore, in continuing with the initial steps of legislative advocacy, his plan was to access the three organizations' Web sites (NFPA, CWLA, NASW) to see what any of them had to say with respect to the issue of sexual orientation and gender identity inclusion. Additionally, he would peruse the U.S House and U.S. Senate Web sites as well as his state and county's legislative branch Web sites to get more information.

Implement the Plan

While Mr. Hanson was dismayed (but not surprised) to find that no bills existed on this issue at any level of government, he was heartened to discover that all three of the national organizations gave strong statements on sexual orientation and gender identity. That National Foster Parent Association states that it is aware that

> gay, lesbian, bisexual, transgender and questioning youth are present in the foster care system and [that the NFPA] encourages and supports establishment of standards, policies, and training programs for foster care providers and professionals based on non-discrimination principles and sensitivity to the sexual orientation of all foster children and youth. (http://nfpainc .org/content/?page=POSITION%20STATEMENTS&pg=1#cp_111_333)

The Child Welfare League of America states that it is working in coalition

> to build the child welfare system's capacity to deal equitably and constructively with young people, family members, and employees who are lesbian, gay, bisexual, transgender, or questioning their sexual orientation (LGBTQ), with particular emphasis on those making the transition to adulthood. (http://cwla.org/programs/culture/glbtqabout.htm)

Finally, the National Association of Social Workers

> supports full civil and human rights for all people and opposes public policies that alienate individuals by race, ethnicity, national origin, gender, age, physical or mental abilities, marital status, sexual orientation, or religious belief. (http://www.socialworkers.org/advocacy/images/ grmaterials/GRLEGAgendaRpt2007.pdf)

While you may not be so fortunate as to have three leading human service organizations giving statements on the topic on which you want to advocate, often at least one major organization will have a statement that is in tandem with the need of the youth in kinship or foster care. It is an unfortunate reality that organizations are often years and sometimes decades ahead of governments with respect to sound, pro-child and pro-family foster care and kinship care policy.

Mr. Hanson did have allies at the national level; he contacted two of these three organizations—those that have local chapters (the NFP and the NASW)—and began to network. He no longer felt alone.

Understand the Legislative Process

Identify the Need

While he vaguely recalled his high school civics class and School House Rock's cartoon "I'm Just a Bill," Mr. Hanson did not really know how the legislative process worked. Understanding this would give him a better appreciation of the process—as well as the timeline—in which a bill becomes a law. He believed that this was an important preparation for his collaboration with the local chapters he would work with.

Analyze the Context

While legislative processes vary by jurisdiction and level of government in terms of names of committees, timelines, and procedures, what they share in common is that a group of people have an idea that they would like to become law. The key is to get at least one current legislator to sponsor the bill and advocate for a hearing on the bill in a committee. This hearing reviews the text of the bill and hears testimony from both supporters and opponents of the proposed legislation.

> The committee ultimately votes to approve the legislation as written, approve with amendments, or vote the bill down. If the bill is approved, either with or without amendments, it will then be referred to the next committee until it reaches the full legislative body of a particular chamber [e.g., U.S. House of Representatives or U.S. Senate]. Generally, once a bill is approved by all governing legislative chambers and signed by the head of the executive branch [e.g., president, governor, or mayor], it becomes law. (pers. comm., Johanna Byrd, Oct. 19, 2008)

Table 9.2 provides detailed information regarding the legislative process in the U.S. Congress.

Because sponsorship is so essential, it is important to find out who your legislative representatives are at the varying levels of government. The U.S. Senate Web site is "senate.gov" and the U.S. House Web site is "house.gov." Foster parents and practitioners can review state and local government

TABLE 9.2 The Legislative Process

INTRODUCTION

Anyone may draft a bill; however, only members of Congress can introduce legislation, and by doing so become the sponsor(s). There are four basic types of legislation: bills, joint resolutions, concurrent resolutions, and simple resolutions. The official legislative process begins when a bill or resolution is numbered - H.R. signifies a House bill and S. a Senate bill - referred to a committee and printed by the Government Printing Office.

STEP 1. REFERRAL TO COMMITTEE

With few exceptions, bills are referred to standing committees in the House or Senate according to carefully delineated rules of procedure.

STEP 2. COMMITTEE ACTION

When a bill reaches a committee it is placed on the committee's calendar. A bill can be referred to a subcommittee or considered by the committee as a whole. It is at this point that a bill is examined carefully and its chances for passage are determined. If the committee does not act on a bill, it is the equivalent of killing it.

STEP 3. SUBCOMMITTEE REVIEW

Often, bills are referred to a subcommittee for study and hearings. Hearings provide the opportunity to put on the record the views of the executive branch, experts, other public officials, supporters and opponents of the legislation. Testimony can be given in person or submitted as a written statement.

STEP 4. MARK UP

When the hearings are completed, the subcommittee may meet to "mark up" the bill, that is, make changes and amendments prior to recommending the bill to the full committee. If a subcommittee votes not to report legislation to the full committee, the bill dies.

STEP 5. COMMITTEE ACTION TO REPORT ON A BILL

After receiving a subcommittee's report on a bill, the full committee can conduct further study and hearings, or it can vote on the subcommittee's recommendations and any proposed amendments. The full committee then votes on its recommendation to the House or Senate. This procedure is called "ordering a bill reported."

STEP 6. PUBLICATION OF A WRITTEN REPORT

After a committee votes to have a bill reported, the committee chairman instructs staff to prepare a written report on the bill. This report describes the intent and scope of the legislation, impact on existing laws and programs, position of the executive branch, and views of dissenting members of the committee.

TABLE 9.2 The Legislative Process (*continued*)

STEP 7. SCHEDULING FLOOR ACTION

After a bill is reported back to the chamber where it originated, it is placed in chronological order on the calendar. In the House there are several different legislative calendars, and the Speaker and majority leader largely determine if, when, and in what order bills come up. In the Senate there is only one legislative calendar.

STEP 8. DEBATE

When a bill reaches the floor of the House or Senate, there are rules or procedures governing the debate on legislation. These rules determine the conditions and amount of time allocated for general debate.

STEP 9. VOTING

After the debate and the approval of any amendments, the bill is passed or defeated by the members voting.

STEP 10. REFERRAL TO OTHER CHAMBER

When a bill is passed by the House or the Senate it is referred to the other chamber where it usually follows the same route through committee and floor action. This chamber may approve the bill as received, reject it, ignore it, or change it.

STEP 11. CONFERENCE COMMITTEE ACTION

If only minor changes are made to a bill by the other chamber, it is common for the legislation to go back to the first chamber for concurrence. However, when the actions of the other chamber significantly alter the bill, a conference committee is formed to reconcile the differences between the House and Senate versions. If the conferees are unable to reach agreement, the legislation dies. If agreement is reached, a conference report is prepared describing the committee members' recommendations for changes. Both the House and the Senate must approve of the conference report.

STEP 12. FINAL ACTIONS

After a bill has been approved by both the House and Senate in identical form, it is sent to the President. If the President approves of the legislation he/she signs it and it becomes law. Or, the President can take no action for ten days, while Congress is in session, and it automatically becomes law. If the President opposes the bill he/she can veto it; or, if he/she takes no action after the Congress has adjourned its second session, it is a "pocket veto" and the legislation dies.

STEP 13. OVERRIDING A VETO

If the President vetoes a bill, Congress may attempt to "override the veto." This requires a two thirds roll call vote of the members who are present in sufficient numbers for a quorum.

Source: courtesy of Congress.org (http://www.congress.org/congressorg/issues/basics/ ?style=legis).

Web sites as well as the blue (government) pages of the phone book to learn the names of their local and state representatives. To use these Web sites, you typically just need to type in your address including your zip code to find out the legislative district you reside in and the legislators who represent you; you will thus obtain the names of your legislators, their contact information, and their political party affiliation. In this era, practically all legislators have Web pages that provide further information on their biography, the committees they serve on, the issues that are important to them, and current news. Caregivers and practitioners can also find out about their state and local government legislative procedures by calling their state or local representatives.

Develop the Plan

After acquainting himself with this process, Mr. Hanson realized that having a legislative sponsor would be an essential component to drafting a bill to expand the state's nondiscrimination law. He did not yet know who his representatives were, and he planned to find not only this but also if the local chapters of the National Foster Parent Association and the National Association of Social Workers knew of particular legislators who either were already, or might be, supportive of a potential bill.

Implement the Plan

Although Mr. Hanson took the opportunity to find out who all his legislators were, his state senator and state representative were most important to him in this case. He discovered, after learning who they were, that his state senator—but not his state representative—was on the state legislative committee that introduced legislation on foster care. However, as Mr. Hanson observed via the senator's Web site, this senator was a member of various religious conservative organizations that tended to be anti-LGBTQ rights. Although it discouraged him to learn that appearances indicated that his own state senator might be (although it was not certain) unsupportive of legal protections for LGBTQ individuals, he was hopeful that the state representative would be supportive and might introduce the bill.

However, when he contacted the two organization's local chapters, his mood lifted. He learned that both organizations had already established good working relationships with two other state senators, who *were* supportive of LGBTQ rights. The organizations said they would consider supporting Mr. Hanson's idea; in particular, the state branch of the National Foster Parent Association would likely support it because it was important to the organization (recall the position statement on LGBT youth from the previous section). Additionally, both organizations encouraged Mr. Hanson to contact his state representative, which he later did, to communicate his position on the idea behind the future bill. Mr. Hanson felt he was making progress.

Gain Familiarity and Use Legislative Advocacy Tools

Identify the Need

This chapter's previous three sections have paved the way to build the important educational foundation upon which legislative advocacy lies. What naturally follows from this educational preparation is a commitment to directly advocating on behalf of the need or cause of interest for youth in care. As you can see from earlier in the chapter, there is a dizzying array of issues (just among the three organizations) from which to choose to advocate. In our vignette, Mr. Hanson was poised to take the next step of legislative advocacy but needed clarification from his board of directors on what role he should play since he believed he was walking a fine line between being an agency director and being an advocate. He also needed to follow particular steps of legislative advocacy to advance the cause of nondiscrimination for LGBT youth.

Analyze the Context

Before he began to actively advocate, it was important that Mr. Hanson resolve a potential ethical dilemma. He knew that, as the director of a nonprofit, 501(c)3 agency, he was not allowed to lobby for a particular issue, but as a professionally trained social worker he had a responsibility to advocate for his clients. Individuals who wish to advocate should check on whether their agencies are legally allowed to do so; this determination is based on their profit status. Nonprofit agencies with a "501(c)(3)" designation can lobby on a particular issue as long as any expenditure associated with lobbying efforts is within the confines of law; further, individuals can advocate as long as they do so in their role as private citizens rather than employees (Tenenbaum 2002).

The vast majority of practitioners are employed by nonprofit organizations; while networking to find like-minded professionals can take place at these agencies, the formal legislative advocacy work has to be conducted outside of the workplace. This means that advocacy cannot be pursued during office hours and that individuals cannot conduct their advocacy in the guise of their official position as a county worker (i.e., they cannot use agency letterhead). Again, it is important to check with the practitioner or supervisor to get more information on the agency's policy on this matter.

Once you have clarified and resolved this dilemma, note that those who advocate for legislative change (in our case as a foster parent, relative caregiver, or a practitioner) are perceived as an interest group, a useful alliance. "Interest groups are also important sources of policy formulation. In addition to identifying problems and applying pressure to have them placed on an agenda, successful interest groups have to supply possible remedies for those problems" (Peters 1999:64). In our example of Mr. Hanson and the state chapters that are supportive of his idea on expanding the state law's nondiscrimination statement, we have a "public interest group" (Peters). A public interest group's purpose is to challenge what is perceived to be unfair or unresponsive and "to attempt to broaden the range of interests represented in the policymaking process. These groups are oriented toward reform of policy and policymaking" (Peters 1999:65). Because the idea of extending nondiscrimination protection to LGBTQ youth can be controversial (although it is slowly becoming more acceptable), it broadens the debate and becomes the focus of change via legislative advocacy.

Develop the Plan

Mr. Hanson's initial research into the status of the law and understanding the legislative process was the beginning of his legislative advocacy. Now he was ready to develop a plan to advance his legislative advocacy with others. Such a plan would consist of three broad steps: (1) organize with others in the advocacy effort; (2) obtain evidence that supports your advocacy position; and (3) communicate with legislators and their aides.

Organizing with others is a foundational step in legislative advocacy. Individuals vary on whether they choose to connect with others when they advocate. While it is admirable to advocate on an individual basis, this section intends to emphasize the importance of collective legislative advocacy. Planning advocacy with others achieves a "strengths in numbers" dynamic (see Shulman 2006); it allows for a coordinated, organized effort that outlines specific strategies to advance a cause; and it serves as mutual reinforcement and energy renewal to those working toward that cause. In the case of caregivers and practitioners, the three national organizations discussed above (NFPA, CWLA, and NASW) are good examples of agencies that promote advocacy. Planning to link to local chapters and colleagues within both your agency and other foster care and child welfare agencies is an important practical step. Organizing can take place through email listservs, meetings, rallies, and work sessions, among other venues. It is important for the caregiver and the practitioner to communicate and collaborate with each other on legislative advocacy. Although sometimes their efforts can diverge, the authors of this book intend to encourage a spirit of collaboration.

Including youth in care as advocates can send a powerful message; such youth must be of the appropriate age and emotional maturity. Of course, the first step is to obtain informed and voluntary consent from the youth as well as from the involved agencies and parents, if necessary. From an ethical perspective, this strategy must involve only youth who are not the particular practitioners' clients, unless the idea comes from the youth themselves. Perhaps the best strategy for recruiting youth in care is to distribute an announcement in a newsletter or listserv for young adults who were recently in foster care to share their stories.

Once individuals have collectively met and strategized about how they each can contribute toward this effort, they must proceed to the second step, which is to ensure that they have good evidence to support their argument. Evidence can take many forms. Most emotionally appealing to legislators are stories of real youth (identifying information removed), often told in their own voices. However, the stories and experiences of foster parents and practitioners also serve as powerful evidence.

Other evidence comes from research and statistics. Referencing journal articles, books, and government reports provides scientific and expert information on the nature and pervasiveness of the problem as well as solutions that can work. Researching and drawing on similar examples of laws that exist in other state or local jurisdictions also can be useful. Such information can be condensed into what are called "talking points"—the main ideas, with supportive details, that outline the argument to be made in advocacy efforts.

The third step is contacting legislators. Communication in this manner is really lobbying—attempting to convince a legislator to support and vote on behalf of the cause. Communication takes several forms (sending faxes and emails, making telephone calls, scheduling in-person appointments [often the most effective strategy]); also required might be testifying in support of the issue before a legislative subcommittee or committee. Table 9.3 provides specific information and advice on communicating with legislators.

TABLE 9.3 Communicating with Your Legislator

BY LETTER

Your purpose for writing should be stated in the first paragraph of the letter. If the letter pertains to a specific piece of legislation, identify it accordingly, e.g., H.R. ___, S. ___ .

Sample text: "As a member of NASW I am writing to [support or oppose] [state the issue]."

Explain your position, and use examples from either your life or the life of your clients.

Ask for the legislator's position, and whether he or she will support your position.

Offer assistance and contact information.

Be courteous, stay to the point, and include key information, using examples to support your position.

Refer to only one issue in each letter and, if possible, keep the letter to one page.

VIA TELEPHONE CALLS

You can get the phone numbers for members of Congress from the U.S. Capitol switchboard at (202)224-3121, the government pages of your phone book, www.house.gov, and www.senate.gov. When you call, share your name and address, identify the bill by both its

---

TABLE 9.3 Communicating with Your Legislator (*continued*)

number and name, and convey your message. You do not have to be an expert; they want to know your opinion.

BY E-MAIL

Use the Congress Web function on NASW's Web site (www.socialworkers. org/advocacy) to send messages instantly to your members of Congress. For the subject line of your e-mail, identify your message by topic or bill number. Always include your address, and never send attachments.

Source: General information courtesy of Congress.org (http://www.congress.org/congressorg/issues/basics/?style=comm); see also http://capwiz.com/socialworkers/issues/basics/?style=comm.

Although we speak of contacting a legislator, in reality it is often the legislator's staff assistants that you will reach; you can leave a message with them to introduce your idea. Contacting the legislative aide can be sufficient for advocacy, as long as the aide passes the information along to the legislator. Checking on the legislator's position on the issue (if not known before) is important in this process. Additionally, reminding the staff member that you are a constituent (and that, through the local chapter of the National Association of Social Workers, for example, you represent *x* number of constituents) can be influential as well (pers. comm., Johanna Byrd, Oct. 19, 2008). Finally, follow up with a thank you note for the legislator's actual or anticipated support—this goes a long way in building a courteous relationship that can make your issue (and any nonwork organization that you are affiliated with) stand out among the sea of requests.

Even when you are collaborating with an organization, your individual legislative advocacy may seem like it is a "drop in the bucket"; however, most legislators and their aides really do pay attention to the amount of public support on a particular topic. They typically believe that every one item of correspondence (email, phone call, mailed letter) they receive represents a number of constituents who share a particular view. And remember that practically all bills face opposition; sufficient preparation, including anticipating and responding to the arguments against the bill, is critical. This is why collaborating with organizations such as the National

Foster Parent Association and others can be very beneficial to your cause; often they have a contact person whose job includes managing legislative affairs (and that organization may also pay a formal lobbyist to act on the agency's behalf).

Implement the Plan

Mr. Hanson was enthusiastic about implementing his plan. He decided to work with the local chapter of NASW and to become an affiliate of the National Foster Parent Association. He was told by his agency's board of directors that while he could not advocate legislatively on work time as an agency director (per both agency policy and the law), he could refer to where he worked when he was advocating off-duty in the role of professional social worker.

Having already made initial contacts when seeking information from the two local chapters (NFPA and NASW), Mr. Hanson now planned to attend each organization's meetings and join several listservs. The staff members at the two organizations agreed to work on Mr. Hanson's behalf with two state senators who they believed would be supportive about putting Mr. Hanson's idea (and now, through their collaboration, the organization's idea) into draft form for a bill. The NFPA chapter's legislative liaison said that this year was a "rallying year," which meant that this was a year to line up additional legislative sponsors (beyond the two senators who had expressed some support) and mobilize foster parents, youth, practitioners, agency administrators, and the community as a whole to become legislative advocates.

It is important to remember, given the different priorities of legislative agendas, that just because an organization is supportive of an issue does not mean that issue is its top legislative priority. In this case, the local chapter of NASW made it a secondary priority; it was supporting the National Foster Parent Association state chapter, which was taking the lead on this issue.

Excited that there was momentum behind his idea, Mr. Hanson wanted to bring some new colleagues on board. He received permission from his board of directors to advertise, via fliers and a notice on a listserv, that the local chapter of NFPA was advocating for the inclusion of LGBTQ youth in the state's nondiscrimination statement (this specific nondiscrimination statement was just one of their priorities); his notice gave the specifics of a meeting on legislative priorities. This advertising allowed networking to occur, and a total of ten practitioners and foster parents agreed to go to the meeting. In fact, the agency director of the public agency (custody agent) that subcontracted Mr. Hanson's agency decided to go as well!

The NFPA chapter developed talking points that incorporated the experiences of their foster parents and practitioners, including Mr. Hanson and the others who chose to join him. Three former youth in foster care also decided to become involved and share their experiences of discrimination. The talking points also detailed research and statistics on the scope of the problem as well as recommendations to improve service delivery for the youth (Rosenwald 2009; Wilber, Ryan, and Marksamer 2006).

The NFPA legislative affairs staff member provided guidance on the best ways to communicate with the legislators in order to get a few more sponsors to introduce the bill in the appropriate subcommittee in the following legislative session. Specifically, they indicated to Mr. Hanson and others which other legislators were supportive, which ones were neutral, and which ones were not supportive. With legislative advocacy it is important to counter your opponents' arguments as well as advance your own cause—and so Mr. Hanson and the other foster parents and practitioners discovered that part of their mobilization effort was to address concerns among some homophobic legislators (one of whom was Mr. Hanson's state senator, who served as co-chair of the committee in which the legislation would need to be introduced). Mr. Hanson learned that part of the strategy was to fight the few but strong voices of the religious community who were opposed to giving "special rights" to youth who identify as LGBTQ.

With these instructions in mind, Mr. Hanson and a coalition from the NFPA, the NASW, and other involved community organizations emailed letters to all legislators in the state and met with several legislators in person. He was excited to be involved in advocacy even though he was not sure what the outcome would be, as he typically was told that legislators were "weighing" their decisions. He realized he had to work on being patient while continuing to remain focused.

In the following legislative session, a total of four co-sponsors in the appropriate state senate subcommittee (including the other committee co-chair) introduced the bill. It passed through the subcommittee (the one co-chair remained against it) in part because of the foresight and determination that Mr. Hanson had shown. It took still one more legislative session (in the subsequent year), but the legislature did pass the bill and the governor signed it into law—some three years after Mr. Hanson had the initial idea. While it had certainly been a long-term project, Mr. Hanson took satisfaction in the knowledge that he had done his part to protect one more group of youth in foster care.

Summary

Legislative advocacy remains an underutilized yet very effective way for many foster parents, relative caregivers, and practitioners to advocate for children in care. The first three items discussed in this chapter (finding out what relevant laws already exist, determining what legislative initiatives/bills are in process, and learning about the nature of the legislative process) provide the important educational foundation on which the actual strategies of legislative advocacy rest.

Nonprofit organizations such as the National Foster Parent Association, the National Association of Social Workers, and the Child Welfare League of America are excellent resources to draw on for assistance with the legislative advocacy process relating to youth in care. Getting a bill introduced and eventually passed is a huge victory, particularly because this is such a long and complex process. Advocating in coalition provides important support for those who care about issues for youth and who believe in the effectiveness of the legislative arena as a way to address these issues.

Discussion Questions

1. What ethical issues exist, with respect to her status as an employee, when a practitioner decides to advocate legislatively?
2. How would you decide on which legislative level (local, state, federal) to advocate?
3. Make a list of foster care and kinship care issues that you believe are candidates for legislative advocacy. How are they similar? How are they distinct?
4. What issues might caregivers and practitioners agree require legislative advocacy? On what issues might there be disagreement? How would you resolve these differences of opinion?

Web Sites

- Child Welfare Information Gateway: http://www.childwelfare.gov/systemwide/laws_policies/state/ (*state statutes*)
- Child Welfare League of America: http://www.cwla.org/childwelfare/fglaws.pdf (*federal laws*); http://www.cwla.org/advocacy/2008legagenda.htm (*legislative agenda*)
- Legal research, forms and other legal information: www.loislaw.com
- Library of Congress: http://thomas.loc.gov/ (*status of pending legislation*)
- National Association of Social Workers: http://www.socialworkers.org/advocacy/images/grmaterials/GRLEGAgendaRpt2007.pdf (*legislative agenda*); http://capwiz.com/socialworkers/issues/ (*legislative advocacy*)
- National Foster Parent Association: http://www.nfpainc.org/content/page=POSITION%20STATEMENTS&nmenu=1&title=NFPA%20Position%20Statements (*position statements*)
- U.S. House of Representatives: house.gov
- U.S. House Subcommittee on Income Security and Family Support: http://waysandmeans.house.gov/committees.asp?formmode=detail&comm=2
- U.S. Senate: senate.gov
- U.S. Senate Subcommittee on Children and Families: http://help.senate.gov/Child+Famlies_sub_index_1.html

[10]

Advocating in Communities

Never doubt that a small group of committed citizens can change the world.

—Margaret Mead

Vignette

Fifty-five-year-old Anna Smith, recently widowed, had been a kinship care provider for her twin eleven-year-old grandsons (Evan and Matt) since her daughter, Ms. Williams, was sentenced to six years in prison for cocaine distribution and conspiracy (the mother did not know who the boys' father was). Because of Ms. Williams' incarceration and substance abuse history, Mrs. Smith decided to initiate proceedings for permanent physical custody of her two grandchildren. She found it difficult to find other kinship care providers with whom she could talk about similar experiences they might share. Specifically, Mrs. Smith sometimes grew tired of explaining her relationship to her grandchildren to her neighbors, school and medical staff, and others. She knew that Evan and Matt were being teased at school both because they were being raised by an "old woman" and because their mother "didn't love them anymore." She also felt the need to talk about the challenges of raising two children at a time when she had been expecting to retire and how she frequently wished for a respite. Occasionally, she thought that unless she received support, the children might have to go to foster care. She hated this thought, but although she loved them very much, she felt like she had underestimated the enormous obligation to which she had agreed.

Mrs. Smith asked Mr. Pick, the caseworker, if there was any support in their fairly rural community for her as a grandmother raising her grandchildren. Mr. Pick checked with his supervisor, who said that unfortunately nothing existed that he knew about. Mr. Pick gave her several books on grandparents who raise grandchildren, and she did appreciate that help. However, Mr. Pick wondered if there was something more he could do to help Mrs. Smith and the children in her care.

Key

Mrs. Smith: grandmother and kinship care provider.
Evan and Matt: grandsons living with Mrs. Smith.
Ms. Abby Williams: birth mother to the boys.
Mr. Pick: caseworker

Margaret Mead's famous quote asserting the power of a small group of people to change the world holds much relevance for this chapter. In addition to legislative advocacy as a specific form of community advocacy (discussed in the previous chapter), advocating in the community can produce the required results when such advocacy in the agency has reached a barrier, or the legislative process has become too slow, or the desired outcome has not occurred. It is at times like these that foster parents and practitioners like Mrs. Smith and Mr. Pike can turn to and utilize the broader community to provide a much-needed anchor in the advocacy process.

Advocacy Checklist

- Address underserved needs of youth in care.
- Reduce the stigma of foster care.
- Obtain support from the community.

Address Underserved Needs of Youth in Care

Identify the Need

As with all advocacy efforts, advocating in the community initially requires the essential step of identifying and assessing the needs that the community has the potential to meet. In the vignette, Mrs. Smith needed additional support as a kinship care provider. New to this role, and still managing both her grief over her husband's death and her unresolved feelings toward her daughter for "abandoning" (in Mrs. Smith's view) her parental duties, Mrs. Smith desperately needed support. What rights did she have as a kinship provider? Were there any services, such as respite or legal assistance, available to help her care for her grandchildren? The caseworker, Mr. Pick, also felt like his hands were tied because information was just not available in the community. Although he had researched the laws and he and a number of fellow practitioners were separately pursuing legislative advocating, he wanted to know what he could do to assist Mrs. Smith in a shorter time period. Although the community sphere is an underused arena for advocacy, it is a place in which these professionals can come to feel the most empowered (see Grover 2004; Pasztor and McFadden 2006). Mr. Pick wanted to explore how the community might be able to help.

Analyze the Context

A number of needs exist that can be addressed in a community context. Although agency policy and local, state, and federal law have many times successfully provided support for the provisions of youth in care, there are times when their attempts are woefully inadequate or simply not present—it is at this juncture that there arises the need to advocate in the community. A sample of these service needs, certainly not exhaustive, is now discussed.

As in the vignette, one service need affecting youth in care that continues to rely on community advocacy is adequately supporting kinship care providers like Mrs. Smith. Kinship care is an increasingly utilized option for foster care placement, and indeed, youth have less behavioral challenges when they directly enter kinship care than when they go into nonkinship foster care placements (Rubin, Downes et al. 2008). However, kinship care providers who are grandparents face additional challenges in this role because they are at greater risk of being poor, not having health insurance (Bryson and Casper 1999), and being in poor health (Hayslip, Shore et al. 1998; Kelley, Yorker et al. 2001; Minkler, Fuller-Thomson et al. 2000). Facing these and other challenges, kinship care providers may need financial assistance, legal information and services (for example, relating to custody), respite, transportation, and general support, among other needs (Rosenwald, Kelchner, and Bartone 2008). The extent to which the community can assist relatives who are raising other relatives' children can strengthen these placements and therefore prevent placement disruption.

Other service needs exist relating to a number of subpopulations of youth who reside in kinship and foster care; these issues present urgent opportunities for advocacy. These groups of youth are marginalized subgroups within the broader population of youth in care because their needs are both historically and currently underserved by agencies. They include older youth, youth with behavioral challenges, youth who are LGBTQ (lesbian, gay, bisexual and transgender), and youth of color.

Older youth in care, those in their late teens up to twenty-one years of age (and in some states a little older), have been undeserved by the foster care system as well as by well-intentioned policies that promote their transition to independent living at the expense of achieving permanency (Nixon 2005). "The number of placements a youth experiences in foster care, and the restrictiveness of those placements, also have a significant negative impact on young people's ability to maintain or establish connections to family members and other supportive adults" (Nixon 2005:573).

Youth with major behavioral challenges are often placed, and sometimes languish, in residential treatment facilities because they have difficulty living in traditional foster or kinship care families. Their behaviors are often dangerous and can include a range of violent acts, such as setting fires, using knives, torturing and killing animals, and physically harming the foster family as well as attempting suicide. While certainly the needs of youth who require such a high level of monitoring cannot be met by a foster family home situation, it is important to maintain a continued awareness of this issue (see Bullard and Johnson 2005 for a discussion of the role of residential treatment centers).

The challenges for lesbian, gay, bisexual and transgender youth (discussed in chapter 9 in a legislative context) comprise another underserved area of youth in care. Heterosexism and transphobia/homophobia in agencies and the lack of uniformity in legal protections continue to affect this population (Rosenwald 2009; Mallon 2001).

The overrepresentation of African-American, Latino, and Native American youth in care remains another large challenge for the foster care system. For example, African-American youth comprise 37 percent of youth in foster care even as they represent only 15 percent of youth in the United States. Outcomes for this population suggest a racist foster care system in which these youth "remain in care longer; are less likely to return home to their families of origin; are less likely to be adopted; and are more likely to [be] emancipated from the child welfare system without permanent connections with at least one adult" (McRoy 2005:624). The gravity of this reality of youth of color in care must continue to be a focus of advocacy. Related to this issue is the increasing prevalence of youth in care with immigrant status, and their accompanying educational, health and mental health, language, and cultural needs (Earner 2005).

As a response to service needs such as those identified above, the "community" provides perhaps the only remaining context in which to address these needs when agencies and the law are unable, unaware, or unwilling. In this context "community" also includes formal organizations, some identified in the last chapter, such as the National Foster Parents Association (NFPA), the Child Welfare League of America (CWLA), the National Association of Social Workers (NASW), the Children's Defense Fund (CDF), and the Foster Family-Based Treatment Association (FFTA). These and other community organizations often take the lead nationally in bringing attention to the issues and therefore serve to shape and influence practice guidelines and policy.

For example, the Child Welfare League of America publishes statements on the disproportionate numbers of African-American, Latino/Hispanic, and Native/Indigenous American youth in care; it also makes recommendations for policy and practice regarding a number of the aforementioned groups, including lesbian, gay, bisexual, and transgender youth (Child Welfare League of America 2003; Wilber, Ryan, and Marksamer 2006).

Another example of a community organization serving in an advocacy role is the National Foster Parent Association, with its "Foster Child Bill of Rights" (see table 10.1). This statement of principles, originally crafted in 1973, represents one community's effort to influence the system's treatment of youth in care by identifying core rights for all of these youth. Foster parent associations are of paramount importance in providing advocacy, empowerment, and support for foster parents (Pasztor and McFadden 2006).

"Community," of course, has a broad meaning going beyond these established organizations; advocating in the community means what you and I and collectivities of all of us can do in smaller and creative ways to address

TABLE 10.1 The NFPA Foster Child Bill of Rights

Even more than for other children, society has a responsibility, along with parents, for the well-being of children in foster care. Citizens are responsible for acting to insure their welfare.

Every child in foster care is endowed with the rights inherently belonging to all children. In addition, because of the temporary or permanent separation from, and loss of, parents and other family members, the child requires special safeguards, resources, and care.

Every child in foster care has the inherent right:

1. To be cherished by a family of his own, either his family helped by readily available services and supports to resume his care, or an adoptive family or, by plan, a continuing foster family.

2. To be nurtured by foster parents who have been selected to meet his individual needs, and who are provided services and supports, including specialized education, so that they can grow in their ability to enable the child to reach his potentiality.

3. To receive sensitive, continuing help in understanding and accepting the reasons for his own family's inability to take care of him, and in developing confidence in his own self worth.

4. To receive continuing loving care and respect as a unique human being...a child growing in trust in himself and others.

4. To grow up in freedom and dignity in a neighborhood of people who accept him with understanding, respect and friendship.

6. To receive help in overcoming deprivation or whatever distortion in his emotional, physical, intellectual, social and spiritual growth may have resulted from his early experiences.

7. To receive education, training, and career guidance to prepare for a useful and satisfying life.

8. To receive preparation for citizenship and parenthood through interaction with foster parents and other adults who are consistent role models.

9. To be represented by an attorney-at-law in administrative or judicial proceedings with access to fair hearings and court review of decisions, so that his best interests are safeguarded.

10. To receive a high quality of child welfare services, including involvement of the natural parents and his own involvement in major decisions that affect his life.

Source: Adapted from National Foster Parents Association 1973. Reproduced by permission of the National Foster Parents Association.

these needs. For example, youth who enter foster care come from environments where abuse and neglect occur. While it is parents and caregivers that directly abuse or neglect, it is essential to examine structural factors in the community at large that may contribute to this abuse and neglect as well. These factors include violence, poverty, homelessness, substance abuse, and teen pregnancy (Barbell and Freundlich 2005:505); becoming aware of such problems and working toward their elimination is an important responsibility we all share.

It should be noted that texts like the one you are reading, as well as peer-reviewed journals like *Child Welfare, Families in Society, Children and Youth Services Review,* and *Journal of Family Social Work,* provide the latest thinking and research on important issues in foster care. And such publications can have a great influence over many years. The power of the book *The Battered Child* by Dr. Kempe and Dr. Helfer, first published in 1968, was to monumentally increase community awareness of child maltreatment; it influenced service delivery in addressing child abuse and continues to make an important impact in its subsequent editions (Kluft 1999). *Grandparents as Parents: A Survival Guide for Raising a Second Family* by S. de Toledo and D. E. Brown is a seminal text for relative caregivers.

Develop the Plan

Returning to the vignette: Mr. Pick, the caseworker, wished to assist Mrs. Smith, as well as other kinship care providers, by creating a specialized service delivery for their needs. In preparation, he reviewed the issues relating to kinship care on the Web sites of the National Foster Parent Association and Child Welfare League of America, and read a few journal articles pertaining to kinship care. Mr. Pick then reviewed and considered three options in developing a plan for an organized community response to assist Mrs. Smith and other kinship care providers. He chose to create one of three entities: a social action group, a coalition, or a delegate council (Toseland and Rivas 2009). These groups vary in respect to their purpose, leadership style, focus, and other variables but share a common investment in addressing unmet or undermet community needs. After reviewing these options, Mr. Pick determined that the best community strategy to help Mrs. Smith and the others would be to create a coalition.

Coalitions—or alliances, as they are sometimes called—are groups of organizations, social actions groups, or individuals that come together to exert influence by sharing resources and expertise. Coalition members agree to pursue common goals, which they believe cannot be achieved by any of the members acting alone.   (Toseland and Rivas 2009:41)

The use of coalitions to meet the needs of kinship care providers can "serve as a springboard for beginning initiatives for an organization of caregivers as well as provide continual feedback and data for new initiatives for existing kinship care coalitions" (Rosenwald, Kelchner, and Bartone 2008:15). Mr. Pick spoke to Mrs. Smith and his supervisor about his ideas, and they were both supportive. Because Mrs. Smith was quite busy with her twin grandsons, she told Mr. Pick that she thought it best for him to coordinate the creation of the coalition and that she would be happy to assist him. His supervisor also supported him professionally and granted him five hours off his regular workload to plan the coalition.

Once the coalition had been established, Mr. Pick went to work on the other important component of developing the plan, which was to plan for a needs assessment. While he had anecdotal information from Mrs. Smith and he had read the literature, he thought it essential to identify the specific needs of kinship care providers in their rural community. Mrs. Smith and Mr. Pick's supervisor were in agreement with him on this decision as well.

Needs assessments determine the existence, scope, and range of a problem as well as what interventions are used and might be useful for a particular population—in our case, kinship care providers (Royse, Thyer et al. 2006). Additionally, they can be of assistance to agency managers and practitioners as they "set priorities, make decisions about the allocation of resources, and identify the gaps between what services exist and what services are needed" (Balaswamy and Dabelko 2002:56). Mr. Pick decided to suggest a particular model of needs assessment—the "stakeholder participatory model"— to the future coalition. This model is guided by the assumption that *everyone* who is affected by the need is invested in crafting and implementing the needs assessment as well as analyzing the data and making recommendations based on this information (Balaswamy and Dabelko 2002; see also Stringer 1999 for a discussion of a related concept, action research).

Specific steps in conducting a needs assessment include identifying all the individuals (stakeholders) affected by the need, planning methods to collect data, and analyzing this information; see table 10.2.

TABLE 10.2 Steps in a Needs Assessment

1. Clearly understand:
   a. The purpose of the needs assessment
   b. The level of assessment: Statewide, community, neighborhood
   c. What stakeholders to include: Clients or potential clients, program staff, key community leaders, state officials, etc.
   d. Budget and available resources
   e. Time allotted for the project
2. Identify the specific information you need to acquire.
3. Determine whether the information already exists or can be obtained with your resources.
4. Design the methodology and instrumentation (if necessary).
5. Collect and analyze the data.
6. Prepare the report.
7. Disseminate preliminary results to key stakeholders to obtain their feedback.
8. Formally disseminate results.

Source: Royse, Thyer et al. 2006:61. Reproduced by permission.

Implement the Plan

Mr. Pick was ready to organize the first meeting of the coalition. Advertising the formation of a kinship care coalition through word-of-mouth, fliers, and emails to interested parties brought in six caregivers (including Mrs. Smith); representatives from three family agencies, a family lawyer, and a professor from the local college all expressed interest in contributing their time. Mrs. Smith and Mr. Pick co-chaired first meeting. Each member introduced himself and stated both his own potential contribution to the coalition as well as a vision of what the coalition could be. After recording these ideas, Mr. Pick proposed conducting a formal needs assessment, and the professor offered to assist with that project. All of the members, and the kinship care providers particularly, expressed excitement that there was now a "community" that was beginning to address needs of kinship care providers that agencies and the law had not been able to meet fully.

Three months passed and data from the needs assessment had been analyzed. Identified needs included legal information, financial assistance, a hotline, respite, and support. To address these needs, the coalition, under the continued leadership of Mr. Pick and Mrs. Smith, formed a few sub-committees. Some of the solutions recommended by subcommittees were implemented, including the securing of a grant that established a kinship care coordinator at a local family services agency; the creation of a hotline for kinship care providers to ask questions (e.g., about custody) and to share their joys and stresses; the onset of a weekly support group; the provision of funds for respite services; and the creation of a quarterly newsletter. Mr. Pick and Mrs. Smith were thrilled with the success they had as they had enlisted the community in advocating for relative caregivers' needs, and by extension, the youth in their care.

Much of the discussion in this section is based on the actual experience one of the authors had with a kinship care coalition in upstate New York. Eventually, that coalition became *the* central clearinghouse for kinship care providers' needs, which shows the promise of coalitions (Rosenwald, Kelchner, and Barton 2008).

Reduce Stigma of Foster and Kinship Care

Identify the Need

Recall from the vignette that Mrs. Smith's grandsons, Evan and Matt, were being teased at school because an "old woman" was raising them and because their mother "didn't love them." Not surprisingly, the boys did not like this—Evan would become angry and get into fights, while Matt would cry and walk away. This greatly disturbed Mrs. Smith, who went to the school and stormed into the principal's office demanding that something be done. She had believed that Mr. Pick's and her interactions with the teachers at the school were confidential, but somehow it had spread around school that the boys were in kinship care with their grandmother; she did not like the adverse effects this was having on them.

Analyze the Context

The need to reduce foster care–related stigma in school touches on the issue of respect for privacy discussed in chapter 5, but here we go further by examining several approaches that can be used in a variety of community settings, including schools, neighborhoods, and recreational facilities. The stigma on children in foster care and, to a lesser degree, kinship care remains despite the fact that in all human societies for hundreds of years children have been raised by relatives and others. There seems to be a stream that runs deep in our society that alternates between rightful compassion for these youth and pity—such an attitude keeps the children in a "suspended" form where they are viewed by many as so unfortunate that they are lucky even to have someone care for them.

Consider this discussion of a child in foster care's experience at school:

> In the early grades of school, names are particularly important. It is not long before the foster child becomes painfully aware that, unlike other children, her name differs from that of the family with whom she lives. Already sensitized to rejection, she soon learns that there is a strong stigma attached to being a foster child, one that reflects the low esteem in which the poor, the failures, and the illegitimate have traditionally been held in our society. The child may seek to avert this stigma by trying to "pass," pretending that her surname is the same as that of the foster family. Even if she succeeds at first, within herself she knows she isn't really a full member of that family, and sooner or later someone—a classmate, a teacher, the foster parents themselves—will confront her with the fraud. The subsequent embarrassment will further emphasize her difference and the vulnerability of her position.   (Steinhauer 1991:67)

Children should never be placed in a position such as the above. Advocates like Mrs. Smith and Mr. Pick have a role to play in reducing the stigma in the community.

Develop the Plan

Developing a plan to reduce such stigma requires a two-tier approach. The first component requires that the adult advocates educate others about foster and kinship care as a necessary and valuable option to keep children safe and help them thrive. It is this strengths-perspective that will help reframe these care options in terms other than a negative stereotypical view. Foster and kinship care needs to be normalized; it should be defined as only one aspect of the child's life, complex as it may be. In fact, referring to "children in care" as opposed to "foster children," as in this book's title and preference, represents an attempt to change this discourse.

Foster parents like Mrs. Smith and practitioners like Mr. Pick might first begin "at home." Believe it or not, prejudice about "foster children" can occur even among well-meaning professionals within the child welfare system. Some of these professionals enter their various professional roles to help children, but the basis of this desire is actually pity. There is an important distinction between pity and compassion: pity manifests as a constant "feeling sorry" for a youth, while compassion reflects an attitude of deep caring. Honest conversations with these practitioners will serve as a good first step in reducing subconscious stigma within the professional community. These conversations can then extend to other professionals, such as family court attorneys, pediatricians, principals, and teachers, who, though child advocates by definition, may need a "refresher" on care-related attitudes. Of course, this educational conversation can then be taken to the general community of family members, friends, neighbors, and the like. Foster parents and practitioners can even write letters to the local paper or blog on the importance of focusing on strengths rather than stigma.

The other component of the plan relates preparing the youth themselves—in our vignette, Matt and Evan—to respond when they are teased at school or in the neighborhood. Planning ahead of time to give specific responses or take certain actions can help reduce the negative consequences of such encounters. An excellent resource here is an online article by Carrie Craft (http://adoption.about.com/od/fostering/a/coverstories.htm), which provides an array of responses to questions that children in care (and children who are adopted as well) can use when approached about this status by others. By using a "cover story," for instance, youth have the freedom to respond in the ways that make them the most comfortable—this also liberates them from the feeling of stigma that is all too common in such situations.

There are any number of different strategies that can help the child establish boundaries, distinguish between secrecy and privacy, and protect him- or herself. Only the caregiver and practitioner, who know the child well, can discern which strategies might work best. Keep in mind that one person who should not be educated on stigma reduction is the child herself or himself. Some youth might internalize any such attempts as tacit confirmation that they *are* worthless and unwanted—assessing for this potential dynamic is another important component of the plan.

Implement the Plan

Mrs. Smith sat down with Evan and Matt one night after school and helped them work out some responses to use to address any unwanted questions. Evan liked saying that his mother was out of town, while Matt felt comfortable with stating he didn't want to talk about it. Mrs. Smith asked them to let her know how any new encounters turned out; she reminded them of the importance, particularly for Matt, of not fighting or otherwise bring themselves down to a teasing child's level. Mr. Pick gave Mrs. Smith several relevant books for the boys, which helped them understand more about foster care; these were: *Maybe Days: A Book for Children in Foster Care* (2002) by Jennifer Wilgocki, Marcia Kahn Wright, and Alissa Imre Geis; *Kids Need to Be Safe: A Book for Children in Foster Care* (2005) by Julie Nelson and Mary Gallagher and *The Star: A Story to Help Young Children Understand Foster Care* (2005) by Cynthia Miller Lovell and Angie J. Przystas.

In addition, both Mrs. Smith and Mr. Pick, in the course of their day-to-day routines, were more vigilant to directly address negative comments when they heard them around their colleagues, collaborating partners, and community members at large. Mrs. Smith, who enjoyed "blogging" (akin to writing a journal on the Internet), started a blog on how wonderful children in care were. She received a number of supportive messages in response. All involved were proud that they were advocating to reduce welfare-related stigma and to change the community perception of kinship and foster care.

Obtain Support from the Community

Identify the Need

Mrs. Smith worked hard to understand the needs of youth in care, who were particularly vulnerable. She also focused on helping Evan and Matt respond to questions they might get about living with their grandmother instead of their mother. Mrs. Smith, in collaboration with Mr. Pick, worked diligently to promote the children's needs at their school, with their pediatrician, and in court. They were both proud of their advocacy efforts.

After a few months of these efforts, however, Mrs. Smith woke up absolutely exhausted one day. She knew that she neither could nor would ever give up custody of the boys to unfamiliar foster parents, because she wanted them to remain important members of their birth family. This day brought the culmination of all the stress she had been under, and she realized she needed more support. She knew of only one other person, an acquaintance, who was raising a grandchild. Mrs. Smith appreciated Mr. Pick's twice a month calls and monthly visit but felt like she needed more help.

At the same time, Mr. Pick was coming to feel that while working as a child welfare practitioner was deeply rewarding (he had been in this role for three years), he felt like he was beginning to burn out on this work and was starting to reconsider his choice of work. While he did have his supervisor to talk with, and she was there when he needed him, she herself was always being pulled in several directions and was unable to give him the depth of support he wanted. Like Ms Smith, Mr. Pick needed more support from his peers.

Analyze the Context

In a sense we conclude this book in the same way it began—by examining individuals' readiness to become foster parents and relative caregivers. Here in this chapter, however, the character in our vignette has already made her decision to embark on this role; she is working to make sure she continues to be ready to foster by finding support from the community that will "shore up" her resiliency. Practitioners like Mr. Pick can also draw on community support to help them stay as satisfied as possible in their jobs.

All parties involved in the child welfare system typically have a deep-felt need to assist youth with vulnerabilities, provide nurturing and care, and contribute to the forming of these children into resilient, strong adults themselves. And indeed, the joys of fostering, caregiving, and serving as a practitioner in this field are many and deep. Yet the need for support when facing stress and challenges will inevitably occur, and it is essential that the community be able to be relied on to provide such support. The importance of providing mutual aid to each other cannot be understated, because unmanaged stress can lead to tense situations, short tempers, and ultimately, at times, to placement disruption and caregivers leaving their role. Additionally, because practitioners in child welfare experience high turnover, addressing systemic factors such as manageable caseload numbers, appropriate and sufficient supervision and training, and fair salaries and benefits is essential in retaining advocates for youth in care. Therefore, advocating for youth in care includes a component in which the practitioners and caregivers themselves network with others in the community to create and provide strategies to facilitate their own support.

What do we mean by community support? First, this must be distinguished from the support that agencies should already have in place, which is not always fully realized because of busy schedules and personality conflicts. While there is certainly the potential for caregivers to receive strong support from their practitioner, and for the practitioner to be supported by her supervisor and coworkers (and these professionals should in turn seek it as they can), this potential may not be fully met. For example, one study surveying agencies found that only half provided space and supervision for these support groups (Bartone, Rosenwald, and Bronstein 2008). As such, the community can provide a good forum for support; one strategy that is highlighted is the specific creation of support groups.

The goals of support groups are "to foster mutual aid, to help members cope with stressful life events, and to revitalize and enhance members' coping abilities so they can effectively adapt to and cope with future stressful life events" (Toseland and Rivas 2009:20). Support groups that are community-based are purposeful gatherings that are free from any agency connection. While support groups for foster parents can certainly be sponsored by agencies, when they are created by a group of foster parents themselves, with no formal agency sponsorship, their potential for creating a complete trusting atmosphere is greater. Among kinship care foster parents, for example, support groups are the most or second-most frequently requested form of assistance (Bartone, Rosenwald, and Bronstein 2008; Woodworth 1996). These groups provide "emotional support, solidarity and advice-seeking" (Woodworth, cited in Bartone, Rosenwald, and Bronstein 2008:226). Consider the following quotes, which showcase the value of a group support setting for foster parents (in case this was a focus group cofacilitated by one of this text's authors, who represented a university).

"I learned that I'm not the only one unhappy right now."

"It's good for your soul. You know, just to come in here and talk to everybody else that's going through the same thing and doing the same thing you are. I can really understand because until you're doing it and live that life, you have no comprehension of what it's like. And I don't care, you know, they say, 'Oh, I know how you feel.' No you don't. You don't do this. You don't know how it feels! So you know, I think it was really good for your soul, to just, even if we didn't accomplish anything we all got to sit here and talk and find out from each other."

"I needed to hear that you had that good story, because I'm not feeling very good right now."   (Rosenwald and Bronstein 2008:296)

Support, of course, is also important to the practitioner. Forming and joining support groups in the professional community can provide practitioners (as well as foster parents) with a source of mutual assistance; a central dynamic of groups is that they offer members the reassurance that they are not alone and that they can bring in individual problems to be solved by the whole (Gitterman and Shulman 2005). Such problems and challenges can include managing high caseloads, negotiating the sometimes delicate relationships between youth, foster parent and birth parent, and juggling a number of case management and crisis intervention priorities. Therefore, support groups for practitioners allow them to speak freely, within the bounds of confidentiality, to other practitioners, who have similar stresses as well as joys to share.

While the emphasis is on support, these groups typically have an educational component as well, such as teaching members about community resources and advocacy strategies. They also can have a "strengths-in-numbers" component—members gain such a sense of unity that they plan to act outside of the group to advance the group's needs (Gitterman and Shulman 2005). An example of this would be a group of practitioners planning a meeting with their legislators to discuss their own issues of caseload and salary as well as to bring up issues on behalf of youth, their birth parents, and their caregivers.

Develop the Plan

Mrs. Smith approached Mr. Pick for advice. He suggested that she form a support group in the community and he offered to provide her with a list of other kinship care providers, including both those who had attended the newly formed coalition and those who did not attend; Mrs. Smith would then call or email them with information about the support group. Mrs. Smith preferred to have the support group meet outside of the agency so that the caregivers could be completely frank with each other. To assist her further, Mr. Pick said he would contact the local chapter of the National Foster Parent Association to secure space for a meeting.

In Mr. Pick's own case, he planned to contact his local chapter of the National Association of Social Workers to see if there was any interest among child welfare practitioners in forming a peer-supervision support group in which they would listen to each other and provide guidance. Once there were even a few other interested practitioners, he would proceed with the logistics in setting up this group.

Implement the Plan

One month after the initial exploration, both a kinship caregiver support group and a peer supervision–based practitioner support group had been formed. The former met weekly at a local church while the latter met monthly at the home of one of the members. Mrs. Smith and Mr. Pick planned the groups' first meetings; as time passed, other members took on leadership roles. This enabled Mrs. Smith and Mr. Pick to devote more time to cofacilitating their kinship care coalition. Although they worked together on the coalition (and Mr. Pick was in the role of Mrs. Smith's grandchildren's caseworker), they each respected the confidentiality that was necessary for these separate support groups. For ethical reasons they did not share with each other the contents of the group discussions— with one exception. In Mr. Pick's group, one member thought it would be instructive to have a few kinship caregivers share their perspectives with group members. Two kinship care parents volunteered to come to the practitioner group and engage in a dialogue about what it is really like to raise grandchildren and other relatives' children when the parent is unable or unwilling.

As a result of the formation of these support groups in the community, Mrs. Smith became reenergized and knowledgeable about community resources (including a transportation resource in the neighboring rural town that she could access). Her group members relied on existing information from their state (via a very useful kinship care Internet resource: http://www.grandfactsheets.org/state_fact_sheets.cfm) and identified other resources for each other. From his group experience, Mr. Pick recommitted to his role and no longer thought about leaving the agency. The community was now providing them with a safety net.

Summary

The following quote summarizes the spirit of this chapter:

> Change requires community problem solving. Abused and neglected children requiring family foster care belong to and in their communities. A community cannot be a place where children are harmed and then cast aside to a different community to be healed. A real community takes care of its own. (Pasztor, McNitt, and McFadden 2005:674)

"Taking care of its own" means that the community must provide both necessary information and the mechanism by which change can occur. Identifying underaddressed needs and drawing upon community organizations that set the standards to address these needs, networking with the community to reduce stigma, and relying on the community as one strategy to receive support are all facets of direct or indirect advocacy. Community-minded foster parents, kinship caregivers, and practitioners should take advantage of this forum to complement their advocacy on behalf of the children in their care.

Discussion Questions

1. This chapter has identified just a few of the needs within foster care and kinship care that should be addressed more than they are currently. Which of these issues do you see as the most important? How well do you think the community responds to those needs? Why?

2. How does advocating in the community align with advocacy for policy change in agencies and in the legislative arena? How might community advocacy conflict with these other advocacy settings?

3. Do you think the stigma surrounding foster care, and to a lesser extent kinship care, can ever be removed? Why or why not?

4. "The availability of support groups can be a central component in working to reduce placement disruption." Please explain this statement.

Web Site

- Carrie Craft, "Teaching foster/adoptive children how to answer questions": http://adoption.about.com/od/fostering/a/coverstories.htm

References

Abramson, J. S., and L. R. Bronstein. 2004. Group process dynamics and skills in interdisciplinary teamwork. In *Handbook of Social Work with Groups*, ed. C. Garvin, M. Galinsky, and L. Gutierrez. New York: Guilford.

Abramson, J. S., and T. Mizrahi. 2003. Understanding collaboration between social workers and physicians: Application of a typology. *Social Work in Health Care* 37.2:71–100.

Administrative Directive. Adam Walsh, Protection and Safety. www.ocfs.state.ny.us/main/policies/external/OCFS_2008/ADMs/08-OCFS-ADM-06%20Criminal%20History%20Record%20Checks%20and%20Mandatory%20Disqualifying%20Crimes%20(Foster%20and%20Adoptive%20Parents).pdf.

"The Adoption Home Study Process." Child Welfare Information Gateway. www.childwelfare.gov/adoption/adoptive/homestudy.cfm.

Advocates for Children of New York, Inc. 2000. July. *Educational Neglect: The Delivery of Educational Services to Children in New York City's Foster Care System.*

American Academy of Pediatrics. Checklist for Child in Foster Care. www.aap.org/sections/adoption/healthtopic/FC_Office_Checklist.doc.

American Psychiatric Association. 2000. *Diagnostic and Statistical Manual of Mental Disorders.* 4th ed., rev. Washington, DC: American Psychiatric Association.

Avery, R. 2000. Perceptions and practice: Agency efforts for the hardest-to-place children. *Children and Youth Services Review* 22.6:399–420.

Balaswamy, S., and H. I. Dabelko. 2002. Using a stakeholder participatory model in a community-wide service needs assessment of elderly residents: A case study. *Journal of Community Practice* 10.1:55–70.

Barbell, K., and M. Freundlich. 2005. Foster care today: Overview of family foster care. In Mallon and McCartt Hess 2005:504–517.

Barker, R. L. 1996. *The Social Work Dictionary.* Washington, DC: National Association of Social Workers Press.

Barth, R. P. 1990. On their own: The experiences of youth after foster care. *Child and Adolescent Social Work Journal* 7:5:419–440.

Bartone, A., M. Rosenwald, and L. Bronstein. 2008. Examining the structure and dynamics of kinship care groups. *Social Work with Groups* 31.3–4:223–238.

Bass, S., M. Shields, R. Lowe-Webb, and T. Lanz. 2004. *Children, Families, and Foster Care: A Synopsis.* Los Altos, CA: David and Lucile Packard Foundation.

Bayless, L., and H. Craig-Oldsen. 2004. *GPSII/MAPP Implementation Guide.* Duluth, GA: Child Welfare Institute.

Bowlby, J. 1980. *Attachment and Loss,* vol. 3: *Loss.* New York: Basic Books.

Bronstein, L. R. 2001. Index of interdisciplinary collaboration. Unpublished manuscript.

——. 2003. A model for interdisciplinary collaboration. *Social Work* 48.3:297–306.

Bronstein, L. R., P. Kovacs, and A. Vega. 2007. Goodness of fit: Social work education and practice in health care. *Social Work in Health Care* 45.2:59–76.

Brown, J., and P. Calder. 2002. Needs and challenges of foster parents. *Canadian Journal of Social Work* 4.1:125–135.

Bruns, E. J., and J. D. Burchard. 2000. Impact of respite care services for families with children experiencing emotional and behavioral problems and their families. *Children's Services: Public Policy, Research, and Practice* 3:39–61.

Bryson, K., and L. M. Casper. 1999. *Coresident Grandparents and Grandchildren.* U.S. Bureau of the Census, Current Population Reports, Special Studies. Washington, DC: U.S. Bureau of the Census.

Buehler, C., M. E. Cox, and G. Cuddeback. 2003. Foster parents' perceptions of factors that promote or inhibit successful fostering. *Qualitative Social Work* 2.1:61–83.

Buehler, C., J. G. Orme, J. Post, and D. Patterson. 2000. The long-term correlates of family foster care. *Children and Youth Services Review* 22:595–625.

Bullard, L. B., and K. Johnson. 2005. Residential services for children and youth in out-of-home care. In Mallon and McCartt Hess 2005:558–572.

Burton, L. M., P. Dilworth-Anderson, and C. Merriweather-de Vries. 1995. Context and surrogate parenting among contemporary grandparents. *Marriage and Family Review* 20.3–4:349–366.

Bush, R. A. B., and J. P. Folger. 2005. *The Promise of Mediation*. Rev. ed. San Francisco: Jossey-Bass.

Casey Family Services. 2001. *The Road to Independence: Transitioning Youth in Foster Care to Independence*. New Haven: Casey Family Services.

Chahine, Z., and S. Higgins. 2005. Engaging families and communities: The use of family team conferences to promote safety, permanency, and well-being in child welfare services. In Mallon and McCartt Hess 2005:118–128.

Chamberlain, P., J. M. Price, J. B. Reid, J. Landsverk, P. A. Fisher, and M. Stoolmiller. 2006. Who disrupts from placement in foster and kinship care? *Child Abuse and Neglect* 30.4:409–424.

Children's Defense Fund. 2008. www.childrensdefense.org/child-research-data-publications/data/FCSIAA-kinship-summary.pdf.

Child Welfare League of America. 1997. *Child Abuse and Neglect: A Look at the States.* Washington, DC: Child Welfare League of America.

——. 2003. Children of color in the child welfare system. Washington, DC: Child Welfare League of America. www.cwla.org/programs/culture/disproportionate statement.pdf.

——. 2003b. *Standards of Excellence for Family Foster Care Services*. Rev. ed. Washington, DC: Child Welfare League of America.

——. 2008. Standards of excellence for health care services for children in out-of-home care. Washington, DC: Child Welfare League of America. www.cwla .org/programs/standards/standardsintrohealthcare.pdf.

Choice, P., A. D'Andrade, K. Gunther, D. Downes, J. Schaldach, C. Csiszar, and M. Austin. 2001. *Education for Foster Children: Removing Barriers to Academic Success*. Berkeley, CA: Bay Area Social Services Consortium, Center for Social Services Research, School of Social Welfare, University of California, Berkeley. cssr.berkeley.edu/research_units/bassc/projects.html.

Clausen, J. M., J. Landsverk, W. Ganger, D. Chadwick, and A. Litrownik. 1998. Mental health problems of children in foster care. *Journal of Child and Family Studies* 7:283–296.

Clements, J. A., and M. Rosenwald. 2007. Foster parents' perspectives on LGBT youth in the child welfare system. *Journal of Gay and Lesbian Social Services* 19.1:57–69.

Cohen, E. P. 2003. Framework for culturally competent decisionmaking in child welfare. *Child Welfare* 82.2:143–152

Collado, C., and P. Levine. 2007. Reducing transfers of children in family foster care through onsite mental health interventions. *Child Welfare* 86.5:133–150.

Costello, E. J., A. Angold, B. U. Burns, D. K. Stangl, D. L. Tweed,, et al. 1996. The Great Smoky Mountains study of youth: Goals, design, methods, and the prevalence of DSM-III-R disorders. *Archives of General Psychiatry* 53:1129–1136.

Courtney, M. E., Terao, S., and Bost, N. 2004. *Midwest Evaluation of the Adult Functioning of Former Foster Youth: Conditions of Youth Preparing to Leave State Care.* Chicago. IL: Chapin Hall Center for Children at the University of Chicago.

Cox, M. E., J. G. Orme, and K. W. Rhodes. 2003. Willingness to foster children with emotional or behavioral problems. *Journal of Social Service Research* 29.4:23–51.

Craft, C. 2008. Teaching foster/adoptive children how to answer questions. adoption.about.com/od/fostering/a/coverstories.htm.

Crosse, S. B., E. Kaye, and A. C. Ratnofsky. 1993. A report of the maltreatment of children with disabilities. Washington, DC: U.S. Department of Health and Human Services, National Center on Child Abuse and Neglect.

Crosson-Tower, C. 2004. *Exploring Child Welfare: A Practice Perspective.* 3rd ed. New York: Pearson Education.

——. 2007. *Exploring Child Welfare: A Practice Perspective.* 4th ed. Boston: Allyn and Bacon.

Crumbley, J. and Little, R. 1997. *Relatives Raising Children: An Overview of Kinship Care.* Washington, DC: Child Welfare League of America.

Czerwinskyj, S. 2003. Reflections of foster parent training and the impact on foster children. *Praxis* 39.2:23–37.

Deihl, R., and C. Fiermonte. n.d. *Legal Resource Manual for Foster Parents.* San Mateo, CA: Legal Advocates for Permanency Planning.

de Toledo, S., and D. E. Brown, D. E. 1995. *Grandparents as Parents: A Survival Guide for Raising a Second Family.* New York: Guilford Press.

Dickerson and Allen. 2007. *Adoptive and Foster Parent Screening: A Professional Guide for Evaluations.* New York: Routledge.

Dolgoff, R., F. M. Loewenberg, and D. Harrington. 2008. *Ethical Decisions for Social Work Practice.* 8th ed. Belmont, CA: Brooks Cole.

Dore, M. M. 2005. Child and adolescent mental health. In Mallon and McCartt Hess 2005:148–172.

Dore, M. M., and N. Feldman. 2005. Generalist practice with abused and neglected children and their families. In *Strengths-Based Generalist Practice: A Collaborative Approach*, ed. J. Poulin, pp. 431–462. 2nd ed. Belmont, CA: Brooks/Cole.

dosReis, S., J. M. Zito, D. J. Safer, and K. L. Soeken. 2001. Mental health services for youths in foster care and disabled youths. *American Journal of Public Health* 91.7:1094–1099.

Dozier, M., D. Grasso, O. Lindhiem, and E. Lewis. 2007. "The Role of Caregiver Commitment in Foster Care: Insights from the 'This Is My Baby Interview.'" In *Attachment Theory in Clinical Work with Children: Bridging the Gap Between Research and Practice*, ed. D. Oppenheim and F. Douglas, 90–108. New York: Guilford.

Duquette, D. N. 1990. *Advocating for the Child in Protection Proceedings.* Lexington, MA: Lexington Books.

Earner, I. 2005. Immigrant children and youth in the child welfare system: Immigrant status and special needs in permanency planning. In Mallon and McCartt Hess 2005:655–664.

Edwards, R. L., and J. A. Yankey. 1991. *Skills for Effective Human Services Management*. Washington, DC: NASW Press.

Elze, D. E., W. F. Auslander, A. Stiffman, and C. McMillen. 2005. Educational needs of youth in foster care. In Mallon and McCartt Hess 2005:185–204.

English, D. J., S. Kouidou-Giles, and M. Plocke. 1994. Readiness for independence: A study of youth in foster care. *Children and Youth Services Review* 16:147–158.

Festinger, T. 1983. *No One Ever Asked Us: A Postscript to Foster Care*. New York: Columbia University Press.

Finn, J. L. 1994. Contested caring: Women's roles in foster family care. *Affilia* 9.4:382–400.

Frey, L. L., S. B. Greenblatt, and J. Brown. 2005. A call to action: An integrated approach to youth permanency and preparation for adulthood. New Haven, CT: Casey Family Services. www.aecf.org/upload/publicationfiles/casey_permanency_0505.pdf.

Garland, A. F., Hough, R. L., Landsverk, J. A., McCabe, K. M., Yeh, M., Granger, W. C. et al. 2000. Racial and ethnic variations in mental health care utilization among children in foster care. *Children's Services: Social Policy, Research, and Practice* 3.3:133–146.

Geenen, S. 2006. Are we ignoring youths with disabilities in foster care? An examination of their school performance. *Social Work* 51.3:233–241.

Gitterman, A., and L. Shulman, eds. 2005. *Mutual Aid Groups, Vulnerable and Resilient Populations, and the Life Cycle*. 3rd ed. New York: Columbia University Press.

Grover, S. 2004. Advocating for children's rights as an aspect of professionalism: The role of frontline workers and children's rights commissions. *Child and Youth Care Forum* 33.6:405–423.

Groza, V., L. Houlihan, and Z. B. Wood. 2005. Overview of adoption. In Mallon and McCartt Hess 2005:687–706.

Gummer, B. 1991. A new managerial era: From hierarchical control to "collaborative individualism." *Administration in Social Work* 15.3:121–137.

——. 1995. Go, team, go! The growing importance of teamwork in organizational life. *Administration in Social Work* 19.4:85–100.

Halfon, N., G. Berkowitz, and L. Klee. 1992. Children in foster care in California: An examination of Medicaid-reimbursed health services utilization. *Pediatrics* 89.6:1230–1237.

Halfon, N., M. Inkelas, R. Flint, K. Shoaf, A. Zepeda, and T. Franke. 2002. *Assessment of Factors Influencing the Adequacy of Health Care Services to Children in*

Foster Care. Los Angeles: UCLA Center for Healthier Children, Families, and Communities.

Hardin, M. 2005. Role of the legal and judicial system for children, youth, and families in foster care. In Mallon and McCartt Hess 2005:687–706.

Hayslip, B., and R. J. Shore. 2000. Custodial grandparenting and mental health services. *Journal of Mental Health and Aging* 6:367–383.

Hayslip, B., R. J. Shore, C. E. Henderson, and P. L. Lambert. 1998. Custodial grand-parenting and the impact of grandchildren with problems on role satisfaction and role meaning. *Journal of Gerontology* 53B.3:S164–S173.

Helfer, M. E., R. S. Kempe, and R. D. Krugman. 1997. *The Battered Child.* 5th ed. Chicago: University of Chicago Press.

Hepworth, D. H., Rooney, R. H., and Larsen, J. 1997. *Direct Social Work Practice: Theory and Skills.* Pacific Grove, CA: Brooks/Cole Publishing Company.

Herman, J. 1997. *Trauma and Recovery: The Aftermath of Violence—from Domestic Abuse to Political Terror.* New York: Basic Books.

Iglehart, A. P. 1994. Adolescents in foster care: Predicting readiness for independent living. *Children and Youth Services Review* 16:159–169.

Jensen, P. S., and K. E. Hoagwood, eds. 2008. *Improving Children's Mental Health Through Parent Empowerment: A Guide to Assisting Families.* New York: Oxford University Press.

Kaplan, C. 2004. Children missing from care: An issue brief. Washington, DC: Child Welfare League of America. www.cwla.org/programs/fostercare/childmiss07.pdf.

Keeping Children and Families Safe Act. 2003. laws.adoption.com/statutes/keeping-children-and-families-safe-act-of-2003.html.

Kelley, S. J., B. C. Yorker, D. M. Whitley, and T. A. Sipe. 2001. A multimodal intervention for grandparents raising grandchildren: Results of an exploratory study. *Child Welfare* 80:27–50.

Kessler, R. C., P. J. Pecora, J. Williams, E. Hiripi, K. O'Brien, D. English, J. White, R. Zerbe, A. C. Downs, R. Plotnick, I. Hwang, and N. Sampson. A. 2008. Effects of enhanced foster care on the long-term physical and mental health of foster care alumni. *Archives of General Psychiatry* 65.6:625–633.

Kets de Vries, M. F. R., and R. S. Carlock. 2007. *Family Business on the Couch.* Hoboken, NJ: Wiley.

Landsverk, J., and A. F. Garland. 1999. Foster care and pathways to mental health services. In *The Foster Care Crisis: Translating Research Into Policy and Practice,* ed. P. A. Curtis, G. Dale Jr., and J. C. Kendall, 193–210. Lincoln: University of Nebraska Press.

LeProhn, N. S. 1994. The role of the kinship foster parent: A comparison of the role conceptions of relative and non-relative foster parents. *Children and Youth Services Review* 16.1/2:65–84.

Lester, P., and C. Vamvas. 2007. Kinship Caregiver Support Act. Washington, DC: Alliance for Children and Families/United Neighborhood Centers of America. www.alliance1.org/Public_Policy/policynews/Kinship_Caregiver.pdf.

Levine, A. 2005. Foster youth: Dismantling educational challenges. *Human Rights: Journal of the Section of Individual Rights and Responsibilities* 32.4:5.

Lewis, J. D., M. D. Lewis, T. Packard, and F. Souflee Jr. 2001. *Management of Human Service Programs*. Belmont, CA: Wadsworth.

Linares, L. O., D. Montalto, M. Li, and V. S. Oza. 2006. A promising parenting intervention in foster care. *Journal of Consulting and Clinical Psychology* 74.1: 32–41.

Love, L., and I. Velasco-Nunez, eds. 2004. *GPSII/MAPP: Group Preparation and Selection II/Model Approach to Partnership in Parenting*. Duluth, GA: Child Welfare Institute.

Lovell, C. M., and A. J. Przystas. 2005. *The Star: A Story to Help Young Children Understand Foster Care*. Battle Creek, MI: Roger Owen Rossman.

Lugaila, T., and J. Overturf. 2004. *Children and the Households They Live In: 2000*. U.S. Bureau of the Census, Census 2000 Special Reports. Washington, DC: U.S. Bureau of the Census.

MacGregor T. E., S. Rodger, A. L. Cummings, and A. W. Leschied. 2006. The needs of foster parents: A qualitative study of motivation, support, and retention. *Qualitative Social Work* 5.3:351–368.

MacLean, I. 1992. "Toward an Effective Parenting Partnership for Children in Child Welfare Agencies and Foster Parent Programs." Master's practicum, Nova University, Sarnia, Ontario.

Mallon, G. P. 1998. After care, then what? Outcomes from a study of an independent living program. *Child Welfare* 77:61–78.

——. 2001. "Sticks and stones can break your bones": Verbal harassment and physical violence in the lives of gay and lesbian youths in child welfare settings. *Journal of Gay and Lesbian Social Services* 13.1–2:63–81.

Mallon, G. P., and P. McCartt Hess, eds. 2005. *Child Welfare for the Twenty-First Century: A Handbook of Practices, Policies, and Programs*. New York: Columbia University Press.

McCarthy, J., and M. Woolverton. 2005. Healthcare needs of children and youth in foster care. In Mallon and McCartt Hess 2005:129–147.

McClelland, M., and R. Sands. 1993. The missing voice in interdisciplinary communication. *Qualitative Health Research* 3.1:74–90.

McFadden, E. J. 1996. Family-centered practice with foster-parent families. *Families in Society* 77.9:545–558.

McGowan, B. G. 2005. Historical evolution of child welfare services. In Mallon and McCartt Hess 2005:10–46.

McKenna, P. J., and D. H. Maister. 2002. *First Among Equals: How to Manage a Group of Professionals*. New York: Simon and Schuster.

McMillen, C., W. Auslander, D. Elze, T. White, and R. Thompson. 2003. Educational experiences and aspiration of older youth in the foster care system. *Child Welfare* 72:475–495.

McRoy, R. G. 2005. Overrepresentation of children and youth of color in foster care. In Mallon and McCartt Hess 2005:623–634.

Minkler, M., E. Fuller-Thomson, D. Miller, and D. Driver. 2000. Grandparent caregiving and depression. In *Grandparents Raising Grandchildren: Theoretical, Empirical, and Clinical Perspectives*, ed. B. Hayslip Jr. and R. Goldberg-Glen, 207–219. New York: Springer.

Mitchell-Clark, K. ed. 2003. *Family Team Conferences in Domestic Violence Cases: Guidelines for Practice*. San Francisco: Family Violence Prevention Fund.

National Association of Social Workers. 1999. Code of ethics. www.socialworkers.org/pubs/code/default.asp.

———. 2003. *Chapter Legislative Operations Manual*. Washington, DC: National Association of Social Workers. www.socialworkers.org/pace/resources/PACE-Chapter LegManual.pdf.

———. 2007. Indicators for the achievement of the NASW standards for cultural competence. Washington, DC: National Association of Social Workers. www.socialworkers.org/practice/standards/NASWCulturalStandardsIndicators2006.pdf.

National Child Traumatic Stress Network. 2008. Intervention descriptions. www.nctsnet.org/nccts/nav.do?pid=ctr_top_trmnt_prom.

National Foster Parent Association. 1973. Foster child bill of rights. Gig Harbor, WA: National Foster Parent Association. www.nfpainc.org/content/page=FOSTERCHILDBILLOFRIGHTS&nmenu=3&title=Foster%20Child%20Bill%20of%20Rights.

———. 2008. Code of ethics for foster parents. Gig Harbor, WA: National Foster Parent Association. www.nfpainc.org/content/?page=FOSTERPARENTCODEOFETHICS.

National Working Group on Foster Care and Education. 2007. *Educational Outcomes for Children and Youth in Foster and Out-of-Home Care*. Seattle, WA: Casey Family Programs.

Nelson, J., and M. Gallagher. 2005. *Kids Need to Be Safe: A Book for Children in Foster Care*. Minneapolis, MN: Free Spirit Publishing.

Netting, F. E., and M. K. O'Connor. 2003. *Organization Practice: A Social Worker's Guide to Understanding Human Services*. Boston: Allyn and Bacon.

Newton, R. R., A. J. Litrownik, and J. A. Landsverk. 2000. Children and youth in foster care: Disentangling the relationship between problem behaviors and number of placements. *Child Abuse and Neglect* 24.10:1295–1318.

New York State Office of Children and Family Services. 2002. *Conditional Surrenders*: 02 OCFS ADM-01. Rensselaer, NY.

Nixon, R. 2005. Promoting youth development and independent living services for youth in foster care. In Mallon and McHartt Hess 2005:573–582.

NSCAW (National Survey of Child and Adolescent Well-Being). 2003a. Baseline report for one-year-in-foster-care sample. www.acf.hhs.gov/programs/opre/abuse_neglect/nscaw/reports/nscaw_oyfc/oyfc_report.pdf.

——. 2003b. Executive summary. www.acf.hhs.gov/programs/opre/abuse_neglect/nscaw/reports/exesum_nscaw/exsum_nscaw.pdf.

——. 2007. Special health care needs among children in child welfare research brief. www.acf.hhs.gov/programs/opre/abuse_neglect/nscaw/reports/special_health/special_health.pdf.

Nugent, C. Special immigrant juvenile status: An ideal path to permanency for vulnerable undocumented abused, neglected or abandoned, youth. *The Judge's Page*. Seattle, WA: National CASA Association. www.nationalcasa.org/Judges Page/Article/special_immigrant_juvenile_status.htm.

O'Connor, M., and K. Barbell. 2001. A guide to special education advocacy for resource families. Washington, DC: Casey Family Programs, National Center for Resource Family Support. www.casey.org/NR/rdonlyres/E7738CD8-828 A-400B-AE22-68A84DD256A2/80/casey_special_education_advocacy.pdf.

Opie, A. 2000. *Thinking Teams/Thinking Clients: Knowledge-Based Teamwork*. New York: Columbia University Press.

Orme, J. G., C. Buehler, M. McSurdy, K. W. Rhodes, M. Cox, and D. A. Patterson. 2004. Parental and familial characteristics of family foster care applicants. *Children and Youth Services Review* 26.3:307–329.

Orme J. G., G. S. Cuddeback, C. Buehler, M. E. Cox, and N. S. Le Prohn. 2007. Measuring foster parent potential: Casey Foster Parent Inventory—Applicant Version. *Research on Social Work Practice* 17.1:77–92.

Pasztor, E., D. Hollinger, N. Halfon, and M. Inkelas. 2006. Health and mental health services for children in foster care: The central role of foster parents. *Child Welfare Journal* 85.1:33–57.

Pasztor, E. M., and E. J. McFadden. 2006. Foster parent associations: Advocacy, support, empowerment. *Families in Society* 87.4:483–490.

Pasztor, E. M., M. L. McNitt, and E. J. McFadden. 2005. Foster parent recruitment, development, support, and retention. In Mallon and McCartt Hess 2005:665–686.

Pecora, P., J. Williams, R. Kessler, E. Hiripi, K. O'Brien, J. Eerson, M. Herrick, and D. Torres. 2006. Assessing the educational achievements of adults who formerly were placed in family foster care. *Child and Family Social Work* 11:220–231.

Peters, B. G. 1999. *American Public Policy: Promise and Performance.* 5th ed. Chappaqua, NY: Seven Bridges Press.

Price, J. M., P. Chamberlain, J. Landsverk, J. B. Reid, L. D. Leve, and H. Laurent. 2008. Effects of a foster parent training intervention on placement changes of children in foster care. *Child Maltreatment* 13.1:64–75.

Quinton, D., A. Rushton, C. Dance, and D. Mayes. 1998. *Joining New Families: A Study of Adoption and Fostering in Middle Childhood.* Chichester: Wiley.

Rae, A., and W. Nicholas-Wolosuk. 2003. *Changing Agency Policy: An Incremental Approach.* Boston, MA: Allyn and Bacon.

Rhodes, K. W., M. E. Cox, J. G. Orme, and T. Coakley. 2006. Foster parents' reasons for fostering and foster family utilization. *Journal of Sociology and Social Welfare* 33.4:105–126.

Rhodes, K. W., J. G. Orme, and C. Buehler. 2001. A comparison of family foster parents who quit, consider quitting, and plan to continue fostering. *Social Service Review* 75.1:84–114.

Rhodes, K. W., J. G. Orme, M. E. Cox, and C. Buehler. 2003. Foster family resources, psychosocial functioning, and retention. *Social Work Research* 27.3:135–150.

Ridding, R. E., C. Fried, and P. A. Britner. 2000. Predictors of placement outcomes in treatment foster care: Implications for foster parent selection and service. *Journal of Child and Family Studies* 9.4:425–447.

Roberts, R. E., C. C. Atkisson, and A. A. Rosenblatt. 1998. Prevalence of psychopathology among children and adolescents. *American Journal of Psychiatry* 155.6:715–725.

Roger, S., A. Cummings, and A. Leschied. 2006. Who is caring for our most vulnerable children? The motivation to foster in child welfare. *Child Abuse and Neglect* 30.10:1129–1142.

Rosenwald, M. 2009. A glimpse within: An exploratory study of child welfare agencies' practices with LGBTQ youth. *Journal of Gay and Lesbian Social Services* 21.4: 1–14.

Rosenwald, M., and L. Bronstein. 2008. Foster parents speak: Preferred characteristics of foster children and experiences in the role of foster parent. *Journal of Family Social Work* 11.3:287–302.

Rosenwald, M., E. Kelchner, and A. Bartone. 2008. Experiences of kinship care providers. Unpublished manuscript.

Royse, D., B. A. Thyer, D. K. Padgett, and T. K. Logan. 2006. *Program Evaluation.* 4th ed. Belmont, CA: Thomson.

Rubin, D. M., K. J. Downes,, A. L. R. O'Reilly, R. Mekonnen, X. Luan, and R. Localio. 2008. Impact of kinship care on behavioral well-being for children in out-of-home care. *Archives of Pediatric Adolescent Medicine* 162.6. www.archpediatrics.com.

Saleeby, D., ed. 2006. *The Strengths Perspective in Social Work Practice*. 4th ed. Boston: Pearson/Allyn and Bacon.

Sanchirico, A., and K. Jablonka. 2000. Keeping foster children connected to their biological parents: The impact of foster parent training and support. *Child Adolescent Social Work Journal* 17.3:185–203.

Sands, R. 1993. Can you overlap here?: A question for an interdisciplinary team. *Discourse Processes* 16.4:545–564.

Schein, R. 1984. An historical perspective of Massachusetts adoption services in the public sector. Unpublished report. Boston: Massachusetts Department of Social Services.

Schneider, R. L., and L. Lester. 2001. *Social Work Advocacy: A New Framework for Action*. Belmont, CA: Wadsworth.

Schooler, J., and K. Jorgenson. 2000. *A System in Transition: Examining Foster Parent Recruitment and Retention in the New Millennium*. Tacoma, WA: National Foster Parent Association.

Seyfried, S., P. J. Pecora, A. C. Downs, P. Levine, and J. Emerson. 2000. Assessing the educational outcomes of children in long-term foster care: First findings. *School Social Work Journal* 24.2:68–88.

Shulman, L. 2006. *The Skills of Helping Individuals, Families, Groups, and Communities*. 5th ed.. Belmont, CA: Thomson.

Simms, M. D., H. Dubowitz, and M. Szilagyi. 2000. Health care needs of children in the foster care system. *Pediatrics* 106.4:909–918.

Stein, T. 1991. *Child Welfare and the Law*. New York: Longman.

Stein, T. J. 1998. *The Social Welfare of Women and Children with HIV and AIDS: Legal Protections, Policy, and Programs*. New York: Oxford University Press.

Steinhauer, P. D. 1991. *The Least Detrimental Alternative: A Systematic Guide to Case Planning and Decision Making for Children in Care*. Toronto: University of Toronto Press.

Stockton, R., R. Rhode, and J. Haughey. 1992. The effects of structured group exercises on cohesion, engagement, avoidance, and conflict. *Small Group Research* 23.2:155–168.

Stoesen, L. 2007. *Children Said at Higher Risk in Red States*. NASW News 52.3. Washington, DC: National Association of Social Workers.

Stringer, E. T. 1999. *Action Research*. 2nd ed. Thousand Oaks, CA: Sage.

Takayama, J. I., E. Wolfe, and K. P. Coulter. 1998. Relationship between reason for placement and medical findings among children in foster care. *Pediatrics* 101:201–207.

Tenenbaum, Jeffrey. 2002. Top ten myths about 501(c)(3) lobbying and political activity. Washington, DC: ASAE and the Center for Association Leadership. www.asae center.org/PublicationsResources/whitepaperdetail.cfm?ItemNumber=12202.

Toseland, R. W., and R. F. Rivas. 2009. *An Introduction to Group Work Practice*. 6th ed. Boston: Allyn and Bacon.

Weaver, C. J., D. W. Keller, and A. H. Loyek. 2005. Children with disabilities in the child welfare system. In Mallon and McCartt Hess 2005:173–184.

Wexler, R. 2002. Take the child and run: Tales from the age of ASFA. *New England Law Review* 36.1:129–152. www.nccpr.org/reports/asfa.pdf.

Wiglocki, J., M. K. Wright, and A. I. Geis. 2002. *Maybe Days: A Book for Children in Foster Care*. Washington, DC: American Psychological Association.

Wilber, S., C. Ryan, and J. Marksamer. 2006. *CWLA Best Practice Guidelines: Serving LGBT Youth in Out-of-Home Care*. Washington, DC: Child Welfare League of America.

Woodworth, R. S. 1996. You're not alone . . . you're one in a million. *Child Welfare* 75.5:619–635.

Zetlin, A. G., L. A. Weinberg, and N. M. Shea. 2006. Improving educational prospects for youth in foster care: The education liaison model. *Intervention in School and Clinic* 41.5:267–272.

Zito, J. M., D. J. Safer, D. Sai, J. F. Gardner, D. Thomas, P. Coombes, M. Dubowski, and M. Mendez-Lewis. 2008. Psychotropic medication patterns among youth in foster care. *Pediatrics* 121.1:157–163.

Index